Harvard Slavic Monographs 1

Osip Mandel'štam and His Age

A Commentary on the Themes of War and Revolution in the Poetry

1913-1923

Steven Broyde

Harvard University Press

Cambridge, Massachusetts

and London, England

1975

To Professor Kiril Taranovsky

Foreword

With this volume Harvard Slavic Studies inaugurates a series of occasional monographs, whose aim is to make available--rapidly, broadly, and as inexpensively as possible--distinguished new scholarship in the area of Slavic literature and culture. Steven Broyde's work exemplifies the qualities we seek: it considers a major figure in modern Russian poetry, illuminating central facets of his method and poetic message through detailed analysis of certain key texts. The result is, in the best sense, a contribution--not simply to individual understanding of Mandel'štam but to that ongoing discussion, in many languages and from many points of view, which constitutes the work of culture. Every monograph seeks to fill some gap; the ambition of such monographs as this is to help move discussion to a new level, through specificity and cogency to prepare the way for responsible generalization.

Donald Fanger

General Editor

Acknowledgments

I would like to acknowledge here my indebtedness in this study to Professor Kiril Taranovsky, my thesis adviser. As a student in his seminars on Mandel'štam, I had the opportunity to share many of his fruitful insights into the poetry; the final chapter on "Našedšij podkovu" had its genesis in one of these seminars. I have learned much from his careful scholarship and wish to thank him for his meticulous reading of my manuscript. I am grateful for his guidance and encouragement.

This work is almost wholly based on my Harvard University doctoral dissertation, January 1973.

The manuscript was completed through the generosity of the Harvard University Russian Research Center, Professor Richard Pipes, director, which provided a fellowship for 1972-73; the Cornell University Committee on Soviet Studies, Walter Pintner, chairman; and the Amherst College Faculty Research Fund.

And lastly, to Susan R. Van Dyne, who has helped me in more ways than I can enumerate.

Contents

Contents

Osip Mandel'štam and His Age

Chapter I

INTRODUCTION

During the last decade the increasing availability of Mandel'štam's
work in the West has awakened widespread, serious interest in his poetry.
Mandel'štam's importance as a major twentieth-century poet hardly needs
to be argued at this time, yet for this very reason it is important to
furnish a concrete, factual examination of the poems on which this reputa-
tion is based. By analyzing in careful detail a number of Mandel'štam's
poems written between 1913 and 1923, a crucial period in Russian history
and in the poet's career as well, we will uncover Mandel'štam's persistent
themes and his characteristic poetic method.

Certain poems from this period are especially fruitful for investi-
gation because they are uniformly considered among the masterpieces in
Mandel'štam's entire career, such as "V Peterburge my sojdemsja snova"
(We Will Meet Again in Petersburg), "Našedšij podkovu" (He Who Found a
Horseshoe), "Vek" (The Age). Yet by seeing these poems in the context of
this decade, we find that these important statements were part of a series
of complicated poetic responses Mandel'štam made to the historical events
of the period. Strangely, a variety of critics have claimed that Mandel'štam was indifferent to his age: "Characteristic of Mandel'štam's
view of the world is a coldness of inner indifference to everything that
occurs. The immense force of inertia which kept Mandel'štam's consciousness intentionally walled off from processes occurring in reality gave
the poet the opportunity of preserving right up until 1925 a position of
absolute social indifference."[1] "He has no social interests."[2] Yet even
this preliminary study of a single decade in Mandel'štam's career

conclusively demonstrates that the poet's consciousness, far from shutting
out contemporary reality, continuously confronted it in an effort to explore the possibilities of art. In his first collection of poems, Kamen',
Stone (1913), Mandel'štam explored the historical context of St. Petersburg in "Peterburgskie strofy," Petersburg Stanzas (1913). This poem has
an added importance because it is organized by a poetic method which he
would continue to utilize in subsequent poems. In 1914 Mandel'štam gave a
lecture no longer extant--"Neskol'ko slov o graždanskoj poèzii" (Some Words
about Civic Poetry)[3]--which we may assume from the title, demonstrated that
he was concerned with the question of the function of the poet in society.
The greatly expanded second edition of Kamen' published in 1916 contains
several poems which examine contemporary subjects as various as Italy and
the war ("Ni triumfa, ni vojny," Neither Triumph nor War, 1913), the changing situation in Europe ("Evropa," 1914), the persecution of the Imjabožcy
("I ponyne na Afone," Even Now on Mt. Athos, 1915). The Russian Revolution provides the central focus for Mandel'štam's next volume, Tristia
(1922), the first poem of which is dated 1916 and includes poems till 1921.
Rather than being unconcerned, Mandel'štam succinctly expressed his belief
in his essay, "O prirode slova," On the Nature of the Word (1922) that
poetry must at times attempt to comprehend and give expression to social
phenomena:

> Akmeizm ne tol'ko liternoe, no i obščestvennoe javlenie v russkoj
> istorii. S nim vmeste v russkoj poèzii vozrodilas' nravstvennaja
> sila. . . . Obščestvennyj pafos russkoj poèzii do six por
> podnimalsja tol'ko do "graždanina", no est' bolee vysokoe načalo,
> čem "graždanin",--ponjatie "muža".
>   V otličie ot staroj graždanskoj poèzii, novaja russkaja poèzija
> dolžna vospityvat' ne tol'ko graždan, no i "muža".[4]

Acmeism is not only a literary, but also a social manifestation in Russian history. Together with it a moral force was revived in Russian poetry. . . . The social spirit of Russian poetry has so far risen only to "citizen"; but there is a more elevated principle than "citizen," the concept of "man."

In contradistinction to the old civic poetry, modern Russian poetry must educate not only "citizens," but "man" too.

Mandel'štam was immensely involved in his age. His poetry represents a continuing commentary on it, an attempt to comprehend and record his reactions to an era which was changing, if not disintegrating, before his eyes. Living at a time of profound social upheaval, Mandel'štam tried in his poetry and prose to understand the changes which were occurring with bewildering rapidity.

One recent scholar has written that "Mandel'štam's purely political poems are, perhaps, his easiest ones, [but] some of his most difficult poems are those which deal with the nature of poetic vision, the social function of poetry, and the relationship between the poet and time."[5] While the meaning of a political poem may be more obvious by providing a particular event on which to focus, the distinction between the two types of poems is not as clear-cut as this statement implies. Mandel'štam's poetry is never easy. Moreover, the political poems to a large extent explore precisely the relationship between the poet and time. By examining many of Mandel'štam's poems written between 1913 and 1923, an especially turbulent period of history which included World War I, the Russian Revolution, and the threat of a second Allied intervention, the present work will explore Mandel'štam's changing and many-faceted responses to his political environment. Primarily, the chapters are arranged chronologically, although within a given chapter poems outside of this order which are related thematically will be discussed. The reason for such an arrangement is twofold. Obviously, we are examining the progression of Mandel'štam's responses to events in the order in which they occurred. But much more importantly, Mandel'štam reacts to events in a varied, complex, and constantly developing way. His responses are never doctrinaire; he does not view things from the vantage point of an already determined framework. Hence, at any point in time a new event can evoke a previously unfelt response. Moreover, it is important to see how Mandel'štam rethought previous solutions in the light of changes in the historical moment.

As will be seen, many of the poems analyzed in this study are ultimately concerned with Mandel'štam's views on the fate of Russian culture, however one chooses to define this elusive word, at a time when the social order was in a state of near chaos; when some people feared for its survival, while others called for its destruction. Mandel'štam's most consistent belief during this period of turmoil was that Russia's cultural heritage must be preserved. However, his belief in the ability of the culture to survive in the midst of an inimical environment fluctuated. If in one poem he views the heritage as threatened and dying ("Na strašnoj vysote bluždajuščij ogon'," At a Fearful Height a Will-'o-the-wisp, 1918), in yet another he can express muted confidence in the likelihood that it will survive, outlasting both those who would destroy it, and those who are attempting to protect it ("V Peterburge my sojdemsja snova," 1920). In "Našedšij podkovu," He Who Found a Horseshoe (1923), the final poem analyzed here, Mandel'štam gives the most complete poetic expression to this theme. Here, his optimism regarding the ability of a vast cultural heritage to endure intact throughout successive social upheavals is most emphatically pronounced. However, as in "V Peterburge my sojdemsja snova," Mandel'štam's almost prescient knowledge about his own fate is most gloomily expressed.

In order to understand Mandel'štam's relation to and involvement with his age, we must examine in considerable detail the poetic artifacts which have survived it. Mandel'štam's poetry rewards and demands detailed analysis; it depends on density of texture and allusion, as well as complexity—it is at once compact and concrete, yet oblique and cryptic, surrendering meaning only after close scrutiny on the part of the reader. For if Mandel'štam's contemporaries often produced undistinguished propaganda, Mandel'štam's poems reveal a breadth of education and a creative genius which give his reactions lasting poetic value. Such analysis will, it is hoped, enable us to understand how he succeeded in transmuting something essentially timebound, a particular response to a particular situation, into something timeless. Mandel'štam himself was aware of this process:

Nastojaščee mgnovenie možet vyderžat' napor stoletij i soxranit' svoju celost', ostat'sja tem že "sejčas". Nužno tol'ko umet' vyrvat' ego iz počvy vremeni, ne povrediv ego kornej—inače on zavjanet. Villon umel èto delat'. Kolokol Sorbonny, prervavšij ego rabotu nad Petit Testament, zvučit do six por.

(II, 349)

The present moment can bear the pressure of centuries and preserve its integrity, remain the same "now." One need only know how to pull it out of the soil of time without harming its roots, otherwise it will wither. Villon knew how to do this. The Sorbonne's bell, which cut short his work on the Petit Testament, still rings.

T. S. Eliot, faced alike with the same disintegration of culture, has observed: "Bad verse may have a transient vogue when the poet is reflecting a popular attitude of the moment; but real poetry survives not only a change of popular opinion but the complete extinction of interest in the issues with which the poet was passionately concerned."[6]

Throughout this period Mandel'štam was able to reevaluate previous
responses. But such shifts, which involved at times apparently contradictory or mutually exclusive responses, do not stem from Mandel'štam's
confusion. Èrenburg, as early as 1920, expressed an opinion which remains
just: "Poets greeted the Russian Revolution with wild shouts, hysterical
tears, laments, enthusiastic frenzy, curses. But Mandel'štam alone understood the pathos of the events, [comprehended] the scale of what was
occurring."[7] Appreciating the significance of the events of his time,
Mandel'štam nonetheless avoided being partisan in most of his poetry. Yet
understanding the issues and remaining detached from factions was not a
position that the poet could maintain without cost. Among the conclusions
to be drawn from the present study are the reasons for the essential ambiguity which characterizes a large part of Mandel'štam's poetic vision.

Chapter II

WORLD WAR ONE

"Zverinec" (The Menagerie) was originally subtitled "oda." One of
the traditional functions of the ode has been to glorify or persuade.
Mandel'štam's poem is an appeal for peace written at the height of World
War I. (The poem is dated January 1916.) At the end of "Zverinec" the
poet is able to envision a future time which will be without war and discord, just as at the beginning of the poem he looked back at a mythological
time of peace when man lived without strife or injustice.

Otveržennoe slovo "mir"
V načale oskorblennoj ěry;
Svetil'nik v glubine peščery
I vozdux gornyx stran -- ěfir;
Ěfir, kotorym ne sumeli,
Ne zaxoteli my dyšat'.
Kozlinym golosom opjat'
Pojut kosmatye svireli.

Poka jagnjata i voly
Na tučnyx pastbiščax vodilis'
I druželjubnye sadilis'
Na pleči sonnyx skal orly, -
Germanec vykormil orla,
I lev britancu pokorilsja,
I gall'skij greben' pojavilsja
Iz petušinogo xoxla.

A nyne zavladel dikar'
Svjaščennoj palicej Gerakla,
I černaja zemlja issjakla,
Neblagodarnaja, kak vstar'.
Ja paločku voz'mu suxuju,
Ogon' dobudu iz nee,
Puskaj uxodit v noč' gluxuju
Mnoj vspološennoe zver'e!

Petux, i lev, i temnoburyj
Orel, i laskovyj medved' -
My dlja vojny postroim klet',
Zverinye prigreem škury,
A ja poju vino vremen-

Istočnik reči italijskoj-
I v kolybeli praarijskoj
Slavjanskij i germanskij len!

Italija, tebe ne len'
Trevožit' Rima kolesnicy,
S kudaxtan'em domašnej pticy
Pereletev čerez pleten'?
I ty, sosedka, ne vzyšči:
Orel toporščitsja i zlitsja.
Čto, esli dlja tvoej prašči
Tjaželyj kamen' ne goditsja?

V zverince zaperev zverej,
My uspokoimsja nadolgo,
I stanet polnovodnej Volga,
I rejnskaja struja svetlej-
I umudrennyj čelovek
Počtit nevol'no čužestranca,
Kak poluboga, bujstvom tanca,
Na beregax velikix rek.

"The Menagerie"

The rejected word "peace"
In the beginning of the offended era;
A lampion in the depth of a cave
And air of mountainous lands--ether;
Ether which we could not,
Did not want to breathe.
The shaggy reed-pipes are again
Singing with a reedy voice.

While the lambs and oxen
Were in the fertile pastures
And the friendly eagles were alighting
On the shoulders of sleepy crags,--
The German reared an eagle,
And the lion submitted to the Briton,
And the Gallic comb appeared
From the rooster's crest.

And now a savage has seized
The sacred club of Hercules,
And the black earth has dried up,
Ungrateful, as of old.
I will take the dry stick,
Will get fire from it,
Let the wild beasts alarmed by me
Go into the dead of night.

Rooster, and lion, and dark brown
Eagle, and affectionate bear--
We will build a cage for war,
We will give shelter to your animal hides,
And I am singing the wine of times--
The source of Italic speech--
And in the proto-Aryan cradle
Slavonic and Germanic flax!

Italy, aren't you tired of
Disturbing the chariots of Rome,
Having jumped over the fence
With the clucking of poultry?
And you, neighbor, don't be offended:
The eagle bristles and is angry.
What if the heavy stone
Isn't suited for your sling?

Having locked the beasts up in the menagerie
We will rest content for a long time,
And the Volga will become deeper,
And the Rhenish water brighter--
And man, having become wiser
Will involuntarily honor the foreigner,
Like a demigod, with the turbulence of dance
On the shores of the great rivers.

"Zverinec" begins with two nominal sentences which are really col-
lapsed similes, each giving a metaphoric equivalent of the concept
"peace." The "offended" era which is mentioned in line 2 can have two
possible references: it can refer to an age in the sense of classical
mythology, a period of the world's history. The era which rejected peace
is probably, in the mythology of Hesiod, the fifth age of man, The Iron
Age, the worst one of all:

    . . . Would that I were not among the men of the fifth generation
    . . . The father will not agree with his children, nor the children
    with their father, nor guest with his host, nor comrade with com-
    rade; nor will brother be dear to brother as aforetime . . .
    Strength will be right and reverence will cease to be.[1]

It is an age characterized by strife and discord; the age most diametrically opposed to the Golden Age, which emerges more clearly in

World War One / 9

stanza two, but which is alluded to here through the image of the cave. Only in the subsequent Silver Age did man begin to build houses: "In that age [the Silver Age] men first sought the shelter of houses. Their homes had heretofore been caves, dense thickets, and branches bound together with bark."[2] More narrowly, the era which rejected peace, in terms of the historical context of this poem, can be the era inaugurated by World War I. For in "Zverinec," Mandel'štam views events not only in terms of a mythological historical continuum, but also in terms of the specific moment.

The metaphor of the fire ("svetil'nik") seems explicit enough. In the depths of the cave, it lights the darkness. It even calls to mind the famous remark made by Sir Edward Grey on the eve of England's entry into the war, "The lamps are going out all over Europe." Air is also used metaphorically for peace. Here it is the ether, in ancient Greek mythology the highest, purest, most transluscent layer of air. Mandel'štam frequently utilized air imagery. Thick, dense dark air usually is part of the negative semantic field, and is analogous to negative concepts, non-peace, non-freedom. A clear example can be cited from a poem written in the same year as "Zverinec." Here the epithet unambiguously delineates the image for us:

> V Petropole prozračnom my umrem,
> Gde vlastvuet nad nami Proserpina.
> My v každom vzdoxe smertnyj vozdux p'em,
> I každyj čas nam smertnaja godina.
>
> (1916; my italics)
>
> In transparent Petropolis we will die,
> Where Proserpina rules over us.
> In every breath we drink deathly air,
> And every hour is our time of death.

The air-peace is rejected ("otveržennyj") because "we" did not know how,
did not want to breathe it. Again, the idea of breathing is a complex
theme in Mandel'štam's poetry. Associated with it are negative possibilities ("Nel'zja dyšat', i tverd' kišit červjami" It's impossible to breathe,
and the firmament swarms with worms ["Koncert na vokzale," Concert at the
Railroad Station, 1925]; "I v trave gadjuka dyšit/Meroj veka zolotoj" And
in the grass a viper breathes/The golden measure of the age ["Vek," 1923
(The Age)]), as well as positive ones (". . . vot vse moi prave,-/I polnoj
grud'ju ix vdyxat' ešče ja dolžen" . . . these are all my rights,-/And I
must breathe them in with full chest ["Razryvy kruglyx buxt i xrjašč i
sineva," Breaches of round bays, and gravel, and blue, 1937]).

Peace in the first quatrain is seen as an all-pervasive possibility,
residing both in the highest stratum, the ether, as well as in the lowest,
the cave. The cave, as we have seen, is a positive image, suggesting a
primordal, mythological Golden Age of mankind, when all lived in harmony.
The "air of mountainous lands" is also a positive image here. This image
becomes more complicated; the phrase "Efir, kotorym ne sumeli,/Ne zaxoteli
my dyšat'" (Ether which we could not,/Did not want to breathe) acts as a
transition to the last two lines in the stanza. We now have a series of
phrases ("vozdux gornyx stran," "kozlinnyj golos," "kosmatye svireli"
[air of mountainous lands, reedy voice, shaggy reed-pipes]) which together
constitute one complex unit. The signals strongly suggest that the
"mountainous lands" is Arcadia, a region which is very mountainous and has
many associations in Greek mythology. Pan was originally an Arcadian
deity. A quotation from the Homeric "Hymn to Pan" clearly shows that it
is Pan who emerges in the second quatrain:

> Muse, tell me about Pan... with his goat's feet and two horns — a
> lover of merry noise. Through wooded glades he wanders
> with dancing nymphs who foot it on some sheer cliff's edge,
> calling upon Pan, the shepherd god.... He has every
> snowy crest and the mountain peaks and rocky
> crests for his domain.... Only at evening, as he returns
> from the chase, he sounds his note, playing sweet and
> low on his pipe of reed....[3]

Pan, a minor deity with mixed attributes, was partly goat-like in form,
and in general amorous. One of his chief functions was to make the flocks
fertile. He invented the musical pipe of seven reeds. The last two lines
of the first stanza do not, however, emphasize Pan's positive characteristics. The tone of the last two lines is conditioned by the two lines which
precede them: "Èfir, kotorym ne sumeli,/Ne zaxotely my dyšat'" (Ether
which we could not,/Did not want to breathe). A conjunctive adverb impli-
citly seems to follow: [Poètomu] kozlinym golosom opjat'. . ." ([There-
fore] the shaggy reed-pipes are again...) It is the negative aspects of
Pan which would logically follow. Pan can induce sudden, groundless fear,
known in consequence as Panic fear. Ovid (Fasti, IV, 761) tells that Greek
shepherds feared to pipe at noon, lest they should wake Pan, who was thought
to be sleeping at that hour. "Kozlinyj golos" as an idiom means reedy
voice. Coming after man's rejection of peace, it sounds ominous--reedy,
perhaps unclear or harsh; Pan seen as a destructive force. "Kozlinyj" itself comes from "kozel" (goat) and connotes the idea of unbridled passions:
satyrs, grotesque creatures, also had goatish features, taken over from Pan,
and were bestial in their desires and behavior. "Kosmatye" (shaggy) is also
in the negative semantic field. It suggests a primordal, primitive condi-
tion; cf. "Čut' mercaet prizračnaja scena" (The phantasmal stage scarcely
glimmers [1920]): "Vse kosmato--ljudi i predmety. . ." (Everything is

shaggy--people and things). In this latter poem, the peace within the

opera is juxtaposed to the rough conditions which reign outside. Thus,

taken together, "reedy voice" and "shaggy reed-pipes" present music as a

discordant force, capable of exciting strong emotions. In this regard,

it is worthwhile to quote from Mandel'štam's essay "Puškin i Skrjabin":

> V drevnem mire muzyka sčitalas' razrušitel'noj stixiej. Élliny
> bojalis' flejty i frigijskogo lada, sčitaja ego opasnym i
> soblaznitel'nym. . . . Nedoverčivoe otnošenie k muzyke, kak k podo-
> zritel'noj i temnoj stixii, bylo nastol'ko sil'no, čto gosudarstvo
> vzjalo muzyku pod svoju opeku.
>
> (II, 358)
>
> Music was regarded as a destructive element in the ancient world.
> The Hellenes feared the flute and Phrygian harmonics, considering
> it dangerous and corrupting. . . . A distrustful attitude towards
> music as a suspicious and dark element was so strong that the state
> took charge of music.

The reed-pipes in this stanza cease being emblematic of an Arcadian

Golden Age. On the contrary, they connote here discord and the martial

aspects of music.

Like stanza one of "Zverinec," stanza two has a dual focus:

> Poka jagnjata i voly
> Na tučnyx pastbiščax vodilis'
> I druželjubnye sadilis'
> Na pleči sonnyx skal orly,--
> Germanec vykormil orla,
> I lev britancu pokorilsja,
> I gall'skij greben' pojavilsja
> Iz petušinogo xoxla.

> While the lambs and oxen
> Were in the fertile pastures
> And the friendly eagles were alighting
> On the shoulders of sleepy crags,--
> The German reared an eagle,
> And the lion submitted to the Briton,
> And the Gallic comb appeared
> From the rooster's crest.

The first quatrain presents Mandel'štam's vision of a Golden Age, this time examined in terms of animals. The second quatrain presents a metamorphosis. The idyllis peace is shattered, and discord once again emerges. Many different writers have presented their concepts of a Golden Age. The best known are Plato's, in Politicus; the prophecies of Isaiah, and the Fourth Eclogue of Virgil. The idea of a once-existing Golden Age of man, and the possibility of a return to it, often emerges during periods of discord. Virgil's wish for a Golden Age was prompted by the calamitous times in which he lived--war (with Persia), famine, political strife. For a considerable period, people had been expecting a new age of the world to begin.[4] Likewise, Mandel'štam's poem was written during the upheavals of World War I. Virgil's Golden Age is described in terms of harmony and peace among animals: "The goats, unshepherded, will make for home with udders full of milk, and the ox will not be frightened of the lion, for all his might. Your very cradle will adorn itself with blossoms to caress you. The snake will come to grief. . . ."[5] Isaiah's uses similar imagery (XI:6): "The wolf also shall dwell with the lamb, and the leopard shall lie down with the kid; and the calf and the young lion and the fatling together, and a little child shall lead them. 7: And the cow and the bear shall feed, their young ones shall lie down together." Mandel'štam's Golden Age, like those of Virgil and Isaiah, is distinguished by harmony. The earth is rich and fertile ("tučnye pastbišča"). The eagle, a symbol of military power since ancient times, is called "friendly" ("druželjubnyj"). In another context this would be interpreted as an oxymoron. As in the first stanza, the peaceful state exists on two strata: on the ground ("na pastbiščax" [in the pastures]--parallels "v peščere" [in a cave]) and

above the ground ("na pleči skal" [on the shoulders of crags]--parallels
"vozdux gornyx stran" [air of mountainous lands]). Even in the midst of
this cosmic harmony, man is sowing the seeds of future discord. The animals are metamorphosed. They cease being emblematic of pastoral peace,
but become, rather, heraldic animals, emblems of individual countries:
the eagle of Germany, Great Britain's lion, the rooster of France. The
idea of a primordal unity among nations, alluded to in stanza four, is
here replaced by nationalism.

The opposition between peace and war is continued into stanza three.
Juxtaposed to the club of Heracles is the dry stick of Prometheus. There
is an implied causal relationship between the second and third stanzas:
"Poka jagnjata i voly . . . vodilis' . . . germanec vykormil orla . . .
a nyne dikar' zavladel palicej Gerakla" (While the lambs and the oxen . . .
were [there] the German reared an eagle . . . and now a savage has seized
the club of Hercules). Heracles' club is called "sacred," because according to some accounts, it was given to him by Hephaestus.[6] Or, it may be
sacred because Heracles lives among the gods: "Now he lives happily in
the glorious home of snowy Olympus."[7] Heracles was the most famous of
Greek heroes, noted for his strength, courage, endurance, good nature, and
compassion. In much of Greek art he was depicted with his club. Hence,
that it is in the hands of a savage implies that all of these positive
qualities associated with Heracles are perverted and that the emblematic
club is consequently no longer used for good ends, but for war, discord.
Moreover, Heracles was venerated in many cult centers not only as a warrior or power who gave aid in war; many prayed to him as a savior who
might help in the deliverance from the perils of war. He was called the

"warder off of the fates and diseases." Equally important, especially in the context of the next two lines, "I černaja zemlja issjakla,/Ne-blagodarnaja, kak vstar'"(And the black earth has dried up,/Ungrateful, as of old), was a later function of Heracles: As the military and civic life of Greek communities waned, the chief significance of Heracles' title "Averter of Evil" shifted from the military sphere to the agricultural and pastoral. The peasant sought his aid in help with flocks and crops. He defended the sheep from their enemy, the wolf. One Attic from the fifth century shows him holding a club and a cornucopia. In other words, as Farnell notes, Heracles underwent a transformation from warrior hero into agricultural shepherd.[8]

The image of the dried-up black earth provides a clear opposition to "fertile pastures" of the Golden Age in stanza two. This line has another dimension, however. For Mandel'štam, black earth ("černaja zemlja," "černozem") has associations with poetry. For example, in "Našedšij podkovu": "[Vozdux byvaet kak] vlažnyj černozem Neèry, každuju noč' raspaxannyj zanovo/. . . plugami. . ." ([The air is like] the moist black earth of Neaira, ploughed anew every night/. . .with plows. . .). This recalls an equation Mandel'štam made earlier: "Poèzija--plug, vzryvajuščij vremja tak, čto glubinye sloi vremeni, ego černozem okazyvaetsja sverxu" (Poetry is a plow which blows up time in such a way that the deep layers of time, its black earth, come to the surface). (II, 266). In this essay, Mandel'štam quotes from "Sestry--tjažest' i nežnost' . . ." (1920): "Vremja vspaxano plugom, i roza zemleju byla," (Sisters-- heaviness and tenderness : Time is blown up by a plow, and the rose was earth). "Černozem" appears in one of Mandel'štam's Voronež poems,

"Stansy" (May–June, 1935), dealing in part with poetry:

> I ne ograblen ja i ne nadlomen,
> No tol'ko čto vsego pereogromlen--
> Kak Slovo o polku, struna moja tuga,
> I v golose moem posle uduš'ja
> Zvučit zemlja--poslednee oruž'e--
> Suxaja vlažnost černozemnyx ga.9

> I am not robbed, nor broken,
> But only made enormous,--
> Like The Tale of Igor's Campaign, my string is taut,
> And in my voice after suffocating
> The earth sounds--the last weapon--
> The dry dampness of blackearth hectares.

Hence, that the rich black earth has dried up shows not only that the Golden Age has been superseded by a harsher, crueler Iron Age. It indicates, too, in Mandel'štam's cosmology, that the times are not propitious for poetry. Poetry is associated with black earth as a rich, life-giving force.

"Ungrateful, as of old" in the third stanza possibly alludes to another myth, the abduction of Persephone by Hades. Heracles' club was stolen by a savage; Demeter's daughter was kidnapped by Hades. Searching for her daughter, Demeter neglected the earth which as a result became barren: "The ground would not make the seed sprout. . . In the fields the oxen drew many a curved plough in vain, and much white barley was cast upon the land without avail."[10] That Mandel'štam may be alluding to this myth becomes more probable if we look at a poem which like "Zverinec," is dated 1916: "V Petropole prozračnom my umrem,/Gde vlastvuet nad nami Proserpina./My v každom vzdoxe smertnyj vozdux p'em,/I každyj čas nam smertnaja godina" (In transparent Petropolis we will die,/Where Proserpina rules over us. In every breath we drink deathly air,/And every hour is our time of death).

The dry stick from which the speaker will get fire is the stick which Prometheus used to bring fire to man: "I hunted down the stealthy fount of fire/In fennel stored, which schooled the race of men/In every art and taught them great resource."[11] The surmise that the dry stick is associated with Prometheus is reinforced when we recall that it was Heracles who freed Prometheus from his punishment. Therefore, when the speaker says that he will take a dry stick, he implies that he will be a Prometheus and will take fire to mankind. With it he will scare the beasts, who will then retreat into the night. By doing this, he will become a benefactor to mankind, as was Prometheus. The positive implications of the fire recall the "svetil'nik" in stanza one: light associated with peace and harmony.

The fourth stanza begins in the vocative. The heraldic animals, which now include the Russian bear, are addressed. The speaker outlines what must be done to curb the warring animals, France, Great Britain, Germany, and Russia being participants in World War I. "My dlja vojny postroim klet'" (We will build a cage for war, "klet'" [cage] used metonymically for "zverinec" [menagerie]); here the animals will presumably be locked up (note the verb "prigret'" used in the sense of "prijutit'" [give shelter to]) to battle among themselves. Once the animals are confined, peace will be restored. A generalized "we," humanity, will perform the action; cf. l. 6 "ne zaxoteli my dyšat'" (We did not want to breathe), l. 42 "My uspokoimsja nadolgo" (We will rest content for a long time [my italics]). Standing somewhat apart, and now concerned with different things, is the speaker. Previously, he had been involved as an agent,

18 / Osip Mandel'štam and His Age

line 21: "Ja paločku voz'mu suxuju" (I will take the dry stick). Now he opposes himself, distances himself from the rest of humanity: lines 27, 29 "My dlja vojny postroim klet'/ . . . A ja poju vino vremen . . ." (We will build a cage for war/. . .And I sing the wine of times) (cf. "Arion": "Nas bylo mnogo na čelne . . ./ A ja . . ./Plovcam ja pel . . ." [There were many of us on the bark . . . And I . . ./I sang to the sailors]). "Wine of times" is perhaps a metaphor for poetry; there are many examples in Mandel'štam's work where poetry is associated with wine, grapes: "Plod naryval, zrel vinograd" ("Grifel'naja oda," 1923) (The fruit was coming to a head, the grapes were ripening [Slate Ode, 1923]); "I otvečal mne oplakavšij Tassa:/—Ja k veličan'jam ešče ne privyk;/Tol'ko stixov vinogradnoe mjaso/Mne osvežilo slučajno jazyk" ("Batjuškov," 1932) And the one who had mourned Tasso answered me this way:/-I haven't yet gotten used to songs of praise;/Only the grape meat of verses/Accidentally refreshed my tongue [Batjuškov, 1932]; "Ja bukvoj byl, byl vinogradnoj stročkoj" ("K nemeckoj reči," 1932 [I was a letter, I was a grape line, To German Speech, 1932]). "Tak i poèt ne boitsja povtorenij i legko p'janeet klassičeskim vinom" ("Slovo i kul'tura," II, 267 [The poet also does not fear repetitions and easily gets intoxicated on classical wine, The Word and Culture]). The "cradle" of the next line is associated on the one hand with the peace and innocence of a child. Also, it was widely used by Romantic historians and poets when referring to the distant past, the urheimat of the nation. Here it is called "proto-Aryan." Proto-Aryan originally referred to peoples speaking languages of the eastern group of Indoeuropean. When Mandel'štam refers to the proto-Aryan cradle, he means that prehistoric time when this one large language family had not yet split up into separate groups, perhaps having a common culture and language, alluding here to a Golden Age of the past. He then continues with a word (flax) which is similar in Slavic (R. "len," Ukr. "len," Czech "len") and Germanic (Gothic "lein," German "Lein"; one should note, too, the etymology of "vino" ["A ja poju vino vremen" (And I sing the wine of times)], which was probably borrowed from the Latin, "vinum," or the German, "Wein"[12]). The similarity of words underpins the idea of the nations having emerged from a common cradle. Significant, too, is the choice of the word flax. It implies the early agricultural nature of the civilization, a time when people cultivated crops, wove, and so on. "In Deutschland verfertigen [sie, the Slavs] Leinwand, beaueten Met, pflanzten Fruchtbäume und führeten nach ihrer Art ein fröliches, musikalisches Leben."[13]

Stanza five begins with a very familiar form of address to Italy, which finally entered the war on the side of the Allies in 1915, having been before that closely tied to Austria–Hungary and Germany (hence, "pereletev čerez pleten'" [having jumped over the fence]). Present-day Italy is juxtaposed to ancient Rome ("Rima kolesnicy," the triumphal chariots of Rome), with its connotations of grandeur and power. Today's Italy ("domašnjaja ptica" [poultry]) is not even given its own heraldic emblem; one wonders, too, whether Mandel'štam, likening Italy to poultry, is not hinting at the belief, held especially by Slavs, that Italians are bad soldiers. In an earlier poem, Italy was again abused:

> Ni triumfa, ni vojny!
> O, železnye, dokole
> Bezopasnyj Kapitolij
> My xranit' osuždeny?

Ili rimskie peruny--
Gnev naroda --obmanuv,
Otdyxaet ostryj kljuv
Toj oratorskoj tribuny;

Ili vozit kirpiči
Solnca drjaxlaja povozka,
I v rukax u nedonoska
Rima ržavye ključi?

      ("Pered vojnoj," (Before the War) <u>Apollon</u> N°N°
      6-7, 1914, p. 12, subsequently entitled "1913")

Neither triumph, nor war!
Oh iron ones, how long are
We condemned to protect
The secure Capitolium?

Or, having deceived the Roman thunderbolts--
The people's anger--
The sharp beak of that
Oratorical tribune is resting;

Or does the sun's decrepit carriage
Carry bricks,
And are the rusted keys of Rome
In the hands of an abortion?

Struve[14] suggests that Mandel'štam's indignation was aroused by Italy's reluctance to enter the war. In "Before the War" Mandel'štam uses pejorative bird imagery ("ostryj kljuv toj oratorskoj tribuny" [the sharp beak of that oratorical tribune]) as he does in "Zverinec" ("domašnjaja ptica [poultry]); he also denigrates Italy through the image of the chariot: Phaethon's sun chariot becomes "Ili vozit kirpiči/Solnca drjaxlaja povozka?" (Or does the sun's decrepit carriage/Carry bricks?). The Roman keys (of power) are rusted in Italy's hands. At any rate, Mandel'štam remained consistent in expressing his scorn for Italy's foreign policy, although others were quick to fall into raptures over Italy's decision to side with the Allies.[15]

If Mandel'štam scorned Italy's military prowess, he respected

Germany's:

> Nemeckaja kaska--svjaščennyj trofej--
> Ležit na kamine v gostinoj tvoej,
> Dotron'sja, ona kak merluška legka,
> Pronizana vozduxom med' šišaka.
>
> V Poznani i Pol'še ne vsem voevat'--
> Svoimi glazami vraga uvidat'
> I, slušaja jader gubitel'nyj xor,
> Sorvat' s neprijatelja gordyj ubor.
>
> (1914)
>
> A German helmet--sacred trophy--
> Lies on the fire-place in your drawing-room,
> Touch it, it's light as lambskin
> The bronze of the spiked helmet is pierced with air,
>
> Not everyone in Poznan and Poland is to fight--
> To see the enemy with his own eyes
> And, hearing the destructive chorus of cannon balls,
> To tear the proud headgear from the enemy.

Lastly, we might mention here Mandel'štam's attitude towards England as
expressed in "1914":

> Sobiralis' èlliny vojnoju
> Na prelestnyj ostrov Salamin,--
> On, ottorgnut vražeskoj rukoju,
> Viden byl iz gavani Afin.
>
> A teper' druz'ja-ostrovitjane
> Snarjažajut naši korabli.
> Ne ljubili ran'še angličane
> Evropejskoj sladostnoj zemli.
>
> O Evropa, novaja Èllada,
> Oxranjaj Akropol' i Pirej!
> Nam podarkov s ostrova ne nado--
> Celyj les nezvanyx korablej.
>
> (1914)
>
> The Hellenes were gathering for war
> Against the lovely island of Salamis,--
> Seized by a hostile hand,
> It was visible from the Athens harbor.

And now our islander-friends
Equip our ships.
Before, the English didn't like
Our sweet European land.

Oh, Europe, new Hellas,
Protect the Acropolis and Piraeus!
We do not need gifts from the island—
A whole forest of unbidden ships.

Terras has written that this poem is an "obvious echo of Solon's Iomen eis Salamina, machesomenoi peri nesou. However, the analogy to the political situation of 1914 is an antithetic one: while the Athenians were called upon by Solon to liberate the island of Salamis, the Russian poet asks Europe to repulse the advances of the insular power and to refuse the dangerous gift of British ships."[16] There was no dearth of anti-British sentiment in Russia on the eve of and during World War I. Great Britain until 1917 pursued a policy of "splendid isolation" (Before, the English didn't like/Our sweet European land) and opposed Russia's policies in Central Asia and the Turkish Straits. Sir George Buchanan notes that anti-British sentiment at the beginning of the war was strong.[17] Count Witte, in March 1914, criticized the Anglo-Russian rapprochement as a "sacrifice of her [Russia's] freedom of action."[18] Later, feelings grew even more bitter, expressed in the often-heard statement that the Allies, especially Great Britain, would fight the war "to the last drop of the Russian soldier's blood."

In the fifth stanza, not only Italy, but Poland as well is addressed in a condescendingly ironic tone; that is, it seems fairly certain that Poland is the "sosedka" (neighbor) referred to in line 37: "A ty, sosedka, ne vzyšči" (And you, neighbor, don't be offended). In "Polacy!" (1914) Poland is addressed directly:

Polaki! Ja ne vižu smysla
V bezumnom podvige strelkov!
Il' voron zakljuet orlov?
Il' potečet obratno Visla?
Ili snega ne budut bol'še
Zimoju pokryvat' kovyl'?
Ili o Gapsburgov kostyl'
Pristalo opirat'sja Pol'še?
I ty, slavjanskaja kometa,
V svoem bluždan'i vekovom,
Rassypalas' čužim ognem,
Soobščnica čužogo sveta!

Poles! I don't see any sense
In the mad exploit of your riflemen!
Or will a raven peck eagles to death?
Or will the Vistula flow backwards?
Or will snow no longer cover
The feather-grass in winter?
Or is it appropriate for Poland to lean on a
Hapsburg crutch?
And you, Slavonic comet,
In your age-old wandering,
Have burst with a foreign fire,
Confederate of a foreign light!

"Polacy!" is full of sarcasm, built on invective and rhetorical questions.
The poem breaks into three parts (ll. 1-2, 3-9, 9-12). Lines 1-2 are a
vocative address to the Poles. The syntagma "bezumnyj podvig" (mad exploit) is ambivalent. The more usual meaning of "podvig" is "an act important in its significance; an action accomplished in difficult circum-
stances, a self-less, heroic deed. Military exploits"; but the word can
have a definite ironical meaning as well: "about any escapades, unseemly
deeds."[19] "Bezumnyj" (mad) in this context is negative (yet the related
word "bezumstvujuščij" need not be pejorative; cf. this word as applied to
Skrjabin, II, 356; also the ambiguous "No, kak bezumnyj, svetel den'" [But
like a madman the day is light "Silentium," 1910]). Together, these words
could suggest awe and incredulity at the feat. The feat, the "podvig
strelkov" (the exploit of your riflemen), refers to a specific historical

act. The "strelki" (Drużyny Strzeleckie") were bands of riflemen formed under the command of Pilsudski:

On the historic day of 6 August 1914 Pilsudski's first small band of ill-armed soldiers from the several pre-war military formations—the cavalry being provided with saddles but not with horses, the infantry armed mostly with obsolete one cartridge rifles, and no artillery at all marched out of Cracow, crossed the frontier of Russian Poland, and soon occupied the town of Kielce in the name of free and independent Poland. In spite of the small size of his force—five batallions in all—this action meant as important a _fait accompli_ as did, say, the first victory of Kościuszko.[20]

The second part illustrates with a chain of implied similes (the exploits are as "mad" as the possibility of . . .) the recklessness of the exploit. The device here is analogous to what is used in a "nebylica" (fable, tall tale): the story does not correspond to reality, the fiction is carried to the absurd. The first one is possible; a raven might peck eagles to death. The raven, clearly, is Poland, the eagle—Russia. If the eagle is usually associated with majesty, omnipotence, power, victory, and so forth, as is befitting the king of birds, then the raven, on the contrary, is traditionally associated with disease, greed, war, ill-omens, the soul of a wicked person; cf. in "Slovo o polku Igoreve" (The Tale of Igor's Campaign) "Togda po Ruskoj zemli rětko rataevě kikaxut', n" často vrani grajaxut', trupia sebě děljače" (Then over the Russian land rarely did the plowman call out, but the ravens cawed often, sharing the corpses); also in "Svetlana." Lines 4-6 are clearly absurd, in the tradition of the nebylica. We escalate from the possible to the impossible. Coming after this, lines 7 and 8 almost appear to be a non sequitur. Seemingly, it is as absurd to imagine the Vistula flowing backward as it is to imagine Poland in league with the Hapsburgs. The entire middle section builds up to this conclusion.

Of course, this is only from a Russian's point of view. For a Pole, it made great sense to side with Austria, "the one partitioning power to give them complete provincial self-government."[21] In the third section, Poland is called "Slavic" to underline its ties to Russia and not with the "Hapsburg crutch" (cf. Brjusov's "Pol'še": "Opjat' rodnogo nam naroda/My stali brat'jami . . ./I kriki 'Pol'ska ne sginela!'/Po-bratski s našim gimnom slej!" [To Poland" "We have again become the brothers/Of a people related to us . . . And the cries, "Poland has not perished"/Fuse in a brotherly fashion with our hymn!][22] Poland is also called a comet, again a negative image. A comet is traditionally an evil omen: "A comet which appears and passes by, and especially one with a tail, among the common people means social misfortune, that is, epidemic, famine, or war, etc."[23] Also, used metaphorically, it describes the course of someone's career; here it would refer to the changeable nature of Poland's power, coming and going like a comet.

If the neighbor of stanza five in "Zverinec" is Poland, the eagle must be Russia. We may read the two sentences as follows: "I ty, sosedka [cf. "I ty, slavjanskaja kometa," "Polacy!"], ne vzyšči: [potomu čto, za to čto] /Orel [Rossija] toporščitsja i zlitsja" (And you, neighbor [cf. And you, Slavic comet, Polacy!] don't be offended: [because] the eagle [Russia] bristles and is angry). A valuable clue for identifying the eagle with Russia is provided in Šum vremeni (The Noise of Time) "v každom dome, v černoj traurnoj ramke, visela kartinka: prostovolosaja devuška Suomi, nad kotoroj toporščitsja serdityj [=zlitsja] orel s dvojnoj golovkoj . . ." (II, 102, my italics; In every home, in a black mourning frame hung a picture: the bareheaded girl Suomi, over whom an angry two-headed eagle

bristled). Poland is likened to a weak David for whom the stone might be
too heavy: "Čto, esli dlja tvoej prašči/Tjaželyj kamen' ne goditsja?"
(What if the heavy stone isn't suited for your sling" (cf. I Samuel 17:49).
In terms of sheer size and strength Poland is to David as Russia is to
Goliath. But Poland is told not to be so arrogant as to think that it
is David; it can not even hold the stone, let alone fling it.

While a Golden Age in the past is alluded to in the first two stanzas, the last stanza provides hope for a future Golden Age. The "klet'"
(cage) of the fourth stanza becomes a "zverinec" (menagerie) in the last
one, a place to exhibit the animals. The animals, two brief portraits of
which were given in the above stanza, showing them to be pitiful and woe-
fully inadequate, are replaced by rivers, the Rhine and the Volga, which
become emblems for Germany and Russia. The emblems have changed from an
expression of war and destruction to one of life and perhaps purification.
The savage, too, has changed, now having grown wiser (l. 17 "dikar'," l. 45
"umudrennyj čelovek"). The military use of music, with its directly stimu-
lating effect, alluded to in the first stanza, has also gone through a
metamorphosis. Here we have dancing, a natural expression of united feeling and action. If we compare the lines from "Zverinec" with corresponding
ones from "Oda Betxovenu" Ode to Beethoven ([1914], "I umudrennyj čelovek/
Počtit nevol'no čužestranca,/Kak poluboga, bujstvom tanca . . ."; "Kto . . .
do tex por ne končil tanca,/Poka ne vyšel bujnyj xmel'?//O Dionis. . ."
[And man, having been made wiser,/Will involuntarily honor the foreigner,
/Like a demigod, with the turbulence of dance; Who . . . did not finish the
dance/Until the turbulent drunkenness was used up?/O Dionysis. . .]), we see
that also present is the motif of religious ecstasy. The Dionysiac rites
made use of wild dance and music with the effect of purgation and

purification.[24] In the first stanza, the negative, harmful aspects of

music are seen, those which contribute to discord and bellicosity. Here

we have music as ritual and religion. The state described in the last

stanza ("I umudrennyj čelovek/Počtit nevol'no čužestranca" [And man, having

become wiser,/Will involuntarily honor the foreigner]) is almost the op-

posite of what is existed in the Iron Age ("The father will not agree with

his children, nor the children with their father, nor guest with his

host."[25] It is practically a prescription of how to avoid war.

The antiwar, antimilitarism sentiment of "Zverinec" was expressed

earlier by Mandel'štam, in "Rejms i Kel'n" (Rheims and Cologne, 1915):

> . . . No v starom Kel'ne tože est' sobor,
> Nekončennyj i vse-taki prekrasnyj,
> I xot' odin svjaščennik bespristrastnyj,
> I v divnoj celosti strel'čatyj bor;
>
> On potrjasen čudoviščnym nabatom,
> I v groznyj čas, kogda gusteet mgla,
> Nemeckie pojut kolokola:
> "Čto sotvorili vy nad Rejmskim bratom!"
>
> . . . But there is a cathedral in old Cologne too,
> Unfinished and nonetheless beautiful,
> At least one unbiased priest,
> And a Gothic-arched pine-forest wonderful in its wholeness.
>
> It is shaken by the monstrous alarm,
> And in the dread hour when the gloom thickens,
> The German bells sing:
> "What have you done to our Rheims brother!"

Here, two famous cathedrals become emblems of two nations which are at

war. The first line seems to contain an implied threat: "But there is

a cathedral in ancient Cologne too [which might equally well be bombed]."

But this is precisely the point; the reader's expectations are frustrated.

The poem does not threaten revenge; it calls for brotherhood, the basis

being two ancient symbols of culture and peace.[26]

Chapter III

REVOLUTION

In a poem printed 15 November 1917 in the Socialist Revolutionary
paper "Volja naroda," Mandel'štam expressed his immediate response to the
fall of the Provisional Government:

> Kogda oktjabr'skij nam gotovil vremenščik
> Jarmo nasilija i zloby,
> I oščetinilsja ubijca-bronevik
> I pulemetčik nizkolobyj,--
>
> --Kerenskogo raspjat'!--potreboval soldat,
> I zlaja čern' rukopleskala:
> Nam serdce na štyki pozvolil vzjat' Pilat,
> I serdce bit'sja perestalo!
>
> I ukoriznenno mel'kaet èta ten',
> Gde zdanij krasnaja podkova;
> Kak budto slyšu ja v oktjabr'skij tusklyj den':
> Vjazat' ego, ščenka Petrova!
>
> Sredi graždanskix bur' i jarostnyx ličin,
> Tončajšim gnevom plameneja,
> Ty šel bestrepetno, svobodnyj graždanin,
> Kuda vela tebja Psixeja.
>
> I esli dlja drugix vostoržennyj narod
> Venki svivaet zolotye--
> Blagoslovit' tebja v dalekij ad sojdet
> Stopami legkimi Rossija.

> When October's favorite was preparing
> A yoke of violence and spite for us
> And the armored-car killer
> And the low-browed machinegunner bristled up,--
>
> "Crucify Kerenskij!"--demanded the soldier,
> And the vicious rabble applauded:
> Pilate allowed us to take the heart on bayonets,
> And the heart ceased beating!
>
> And reproachfully the shade flits by
> Where the red horseshoe of buildings is located,
> As if I hear on a dull October day:
> "Bind him, Peter's whelp!"

> Among civic storms and fierce masks,
> Blazing with the subtlest anger,
> You went dauntlessly, a free citizen,
> Where Psyche led you.
>
> And though the enraptured people
> Weaves gold wreathes for others—
> Russia will descend into distant hell
> With light steps to bless you.

Lenin is obviously "October's favorite" (vremenščik; the word is used in the historical sense of one who has gained power by questionable means). The revolutionaries are portrayed in the most derogatory terms: "pulemetčik nizkolobyj" (low-browed machinegunners) "zlaja čern'" (vicious rabble). At the other extreme, Kerenskij's fall is likened to Christ's crucifixion: "—Kerenskogo raspjat'!—potreboval soldat" ("Crucify him!"—demanded the soldier). Moreover, as has been shown,[1] "Vjazat' ego, ščenka Petrova!" (Bind him, Peter's whelp) is a ciphered citation from Boris Godunov: "Vjazat' Borisova ščenka!" (Bind Boris' whelp!). This subtext simultaneously suggests several things: that the mob, as in Boris Godunov, is fickle and easily manipulated. Moreover, the change of "Borisova ščenka" to "ščenka Petrova" implies that Kerenskij is in a sense a continuer of the line begun by Peter, the true Russian tradition. Freedom is associated with Kerenskij ("svobodnyj graždanin" [free citizen]) and is contrasted to Lenin's repression ("jarmo nasilija" [yoke of force]). The conclusion of the poem states that Russia may yet rue the choice of Lenin, but by then it will be too late.

The same tone of bitterness is to be found in another poem published shortly after the Bol'ševik revolution, "Kassandre" (To Cassandre):

Ja ne iskal v cvetuščie mgnoven'ja
Tvoix, Kassandra, gub, tvoix, Kassandra, glaz,
No v dekabre—toržestvennoe bden'e—
Vospominan'e mučit nas!

I v dekabre semnadcatogo goda
Vse poterjali my, ljubja:
Odin ograblen voleju naroda,
Drugoj ograbil sam sebja. . .

No, esli èta žizn'—neobxodimost' breda,
I korabel'nyj les—vysokie doma—
Leti, bezrukaja pobeda—
Giperborejskaja čuma!

Na ploščadi s bronevikami
Ja vižu čeloveka: on
Volkov gorjaščimi pugaet golovnjami:
Svoboda, ravenstvo, zakon!

Kasatka, milaja Kassandra,
Ty stoneš', ty goriš'—začem
Stojalo solnce Aleksandra
Sto let nazad, sijalo vsem?

Kogda-nibud' v stolice šaloj,
Na skifskom prazdnike, na beregu Nevy,
Pri zvukax omerzitel'nogo bala
Sorvut platok s prekrasnoj golovy. . .

                              (pub. 31 December 1917)

I did not seek in blooming moments
Your, Cassandra, lips, your, Cassandra, eyes,
But in December there is a solemn vigil—
Remembrance torments us.

And in December of seventeen
We lost all, loving:
One robbed by the will of the people,
Another robbed himself.

But if this life is the unavoidability of delerium,
And the tall houses are a forest of ships,
Fly, armless victory,
Hyperborean plague!

On a square with armored cars
I see a man: he
Is frightening wolves with burning logs:
Freedom, equality, law!

My darling swallow, dear Cassandra,
You moan, you burn: why
Did the sun of Alexander stand
A hundred years ago, shine to all?

Sometime in the mad capital,
At a Scythian feast, on the bank of the Neva,
To the sounds of a sickening ball
They'll tear your kerchief from your beautiful head. . .

In this poem, too, the political invective is unambiguous. The
revolutionaries are called "wolves" (l. 15; cf. Majakovskij's "Skazka o
krasnoj šapočke" [published 31 July 1917 in "Novaja žizn'"], against which
Mandel'štam is perhaps in part polemicizing: "A videvšie èto/volki
revoljucii scapali kadeta.//Izvestno, kakaja u volkov dieta./Vmeste s
manžetami sožrali kadeta." [The Tale of the Red Cap: And the wolves of the
revolution who saw this seized the Cadet.// It is well known what kind of
a diet wolves have./ Along with the cuffs they gobbled the Cadet]). They
are frightened by "freedom, equality, law"; the substitution of "law" in
the traditional formula "freed, equality, brotherhood" is striking. It is
precisely a concept of "law" which is absent from the chaos being portrayed: "Odin ograblen voleju naroda [perhaps a pun: this poem was
published in the Socialist Revolutionary "Volja naroda" The Will of the
People; it also suggests the terrorism of Željabov's "Narodnaja volja,
People's Will],/Drugoj ograbil sam sebja" (One robbed by the will of the
people,/Another robbed himself). The ending of this poem is even stronger
than that of "Kogda oktjabr'skij nam gotovil vremenščik": "Na skifskom
prazdnike . . . sorvut platok s prekrasnoj golovy. . . ." (At a Scythian
feast . . ., they'll tear your kerchief from your beautiful head). The
Scythians were barbaric and primitive (cf. "O vremenax prostyx i grubyx"
[1914]: "Ovidij pel arbu volov'ju/V poxode varvarskix teleg" Of times

simple and coarse; Ovid sang the bullock cart/In the march of barbarian

waggons); the Scythian feast, where Axmatova's kerchief will be torn

off,[2] suggests the destruction of beauty by those who do not comprehend

it (cf. earlier, in "Axmatova" [1914]: "V pol-oborota, o pečal',/Na

ravnodušnyx pogljadela./Spadaja s pleč, okamenela/Ložno-klassičeskaja

šal'.//Zloveščij golos--gor'kij xmel'--/Duši raskovyvaet nedra:/Tak--

negodujuščaja Fedra--/Stojala nekogda Rašel'" (With a half-turn, oh grief,

/She glanced at the indifferent./Falling from her shoulders,/The pseudo-

classical shawl turned to stone.//An ominous voice--bitter intoxication--

/Unfetters the depths of the soul:/So,--an indignant Phaedra--/Rachel

once stood).[3]

"Dekabrist" (The Decembrist) was published one week earlier than

"Kassandre." Here, however, the message is much more subtle and ambiguous:

> -Tomu svidetel'stvo jazyčeskij senat-
> Sii dela ne umirajut!
> On raskuril čubuk i zapaxnul xalat,
> A rjadom v šaxmaty igrajut.
>
> Čestoljubivyj son on promenjal na srub
> V gluxom uročišče Sibiri,
> I vyčurnyj čubuk u jadovityx gub,
> Skazavšix pravdu v skorbnom mire.
>
> Šumeli v pervyj raz germanskie duby,
> Evropa plakala v tenetax.
> Kvadrigi černye vstavali na dyby
> Na triumfal'nyx povorotax.
>
> Byvalo, goluboj v stakanax punš gorit.
> S širokim šumon samovara
> Podruga rejnskaja tixon'ko govorit,
> Vol'noljubivaja gitara.
>
> -Ešče volnujutsja živye golosa
> O sladkoj vol'nosti graždanstva!
> No žertvy ne xotjat slepye nebesa:
> Vernee trud i postojanstvo.

Vse pereputalos', i nekomu skazat',
Čto, postepenno xolodeja,
Vse pereputalos' i sladko povtorjat':
Rossija, Leta, Loreleja.

"The Decembrist"

"The pagan senate is witness to the fact that—
These deeds do not die!"
He puffed at his <u>chibouk</u> and drew up his dressing gown,
And close by they were playing chess.

He exchanged an ambitious dream for a hut
In a remote place in Siberia,
And for a fancy <u>chibouk</u> at his poisonous lips
Which had told the truth in the sorrowful world.

German oaks stirred for the first time,
Europe wept in nets.
Black quadrigas reared up
On triumphal bends.

In former times blue punch burned in glasses.
The Rhenish friend,
The freedom loving guitar,
Speaks with the broad noise of the samovar.

"Lively voices are still excited
About the sweet liberty of citizenship.
But the blind heavens do not want sacrifice:
Labor and constancy are more sure.

Everything got entangled and there is no one to tell
That, gradually growing colder,
Everything got entangled and it is sweet to repeat:
Russia, Lethe, Lorelei.

"Dekabrist" consists of six four-line stanzas of alternating six-
and four-foot iambic lines, rhyming aBaB (where B is feminine). This
strophic form is often associated with the genre of elegies, and in particular, with such elegies of Puškin as "Pod nebom golubym,"
"Vospominanie," "Na xolmax Gruzii. . ." (Under the Blue Sky, Remembrance
On the Hills of Georgia). As Tomaševskij has written,[4] these three
elegies are united by a common theme: remembrance. While we would not

say that "Dekabrist" is an elegy, it has, to some extent, elegaic characteristics. We are given the reminiscences of a Decembrist, whose thoughts
are presented in lines 1-2, 17-27. More broadly speaking, the entire poem,
on one level, is a kind of poetic remembrance of Decembrism, its ideals
and the milieu in which it was fostered. From this point of view, the meter
may be perceived as a signal. For the elegaic lyric was widely cultivated
at the beginning of the nineteenth century. It was a genre which some
Decembrist poets rejected (Kjuxel'beker, for example), but which others
utilized in a new way, turning the sentimental, personal elegy into a
vehicle for philosophical or political meditations (Raevskij's elegies,
Glinka's elegaic psalms).

Mandel'štam's poem, through the use of certain signal words, may be
comprehended as a composit of discrete elements which serve to recreate
the essence of Decembrist thought and aesthetics. One of these elements
is lexical. Substantives, for example, can for the most part be assigned
to one of three possible strata: Classical ("senat," "kvadrigi,"
"[triumfal'nye] povoroty," "Leta" senate, quadrigae [triumphal] bends,
Lethe), Russian ("senat," "čubuk," "xalat," "šaxmaty," "Sibir'," "punš,"
"samovar," "žertvy," "Rossija" senate, chibouk, dressing gown, chess,
Siberia punch, samovar, sacrifices, Russia), German ("[germanskie] duby,"
[rejnskaja] podruga," "gitara," "Loreleja" [(German) oaks, (Rheine) friend,
guitar, Lorelei]). In well-developed poetic styles, certain characteristic
words have the ability to evoke for the reader a set of habitual associations.[5] The term "word signals" are particularly apt in this connection,
insofar as the term was used by V. Gofman in his article in Ryleev's
poetry:

The roots of the political phraseology which Ryleev utilized as a signal system heightening the agitational meaning of a poem go back to the Great French Revolution. The signals were the most general elements of the general liberation slogans of the bourgeoisie: 'freedom' ['svoboda'], 'love for fatherland' ['ljubov' k otečestvu'] 'rights of citizenship' ['prava graždanstva'], 'citizen' [graždanin'] 'social good' ['obščestvennoe blago'], 'popular good' ['narodnoe blago'], 'tyranny' ['tiranstvo'], 'autocracy' ['samovlastie'].

These were elements current in the political language of certain circles, even high ones, at the beginning of the XIX century . . . Such elements, which became phraseological units, formulas, signalized a certain order of 'shocking' ideas and concepts in whatever context they happened to fall.[6]

Another essential element in this poem is the archaic thrust of the Decembrist's words. As has been shown,[7] Decembrist poets frequently made use of lofty words, favoring an abundance of Slavonicisms and biblicisms. Along with this, there is a definite oratorical, rhetorical tendency. Lastly, Decembrist poetry freely drew upon motifs from classical (Greek and Roman) literature and history. As Tynjanov has observed: "Classical material was a conventional semantic tint in the current artistic and political speech. . . Antiquity in the 1820s was a simple mask of contemporary themes which fooled no one, a mask, to be sure, which was not accidental, if one takes into account that the revolutionaries of the twenties searched far and wide for their traditions, including in antiquity."[8]

All of these elements, to a greater or lesser extent, are present in Mandel'štam's poem. The first two lines of the poem present the direct speech of the Decembrist. The oratorical orientation of his words is obvious. "Senat" (senate) and "sii dela" (these deeds) are elements from a Decembrist's vocabulary. The word senate works on at least two historical levels. For a contemporary, the senate was the symbol of Republicanism, what Kerensky stood for. It also evokes the scene of the Decembrist uprising. However, the adjective "pagan" (jazyčeskij) suggests that we go back further in time, to a pre-Christian senate of Rome. This senate, for a Decembrist, would have these associations. It was the place where Julius Caesar was murdered and hence is inextricably bound with the name of Brutus. Brutus was, for a Decembrist, the person who toppled the power of kings: "On a table in my room was a book from which I read to Grabbe several letters of Brutus to Cicero, in which the former, having decided to act against Octavius, accuses the latter of cowardice."[9] His name figures prominently in Decembrist poetry. The word "vol'nost'" (freedom) is obviously from the lexical stock of Decembrist poetry, as are "graždanstvo," and "pravda" (citizenship, truth). Very important, too, is the word "žertva" (sacrifice), which occurs throughout the poetry of the Decembrists and those who wrote about them.[10] The word "sladkij" (sweet) ("O sladkoj vol'nosti graždanstva," ". . . i sladko povtorjat'" [about the sweet liberty of citizenship; it's sweet to repeat]) is also significant; it conveys the tonality of the elegaic style of early romantic poetry. "This epithet--'sladkij,' 'sladostnyj,'--became one of the signs of the style of elegaic . . . romanticism of the years 1800-1820. It was repeated literally hundreds of times."[11] The word "skorbnyj" (sorrowful) ("v skorbnom mire" [in the sorrowful world]) is also characteristic.

As stated, Mandel'štam's poem not only recreates the style of Decembrist poetry, but elements of the Decembrists' life style, the historical factors which contributed to the Decembrist movement, and the fate of the Decembrists. Thus, line 4 focuses on a scene characteristic of the Decembrists' life style ("A rjadom v šaxmaty igrajut" [And close by they were playing chess]). Jakuškin wrote:

In the Semenov regiment an artel was formed: about fifteen or twenty officers got together in order to have the opportunity of dining together every day; not only those who were in the artel dined, but everyone who was obliged by duties to spend the entire day in the regiment. After dinner some played chess, others read loudly foreign newspapers and followed events in Europe -- such a pastime was a decided innovation. In 1811, when I entered the Semenov regiment, officers who gathered together either played cards, remorselessly swindling each other, or drank and caroused.[12]

Many Decembrists seem to have smoked a chibouk, as can be ascertained from the numerous pictures in which they are shown holding or smoking one (see, for example, those reproduced in Literaturnoe nasledstvo, vol. 60, bk. 2 M., 1956, pp. 316, 365, 366, 393). A picture which might serve as a source for the lines "On raskuril čubuk i zapaxnul xalat,/A rjadom v šaxmaty igrajut" (He puffed on his chibouk and drew up his dressing gown/And close by they are playing chess) can be found in a collection of pictures about the Decembrists and their way of life.[13] It is a tableau with six Decembrists at ease in a one-room wood-frame cottage. All are wearing dressing-gowns; four smoke chibouks. The focal-point of the picture is a group of three in the center foreground, two playing chess and one standing, gazing forward to the right, chibouk in hand. On the right extreme is a pair of men smoking and apparently engaged in conversation. At left and to the rear, a reclining man is reading in bed.

The first two lines, then, focus on the Senate, realistic and metaphoric, from the vantage point of Siberia. Lines 3-8 describe the cite of the Decembrists' exile--Siberia. The third and fourth stanzas succinctly characterize the historical situation at the time of Decembrism. Line 9, "Šumeli v pervyj raz germanskie duby" (German oaks stirred for the first time) may be understood as referring both to early romanticism and revolutionary tendencies, both associated with Germany. Germany was very important, for a number of reasons, in helping to form the Decembrists' views. As Jakuškin wrote: "A whole year's stay in Germany and then several months in Paris could not but change, if only a little, the opinions of thinking Russian youth. . . ; each of us grew somewhat."[14] Puškin's characterization of Lenskij, albeit in a decidedly ironic tone, shows how important Germany was:

> On iz Germanii tumannoj ["svobodnoj" in the rough draft]
> Privez učennosti plody:
> Vol'noljubivye mečty,
> Dux pylkij i dovol'no strannyj,
> Vsegda vostoržennuju reč'
> I kudri černye do pleč.
>
> (<u>Evgenij</u> <u>Onegin</u>, II, 6)
>
> From misty Germany ["free" in the rough draft]
> He brought the fruits of learning:
> Freedom-loving dreams,
> An ardent and rather strange spirit,
> Always enthusiastic speech,
> And black curls to his shoulders.

"Kinžal" (The Dagger) too, shows what Germany meant at the time in which Decembrism matured.

If Line 9 may be understood as referring to the revolutionary and nationalistic tendencies fostered in German intellectual circles, then line 10, "Evropa plakala v tenetax" (Europe wept in nets) surely refers to the conservative reaction that was overtaking Europe in the beginning of the nineteenth century: the banning of the Tugenbund, the Carlsbad decrees, the antirevolutionary alliance of Austria, Russia, and possibly as well to the despotic autocracy that came to Russia in the wake of the abortive Decembrist revolt. Lines 12-13 support this interpretation. A quadriga was a four-horsed chariot used by Roman generals in their

triumphs. On it, they would enter Rome to shouts of "Io Triumphe" to receive a laurel branch (see Ovid, Tristia, IV, 251ff). This is the first
impression created by the image of the rearing quadrigas. It is part of
the network of classical allusions which are found in this poem. "Povorot"
can refer to a figurative change in direction, a change in the development
of something (n.b. "povorot rulja" [turn of the rudder] in "Sumerki
svobody" [Dawn of Freedom]). It is the word "povorot" which is modified
by the adjective "triumfal'nyj" (triumphal).[15] This triumphal change refers to the change in the direction of European policies, a change from
left to right, from liberal to conservative, which swept over Europe. In
"Krovavaja misterija 9-go janvarja" (The Bloody Mystery Play of January 9)
Mandel'štam uses the image of a rearing four-horsed chariot in relation
to another abortive revolution, that of 1905:

> Peterburg estestvenno tečet v moščnyj
> granitnyj vodoem Dvorcovoj ploščadi, k krasnoj
> podkove zdanij, rassečennoj nadvoe glubokoj
> mednobitnoj arkoj s vzvivšejsja na dyby
> ristališčnoj četverkoj.
>
> (III, 130; this is an accurate description of the
>   architecture.)
>
> Petersburg flows naturally into the mighty
> granite reservoir of the Palace Square, toward
> the red horseshoe of buildings, which is cleft in
> two by a deep, beaten-copper arch with a team of
> four rearing hippodrome horses.

The fourth stanza connects Russia ("širokij šum samovara" [the broad
noise of the samovar]) and Germany ("podruga rejnskaja," "vol'noljubivaja
gitara" [Rhenish friend, freedom-loving guitar]). The punch, the samovar,
the guitar place us in the social milieu of the time, suggesting, on the
one hand a German student society. Then, the German fraternities (e.g. the

Tugenbund) were progressive and in opposition to reactionary elements. But note too that line 13, "Byvalo, goluboj v stakanax punš gorit" (in former times, blue punch burned in glasses), recalls the party described in "Mednyj vsadnik": "A v čas piruški xolostoj/Šipen'e penistyx bokalov/ I punša plamen' goluboj" [And at the hour of a bachelor party/The sputtering of foamy goblets/And the blue flame of punch]). Even drinking songs could be transformed into political hymns—as, for example, Jazykov's "My ljubim šumnye piry" (We love noisy banquets) which combines hedonism with politically radical motifs.[16] Such a poem as Puškin's "Veselyj pir" (Gay Banquet) (Ja ljublju večernij pir,/Gde vesel'e predsedatel',/A svoboda, moj kumir,/Za stolom zakonodatel'. ." [I love an evening banquet/Where merriment is the chairman,/ And Freedom, my idol,/ Is the legislator at the table] can be read within this context. This stanza expands what was left implicit in the preceding one: that there was an intimate connection between early German freedom-loving ideals and the emergence of Russian liberalism. One helped give birth to the other.

"Ešče volnujutsja živye golosa" (Lively voices are still agitated) returns us to the direct speech of the Decembrist. His words here, as well as in line 2, "Sii dela ne umirajut" (These deeds do not die) are important in focusing on the continuing nature of the Decembrist movement. From this point of view, the poem, to a certain extent, may be understood as polemicizing against some of those who had written about Decembrism before Mandel'štam. Stated simply, there were two responses to the Decembrist revolt. Some understood it as an act whose meaning would continue to reverberate into future generations. Nekrassov's "Russkie ženščiny" (Russian Women) (see 11. 861–868) typifies this view; Puškin's "Vo glubine sibirskix rud" (In the depth of Siberian mines) (1827) also conveys such an under-

standing. But other poets understood the significance of the Decembrists

differently. Lermontov, for example, in "Pamjati A. I. O[doevsko]go" (To

the Memory of A. I. O-go) was very pessimistic in feeling that the Decem-

brists' work would die with them. However, it is against Tjutčev, we

feel, that Mandel'štam is polemicizing. "Dekabrist" sounds like a rejoinder

to Tjutčev's "14-oe dekabrja 1825" ("14 December 1825"—which was entitled

"Dekabristam" ["To the Decembrists"] in the 1886 edition of his works):

> Vas razvratilo Samovlast'e,
> I meč ego vas porazil,—
> I v nepodkupnom bespristrast'e
> Sej prigovor Zakon skrepil.
> Narod, čuždajas' verolomstva,
> Ponosit vaši imena—
> I vaša pamjat' ot potomstva,
> Kak trup v zemle, sxoronena.
>
> O žertvy mysli besrassudnoj,
> Vy upovali, možet byt',
> Čto stanet vašej krovi skudnoj,
> Čtob večnyj poljus rastopit'!
> Edva, dymjas', ona sverknula
> Na vekovoj gromade l'dov,
> Zima železnaja doxnula—
> I ne ostalas' i sledov.

> Autocracy has corrupted you,
> And its sword has struck you —
> And in incorruptible impartiality
> The Law has ratified this sentence.
> The people, shunning perfidy,
> Abuse your names —
> And your memory, for posterity
> Is buried like a corpse in the earth.
>
> O victims of reckless thought,
> You hoped, perhaps,
> That there would be enough of your meagre blood
> To melt the eternal pole!
> Smoking, it had scarcely flashed
> On the ancient bulk of ice,

> Iron winter breathed --
> And no traces remained.

Tjutčev's poem presents the Decembrist revolt as being without purpose, an act which would have no further consequences. The Decembrists' attempt was vain and senseless; they and their act are fleeting. The permanency of autocracy, given in allegorical images ("večnyj poljus," "vekovaja gromada l'dov," "železnaja zima" [eternal pole, ancient bulk of ice, iron winter]) is juxtaposed to the Decembrist revolt, which is condemned by the people. To the lines "Vaša pamjat' ot potomstva,/Kak trup v zemle, sxoronena" (And your memory, for posterity, is buried like a corpse in the earth) and "I ne ostalos' i sledov" (And no traces remained) Mandel'štam seems to reply through the Decembrist's "Sii dela ne umirajut," "Ešče volnujutsja živye golosa" (These deeds do not die; Living voices are still agitated).

It is impossible to state conclusively who utters the words in stanza six:

> Vsë pereputalos', i nekomu skazat'
> Čto, postepenno xolodeja,
> Vsë pereputalos' i sladko povtorjat':
> Rossija, Leta, Loreleja.

> Everything got entangled and there is no one to tell
> That, gradually growing colder,
> Everything got entangled and it is sweet to repeat:
> Russia, Lethe, Lorelei.

It might be the Decembrist, continuing his soliloquy. The phrase "sladko povtorjat'" (it is sweet to repeat) recalls "sladkaja vol'nost'" (sweet freedom)— such a modifier being characteristic of the Decembrist's speech pattern. Yet Mandel'štam himself could easily have uttered such words; cf. "O svobode nebyvaloj/Sladko dumat' u sveči" (Near the candle it's sweet to think/About imaginary freedom) (1915; my italics); this poem, incidentally, expresses sentiments similar to those voiced by the Decembrist: "Nam li, brošennym v prostranstve,/Obrečennym umeret',/O prekrasnom postojanstve/ I o vernosti žalet'!" (Should we, abandoned in space,/Doomed to die,/Regret beautiful constancy/And faithfulness?); cf. lines 19-20: "No žertvy ne xotjat slepye nebesa:/Vernee trud i postojanstvo" (But the blind Leavens do not want sacrifice:/Labor and constancy are more sure). "Gradually growing colder" might seem to refer to the person who is speaking, i.e. metaphorically to a loss of hope, ardor, emotional energy. However, this gerund governs the subject of the phrase "vsë pereputalos'" (i.e. vsë pereputalos' i nekomu skazat', čto vsë, postepenno xolodeja, pereputalos' [Everything got entangled and there is no one to tell that everything, gradually growing colder, got entangled]). Might this ("vsë pereputalos'") not refer to the events which took place on the day of 14 December? Cf. "Peterburgskie strofy" ([Petersburg Stanzas] 1915): "Na ploščadi senata-- val sugroba,/Dymok kostra i xolodok styka" (On the square of the senate-- the billow of a snow drift,/Smoke of a bonfire and bayonet's cold)--the cold referring here to the atmosphere, both real and metaphoric.

The last three words of "Dekabrist," "Russia, Lethe, Lorelei," restate all of the themes in the poem. Russia is what the Decembrist was dedicated to; it includes both the Senate Square, the site of the uprising, and Siberia, the place where the Decembrist was exiled after the revolt. Lethe completes the network of classical associations. It is the river from which souls drink after their death, and hence may be understood as relating to the death of the Decembrist. Lorelei, the name of a rock on the Rhine, was the subject of many German romantic works (Clemens Brentano, Godwi; Josef Eichendorff, Ahnung und Gegenwart; Otto Heinrich von Leben, "Die Lorelei"; Heinrich Heine, "Die Lorelei"). It recalls the "Rhenish friend" and completes the theme of German romanticism. We may be justified in reading still more into these last two words. Lethe's water was drunk by souls about to be reincarnated, so that they forgot their previous existence. Might this therefore not refer to the reincarnation of the Decembrist, his reemergence in modern times? "Dekabrist" was, after all, published on 24 December 1917, some two months after the Bol'ševik takeover.

The association of Lorelei to Russia must be considered since they are emphatically juxtaposed in the concluding triad. What is basic to the various romantic reworkings of the old Rhine legend of Lorelei is that she causes destruction. This is clearly evident in Heine's "Die Lorelei," the most famous poem on this subject:

> Ich weiss nicht, was soll es bedeuten,
> Dass ich so traurig bin;
> Ein Märchen aus alten Zeiten,
> Das kommt mir nicht aus dem Sinn.
>
> Die Luft ist kühl und es dunkelt.
> Und ruhig fliesst der Rhein;
> Der Gipfel des Berges funkelt
> Im Abendsonnenschein.
>
> Die schönste Jungfrau sitzet
> Dort oben wunderbar,
> Ihr goldnes Geschmeide blitzet,
> Sie kämmt ihr goldenes Haar.
>
> Sie kämmt es mit goldenem Kamme,
> Und singt ein Lied dabei;
> Das hat eine wundersame,
> Gewaltige Melodei.

Den Schiffer im kleinen Schiffe
Ergreift es mit wildem Weh;
Er schaut nicht die Felsenriffe,
Er schaut nur hinauf in die Hoh.

Ich glaube, die Wellen verschlingen
Am Ende Schiffer und Kahn;
Und das hat mit ihrem Singen
Die Lorelei getan.

(In his Voronež "Stansy" (1935), Mandel'štam again used the image of Lorelei: "Ja pomnju vse—nemeckix brat'ev šei/I čto lilovym grebnem Lorelei/Sadovnik i palač [=Hitler] napolnil svoj dosug" [I remember everything—the necks of German brothers/and that the gardener and executioner [=Hitler] filled his leisure with Lorelei's lilac comb]) Heine's Lorelei has been interpreted as being a symbol of the destructive strength of love or beauty. What is germane to our understanding of "Dekabrist" is the fact that her singing brings catastrophe to the boatman and his boat; the boatman, instead of paying attention to the submerged rocks, listens to Lorelei, and thus is destroyed.

Like "Dekabrist," the message conveyed in "Sumerki svobody" (The Dawn of Freedom) is neither simple nor overt:

Proslavim, brat'ja, sumerki svobody,—
Velikij sumerečnyj god.
V kipjaščie nočnye vody
Opuščen gruznyj les tenet.
Vosxodiš' ty v gluxie gody,
O solnce, sudija, narod.

Proslavim rokovoe bremja,
Kotoroe v slezax narodnyj vožd' beret.
Proslavim vlasti sumračnoe bremja,
Ee nevynosimyj gnet.
V kom serdce est', tot dolžen slyšat', vremja,
Kak tvoj korabl' ko dnu idet.

My v legiony boevye
Svjazali lastoček-i vot
Ne vidno solnca; vsja stixija
Ščebečet, dvižetsja, živet;
Skvoz' seti -- sumerki gustye --
Ne vidno solnca i zemlja plyvet.

Nu čto ž, poprobuem: ogromnyj, neukljužij,
Skripučij povorot rulja.
Zemlja plyvet. Mužajtes', muži.
Kak plugom, okean delja,
My budem pomnit' i v letejskoj stuže,
Čto desjati nebes nam stoila zemlja.

Let us glorify, brothers, the dawn of freedom,--
The great crepuscular year.
Into the seething night waters
The massive forest of hunting-nets is lowered.
You are rising in forlorn years,
Oh sun, judge, people.

Let us glorify the fateful burden
Which the people's leader assumes in tears.
Let us glorify the somber burden of power,
Its intolerable weight.
He who has a heart must hear, O time,
Your ship going to the bottom.

We have bound swallows
Into battle legions--and now
The sun is not visible, the whole element
Twitters, moves, lives;
Through the nets--dense dawn--
The sun is not visible and the earth floats.

Well, then, let's try: an enormous, clumsy,
Creaking turn of the rudder.
The earth floats. Courage, men.
As with a plough, dividing the ocean,
We will remember even in Lethe's extreme cold
That the earth cost us ten heavens.

"Sumerki svobody" was first published in "Znamja truda," 24 May
1918, with the subtitle "hymn." A hymn (from Greek "hymnos," festive
song, ode) originally was a festive song in praise of gods; it was in time
expanded to include festive songs glorifying persons or events. The

communist hymn, for example, is the "Internationale." As we will see, the subtitle "hymn," as used here, should not be taken wholly at face value; indeed, in the context of the entire poem, "hymn" becomes decidedly ironic.

The ambiguous nature of this poem is obvious both in the title and the theme of the first stanza, Sumerki; it means either semidarkness coming after sunset (twilight), or semidarkness preceding sunrise (dawn). Normally,[17] unless the word "sumerki" appears with a modifier specifying morning ("sumerki utra," "predrassvetnye sumerki"), it primarily indicates evening twilight. In addition to the expected usage of this word, the signals given in the first four lines of Mandel'štam's poem would tend to underline the assumption that "sumerki" here is twilight: sumerki--sumerečnyj god--nočnye vody--opuščen ("sumerki," crepuscular year, night waters, lowered). But I believe that Mandel'štam's choice of the word "sumerki" is calculatedly ambiguous. The ambiguity is resolved in line five with the appearance of the word "vosxodiš'" (you are rising [sun]) which clearly signifies that "sumerki" means "utrennie sumerki" (morning "sumerki," dawn)--yet the previous signals remain.[18]

The first word of the poem is "proslavim" (let us glorify), which re-iterates the subtitle, "hymn." The form of the verb is first person imperative, thus including the speaker, the poetic "I," among those who should praise. Similarly, the second word, "brat'ja" (brothers), a vocative address, emphasizes the communal nature of the exhortation. The poem thus begins with two marked forms, the imperative and the vocative.

The syntagma "gluxie gody" in line five is difficult. The epithet "gluxie" clearly connotes more than the idea of deaf; rather, it implies something god-forsaken, remote. These are the same words with which

Mandel'štam begins Šum vremeni: "Ja pomnju xorošo gluxie gody Rossii--
devjanostye gody, ix medlennoe opolzanie, ix boleznennoe spokojstvie, ix
glubokij provincializm--tixuju zavod': poslednee ubežišče umirajuščego
veka." (I remember well the forlorn years of Russia -- the decade of the
nineties, their slow sliding, their morbid quiet, their deep provincialism
-- a quiet backwater: the last refuge of a dying age.) In this instance,
Mandel'štam has in mind the idea of "gluxaja pora"--a time characterized
by the absence of any activity (see Aseev's "Pervomajskij gimn" [(May 1st
Hymn) 1920]: "Byla pora gluxaja,/byla pora nemaja,/no cvel, blagouxaja,/
rabočij prazdnik maja." [It was a deaf time (stagnant time), it was a dumb
time,/but you bloomed, fragrant,/worker's holiday of May]). Also possible
is an allusion to Blok's poem: "Roždennye v goda gluxie/Puti ne pomnjat
svoego./My--deti strašnyx let Rossii--/Zabyt' ne v silax ničego" (my
italics) [Those born in forelorn years/Do not remember their path./ We --
children of the terrible years of Russia --/ Are unable to forget anything].
Thus the almost stereotyped equation of the three nouns in line 6, "solnce,"
"sudija," "narod" (sun judge, people), which would seem unquestionably
positive without the preceding phrase "gluxie gody," is noteworthy and unexpected. (In a "normal" hymn, God, judge, people is clear. Here the
phrase is surrounded by negative or ambivalent things. Both responses are
called for by Mandel'štam's usage.

The revolution is ideally the assumption of power by the people;
hence they are the judge. Mandel'štam, even in exile in Voronež, continued to assert this belief: "Esli b menja naši vragi vzjali/I perestali
so mnoj govorit' ljudi;/Esli b lišili menja vsego v mire--/Prava dyšat' i
otkryvat' dveri/I utverždat', čto bytie budet,/I čto narod, kak sudija,

sudit. . ." (1937 [If our enemies took me/And people stopped talking to me;/If I was deprived of everything in the world--/The right to breathe and open doors/And affirm that being will be/And that the people, like a judge, judge]). As Axmatova wrote, "Mandel'štam was one of the first to begin writing verses on civic themes. For him the revolution was an enormous event and the word 'people' does not figure in his verse accidentally."[19] The idea of the people as light and judge can be found frequently in poetry written at the time of the revolution. See, for example, V. T. Kirillov's "My" (We): "Vsë--my, vo vsem--my, my plamen' i svet pobeždajuščij,/Sami sebe Božestvo, i Sud'ja, i Zakon" (Everything -- we, in everything - we, we are the flame and conquering light,/We are our own Deity, Judge, and Law).

Lines 7 through 10 seem fairly straightforward. Mandel'štam elaborates on what is to be praised. The "leader" referred to is undoubtedly Lenin. The Dictionary of the Contemporary Russian Literary Language provides the following definition of "vožd'": "Political leader and teacher of the Communist Party and working people, who is the spokesman of its will, strivings, desires. . . .'Lenin was the leader not only of the Russian proletariat, not only of the European workers . . . but of all the workers of the world.' Stalin. Speech at the Second All-Union Congress of Soviets 26 Jan. 1924." (See Bednyj's "Voždju (Tov. Leninu v den' rabočej pečati posvjaščaju [To the Leader (To Comrade Lenin on the day of the worker's press I dedicate this)] Pravda, 4 May 1918). Mandel'štam provides his own gloss on these lines in "Slovo i kul'tura" The Word and Culture (1921): "Net ničego bolee golodnogo, čem sovremennoe gosudarstvo, a golodnoe gosudarstvo strašnee golodnogo čeloveka. Sostradanie k gosudarstvu, otricajuščemu slovo—obščestvennyj put' i podvig sovremennogo

poèta" (There is nothing hungrier than the contemporary government, and a

hungry government is more terrible than a hungry person. Compassion for a

government which denies the word is the social path and exploit of the con-

temporary poet; lines 7-10 of "Sumerki svobody" follow [II, 268]). The

phrase "in tears" points to the highly emotional nature of Lenin's assump-

tion of power and probably should not be interpreted as having any ironic

overtones. The "sombre burden of power" ("vlasti sumračnoe bremja") may

also characterize the leader's view of his responsibilities. The second

stanza closes with an image of a sinking ship. Viewed as representing time

("Vremja. . .tvoj korabl'"), the ship is going to the bottom because with

the revolution the continuum represented by Czarist Russia came to an end

(cf. "Našedšij podkovu": "Xrupkoe letoisčislenie našej èry podxodit k

koncu." [The fragile chronology of our era is coming to an end]).

The third stanza opens with the image of swallows. In traditional

folklore, the swallow has several associations: a builder, contentment in

poverty, diligence; also, hopefulness, rebirth, spring. Significantly,

the image of swallows suggests both hopefulness and the capacity to build;

bound together in large numbers, they might be capable of great strength.

In the context of this poem swallows might be equated with the Russian

people. There are numerous instances where birds are metaphoric for the

Russian people. Gogol's famous troika apostrophe from Dead Souls immediate-

ly comes to mind. "Ex, trojka! ptica trojka, kto tebja vydumal? (Eh,

trojka! bird trojka, who invented you?). Mandel'štam, in "Xolodnoe leto"

(Cold Summer) saw Russians as a flock of birds: "Malen'kie prodavščicy

duxov stojat na Petrovke, protiv Mjur-Merliza—prižavšis' k stenke, celym

vyvodkom lotok k lotku. Ètot malen'kij otrjad prodavščic--tol'ko stajka.
Vorob'inaja, kurnosaja armija moskovskix devušek. . ." (Small vendors of
perfumes stand on the Petrovka, opposite Mjur-Merliza -- pressed up to the
wall, a whole brood, hawker's tray to hawker's tray. This small detachment
of vendors is only a little flock. A sparrow, snub-nosed army of Moscow
girls. . . . II, 167). Further on in this essay, Mandel'štam uses the
word swallow ("kasatka") in referring to the French revolutionaries giving
as a framework a paraphrase from Barbier:

> Vspominaju jamb Barb'e: "Kogda tjaželyj znoj prožeg bol'šie kamni".
> V dni kogda roždalas' svoboda--"èta grubaja devka, bastil'skaja
> kasatka" [cf. Barbier, "C'est la vierge fouguese, enfant de la
> Bastille. . .," "La Curée"] --Pariž besnovalsja ot žary--no žit'
> nam v Moskve, seroglazoj i kurnosoj, s vorob'inym xolodkom v
> ijule. . . . (II, 168

> I recall Barbier's iamb: "When the severe heat burned through the
> large stones." In the days when freedom was being born -- "This
> coarse girl, the Bastille swallow. . ." -- Paris was raging from the
> heat -- but we must live in Moscow, gray-eyed and snubnosed, with a
> sparrow-like chill in July. . .).

Another possibility which needs to be considered is the connection
between the swallow and the soul. In Mandel'štam's poetry we have this
equation in, for instance, "Kogda Psixeja žizn' spuskaetsja k tenjam"
(When Psyche-life descends to the shades) and "Ja slovo pozabyl, čto ja
xotel skazat'" (I forgot the word I wanted to say).[20] (Also, even earlier,
in "Pod grozovymi oblakami" [Under thunder clouds; 1909]: "V svjaščennom
straxe tvar' živet,/I každyj soveršit dušoju,/Kak lastočka pered grozoju,/
Neopisuemyj polet" [A creature lives in sacred fear,/ And each performs
with its soul,/ Like a swallow before the storm,/ An indescribable flight]).
The prototype is perhaps Deržavin's "Lastočka" (Swallow). Swallow-soul

and swallow-Russian people reinforce rather than exclude each other.
Finally, one should note Mandel'štam's comments in "Razgovor o Dante"
(Talking about Dante):

> Dantovskie sravnenija nikogda ne byvajut opisatel'ny, to est'
> čisto izobrazitel'ny. Oni vsegda presledujut konkretnuju zadaču
> dat' vnutrennij obraz struktury ili tjagi. Voz'mem obširnejšuju
> gruppu "ptič'ix" sravnenij—vse èti tjanuščiesja karavany to
> žuravlej, to gračej, to klassičeskie voennye falangi lastoček. . .
> (II, 416)
>
> Dante's similes are never descriptive, that is, purely depicting.
> They always pursue the concrete task of giving the inner image of
> the structure or the tractive force. Let us take the rather large
> group of "bird" similes — all these extended caravans now of
> cranes, now rooks, now classical military phalanxes of swallows. . . .

What Mandel'štam had in mind in the last instance is not clear; a careful
check of Dante's Comedy reveals no such imagery.

The swallows are bound together with mesh, nets ("skvoz' seti,"
1.17). This image is extremely complex and seems to allow two mutually
contradictory interpretations, which need to be explored. Of primary importance is that the swallows, so bound, would obscure the sun. Before
instruments were invented, the sun was essential for navigating ships.
With the sun obscured ("i vot/Ne vidno solnca") the ship cannot steer a
true course; this is clearly the idea of line 18: "Ne vidno solnca i
zmelja plyvet" (The sun is not visible and the earth floats). Hyperbolically, the ship is the earth, afloat, without direction. Omry Ronen[21] has
found in this poem a possible allusion to the Acts of the Apostles (XXVII:9)
which substantiates this interpretation:

> XXVII:9 Now when much time was spent, and when sailing was now
> dangerous, because the fast was now already past, Paul admonished

them, 10. And said unto them, Sirs, I perceive that this voyage
will be with hurt and much damage, not only of the lading and ship,
but also of our lives. 20: And when neither sun nor stars in many
days appeared [No kak mnogie dni ne vidno bylo ni solnca, ni zvezd],
and no small tempest lay on us, all hope that we should be saved was
taken away.

In Mandel'štam's "XIX vek" (XIX Century), the absence of the sun is seen

as a negative phenomenon: "Irracional'nyj koren' nadvigajuščejsja èpoxi,

gigantskij, neizvlekaemyj koren' iz dvux, podobno kamennomu xramu čužogo

boga, otbrasyvaet na nas svoju ten'. V takie dni razum enciklopedistov—

svjaščennyj ogon' Prometeja." (II, 325, my italics [The irrational root

of the approaching epoch, the gigantic, inextractable root of two, like

the stone temple of an alien god, casts its shadow on us. In such days,

the reason of the Encyclopediasts is the sacred fire of Prometheus.]; cf.

"Gumanism i sovremennost'" [Humanism and the Present]: "Vse čuvstvujut

monumental'nost' form nadvigajuščejsja social'noj arxitektury. Ešče ne

vidno gory, no ona uže otbrasyvaet na nas svoju ten' i. ..my dvižemsja v

ètoj teni so straxom i nedoumeniem." [Everyone feels the monumentality

of the forms of the approaching social architecture. The mountain is not

yet visible, but it already casts its shadow on us . . . and we move with-

in this shadow with fear and wonder. II, 394] Mandel'štam, of course, was

not alone in using such imagery; Blok, too, for example, equated the ab-

sence of the sun with negative omens as in "Dvenadcat'" (The Twelve)

"Černoe, černoe nebo" (Black, black sky).

The swallows — that is, the Russian people — bound together into

nets, constitute a complex, ambivalent image. On the one hand, the fact

that they are bound has the potential of multiplying their strength as

individuals; united they are capable of tremendous force. On the other hand, the nets can be viewed as something which hinders freedom, thus forming part of the semantic field of constraint, inhibition: gruznyj les tenet (massive forest of hunting nets) (cf. "Dekabrist": "Evropa plakala v tenetax" [Europe wept in hunting nets])—nevynosimyj gnet—svjazali lastoček—skvoz' seti (intolerable weight—bound swallows—through nets). If, in addition, one accepts the suggestion that the swallows are souls bound together, then a further possibility arises which complements the positive side of this complex image. That is, the souls of line 14 recall the nets cast into the waters in lines 3 and 4; the water may be understood as the sea of life, a metaphor found throughout Mandel'štam's work. The nets are used to catch fish—metaphorically, men's souls. Such imagery is, of course, abundant throughout the New Testament. See, for example, Matthew 4:18-19; 13:47 (cf. Esenin, "Inonija": "I zarja, opuskaja veki,/Budet zvezdnyx lovit' v nix [v rekax] ryb." [And the dusk, lowering its eyelids,/ Will catch starry fish in them (rivers)]. The first and third stanzas may therefore be viewed as partially analogous, in that in one water is the metaphoric element, in the other—air.

While one may object to the fact that a single image seems to be supersaturated with ostensibly diametrically opposed possibilities of interpretation, we should again point out that the poem as a whole posits an extremely ambivalent attitude toward the revolution and its potential, an ambivalence that is inherent in the first word of its title, "sumerki."

"The whole element/ Twitters, moves, lives" refers to the revolution and suggests the energy which it produces. In another poem by Mandel'štam, "Našedšij podkuvu," the same thought is expressed in the section which

begins "S čego načat'?/Vse treščit i kačaetsja." (What to begin with?/
Everything cracks and rocks) The bound swallows of "Sumerki svobody" appear here, in "Našedšij podkovu," simply as birds bound together: "V
broskoj uprjaži gustyx ot natugi ptič'ix staj." (In a bright harness of
flocks of birds thick from strain). Here, however, the image is overtly
ominous, because the birds are harnessed to chariots which smash themselves to pieces.

Mandel'štam provides yet additional levels of meaning for the original term sumerki. The "gustye sumerki" in line 17 suggest the idea of
thick, dense air; air which is difficult to breathe — the air of the historical moment. Blok used this metaphor to describe the atmosphere of the
revolution: "We know that our comrades entered the revolutionary epoch
each by their own path, that they breathe air smelling of the sea and the
future; the present is practically impossible to breathe; it's possible
to breathe only the future. "[Speech at the Poets' Union]" (1920)[22] and
later on in his "About the Poet's Mission": "Puskin was not killed by
D'Anthès bullet. He was killed by the absence of air. His culture was
dying with him." Mandel'štam often used this image: "My v každom vzdoxe
smertnyj vozdux p'em" (In every breath we drink deathly air) ("V Petropole
prozračnom my umrem" [In transparent Petropolis we will die], 1916);
"Vozdux zamešan tak že gusto, kak zemlja.--/Iz nego nel'zja vyjti, a v
nego trudno vojti." (The air is mixed as thickly as earth,--/It is impossible to leave and difficult to enter it.) ("Našedšij podkovu" 1923),
and so forth.

Not only is the sun obscured and the air dense, but the earth is
afloat, without direction; hence it is necessary to turn the rudder.

Mandel'štam says "Nu čto ž, poprobuem" (Well, then, let's try). This expresses perhaps his reluctant agreement, his acceptance without willing-
ness. The same resigned intonation is heard in the poem "Net, nikogda
ničej ja ne byl sovremennik" (No, never was I anyone's contemporary,
1924): "Nu čto že, esli nam ne vykovat' drugogo,/Davajte s vekom vekovat'"
(Well, if we can't forge another one,/Let's live this age); similarly in
"Čut' mercaet prizračnaja scena" (The phantasmal stage scarcely glimmers;
1920): "Ničego, golubka Evridika,/Čto u nas studenaja zima" (It's all
right, Euridice, my dove,/That it's freezing cold winter) and in "V Peterburge my sojdemsja snova" (We will meet again in Petersburg; 1920): "Čto
ž, gasi, požaluj, naši sveči. . ." (Well, blow out our candles). Noting,
however, the string of three epithets which modify "turn of the rudder"
("enormous," "clumsy," "creaking"), one may well doubt the efficacy of the
attempt to steer the ship successfully. Line 21 repeats line 18: "Zemlja
plyvet" (The earth floats). Despite efforts the situation is the same:
the earth is sailing, but still with no known direction. The urgency and
perhaps desperation of the situation is eloquently expressed in the imperative "Mužajtes', muži" (Courage, men). The speaker's response to the
situation is expressed in a phrase typical of patriotic odes.[23] This is
the only instance of second person imperative in the poem; previously, the
speaker clearly included himself in the exhortation ("proslavim,"
"poprobuem" [let's glorify, let's try]) or the accomplished fact ("My . . .
svjazali lastoček" [We have bound swallows]). Here the speaker exhorts
others to take courage: implicit is that he does not lack courage, but
has enough so that he can even urge others on. (Or might the use of this
stock phrase, a "speech gesture," as Nilsson called it, aesthetically

distance the speaker from his addressees? Such a phrase might be used with "believers," but he, being doubting and ambivalent, does not include himself in the imperative.)

The poem concludes with two hyperboles: we will remember even in Lethe's cold, and the earth has cost us ten heavens. Lethe is called cold possibly because the act of forgetting is viewed as something which numbs; but even Lethe will not erase the memory. The last line, "desjati nebes nam stoila zemlja" (the earth cost us ten heavens), includes the speaker among those who have paid the price of the revolution.

In "Sumerki svobody" we have two dominant signal systems of imagery. First, ship imagery: lines 3-4: ship lowering its nets into the seething night waters; lines 11-12: ship of time sinking; lines 17-18: earth ship afloat; lines 19-20: clumsy turn of the rudder; line 21: earth still afloat. Second, imagery relating to the sun: line 1: "sumerki," line 2: crepuscular year, line 3: night waters, line 5: you (sun) are rising, lines 14-15: the sun is not visible, line 16: dense "sumerki," lines 17-18: the sun is not visible. The ship imagery which Mandel'štam uses in this poem relates either to the ship of time or the ship of state. The ship of state has a long poetic history, and Mandel'štam here equates it with the Russian government, which he feels is undergoing a (dangerous) change in course.

The sun as a positive, life-giving symbol has a long tradition, too. In pre-revolutionary Russian poetry, one may cite, for example, Bal'mont's Budem kak solnce (Let's Be Like the Sun).

What concerns us here is that both of these images, the ship of state and the sun, were extensively used, especially by the Proletkul't poets, in the years immediately before and after the revolution; this has

been shown by Z. Papernyj in his Poètičeskij obraz u Majakovskogo

(Majakovskij's Poetic Image) (Moscow, 1961).[24] In fact, by as early as

1919, so widespread was this imagery that one commentator felt prompted

to write:

> One encounters poems with an allegoric content. The ship skimming
> proudly along the rough waves is the proletarian revolution. Day-
> break with bright rays is the coming life of the toiling masses. A
> threatening storm breaking century-old oaks is the proletarian revo-
> lution. Dusk is our burning out life. But all of this is old.[25]

In order to see the distinctive way in which Mandel'štam used this imagery,

it will be helpful to cite typical examples from some other poets: "My v

burnom okeane/Plyvem . . . My u rulja./Vdali, v gustom tumane/Zavetnaja

zemlja . . .//Vse nebo v groznyx tučax,/Vse v molnijax blestit./ Pod rev

valov kipučix/Korabl' streloj letit . . ." (We are sailing in the rough

ocean . . ./ We are at the rudder./ In the distance, in the dense fog/ Is

the cherished land . . .// The whole sky is in thunderclouds,/ Everything

flashes with lightning./ To the roar of the seething billows/ The ship

flies like an arrow . . .);[26] "My v puti svoem nemalom/Mnogo vyderžali

groz./Za poslednim perevalom/Vstanet ostrov vol'nyx grez!" (On our con-

siderable path we/ Endured many thunderstorms./ After the last pass/ An

island of free dreams will arise.).[27] Kirillov, especially, one of the

most popular proletarian poets, used this imagery: "Plovec" (The Sailor,

1918):

> Smelej vpered, plovec otvažnyj,
> K bregam lazorevym tvoj put'.
> Pust' škval bušujuščij, almaznyj
> Otvagoj napolnjaet grud'.

Vstrečaj grozu zvenjaščej pesnej,
Kto serdcem smel, tot pobedit,
Tam ostrov, vsex zemel' čudesnej,
Za gran'ju sineju ležit.

Svoboda--Deva ognevaja
Plovca otvažnogo tam ždet.
Ee dyxan'e--rozy maja,
Ee usta--volšebnyj med.

Smelej rasprav' polotna-kryl'ja,--
On blizok, ostrov zolotoj.
Ešče, ešče odno usil'e,
I raj čudesnyj budet tvoj.[28]

Go forward more boldly, courageous sailor,
Your path is to the azure shores.
Let the raging, diamond squall
Fill your breast with courage.

Meet the thunderstorm with a ringing song,
He whose heart is bold will conquer,
There an island, more marvelous than all the lands,
Is located beyond the blue border.

Freedom -- fiery Maiden,
Waits for the courageous sailor there.
Her breath -- roses of May,
Her lips -- magical honey.

Spread more boldly the canvas-wings, --
It's close, the gold island.
Yet one more effort,
And a miraculous paradise will be yours.

At least as common an image was the bright light of the revolutionary
sun. Majakovskij in Misterija-buff saw the revolution in a halo of
light, the victory of the sun: "Gimn (toržestvenno): 'Son vekovoj
raznesen--/celoe more utr./Xutor mira, cveti!/Ty naš!/A nad nami solnce,
solnce i solnce./. . . ./Grej! Igraj! Gori!/Solnce--naše solnce!/. . . .
/Slav'sja!/Sijaj,/solnečnaja naša/Kommuna!'" (Hymn (triumphantly): 'The
age-old sleep is dispersed --/ A whole sea of mornings./ Farmstead of

the world, blossom!/ You are ours!/ And above us is sun, sun, and sun./
. . . ./ Warm! Play! Burn!/ Sun - our sun!/ . . . ./ Be renowned'/ Shine,
/ our sunny/ Commune!') Examples from Kirrilov may also be cited: /Ėti
pesni--zov mogučij k solncu, žizni i bor'be." "Novoe solnce miru neset,/
Rušit trony, temnicy,/K večnomu bratstvu narody zovet,/Stiraet čerty i
granicy."[29] (These songs are a powerful call to the sun, to life, to battle; [He] carries a new sun to the world,/ Pulls down Thrones, dungeons,/
Calls people to eternal brotherhood,/ Erases boundaries and borders.).

Mandel'štam's choice of imagery indicates that he was aware of the
stereotyped allegorical imagery that was so common at the time of the revolution. He seems to be polemicizing against those who expressed blind optimism in the future. To the Proletarian poets' ship, sailing resolutely
on course, he counterposes a ship adrift, a ship in need of steering. To
the bright revolutionary sun he opposes a state of half-light, dawn, and a
sun which is obscured. To the poet Kirillov, who cries out "Kto serdcem
smel, tot pobedit" (He whose heart is bold will conquer), he seems to reply, "V kom serdce est', tot dolžen slyšat', vremja,/Kak tvoj korabl' ko
dnu idet" (He who has a heart must hear, O time,/Your ship going to the
bottom). The basic thrust of the poem is decidedly ambivalent; the sun
rises, but the ship sinks. The revolution has both negative and positive
potential; it does represent a new course, but one fraught with dangers:
it may lose its course, it may take away freedom. The very choice of the
word "sumerki" signals the ambivalent nature of Mandel'štam's attitude
toward the revolution. The fact that the title and the first two lines
were subsequently removed supports this hypothesis. Either the censors
found this too ambiguous or Mandel'štam himself did; although one would

suppose the former.

In another poem written in the same year (1918), Mandel'štam was more straightforward in revealing his doubts and misgivings. Here the main difficulty in understanding the poem involves the punctuation of the text:

Na strašnoj vysote bluždajuščij ogon',
No razve tak zvezda mercaet?
Prozračnaja zvezda, bluždajuščij ogon',
Tvoj brat, Petropol', umiraet.

Na strašnoj vysote zemnye sny gorjat,
Zelenaja zvezda letaet.
O, esli ty zvezda,--vody i neba brat,
Tvoj brat, Petropol', umiraet.

Čudoviščnyj korabl' na strašnoj vysote
Nesetsja, kryl'ja raspravljaet --
Zelenaja zvezda, v prekrasnoj niščete
Tvoj brat, Petropol', umiraet.

Prozračnaja vesna nad černoju Nevoj
Slomalas', vosk bessmert'ja taet,
O, esli ty zvezda--Petropol', gorod tvoj,
Tvoj brat, Petropol', umiraet.

At a fearful height a will-'o-the-wisp,
But does a star twinkle like this?
Transparent star, will-'o-the-wisp,
Your brother, Petropolis, is dying.

At a fearful height earthly dreams burn,
A green star flies.
Oh, if you are a star,--the brother of water and sky,
Your brother, Petropolis, is dying.

A monstrous ship at a fearful height
Is speeding, spreading its wings--
Green star, in beautiful poverty
Your brother, Petropolis, is dying.

Transparent spring over the black Neva
Has shattered, the wax of immortality melts,
Oh, if you are a star--Petropolis, your city,
Your brother, Petropolis, is dying.

The poem is cited with the punctuation given in <u>Tristia</u> (Peterburg-Berlin, 1922, p. 69). The punctuation found in <u>Vtoraja kniga</u> (Moskva-Peterburg, 1923, p. 31) differs in significant ways: line 7: "O esli ty, zvezda, vody i neba brat"; line 15: "O esli ty, zvezda, Petropol'--gorod tvoj." The punctuation in <u>Tristia</u> clearly makes most sense: "Oh, if you [really] are a star, [then look,] the brother of water and sky,/Your brother, Petropolis, is dying." (instead of "Oh, if you, star, are the brother of Petropolis").[30] In <u>Vtoraja kniga</u> (Second Book), "star" is vocative, and even though it is feminine gender, it is called "brother" (masculine).[31] Lines 15-16 in the <u>Vtoraja kniga</u> version, similarly, make "star" a vocative: "Oh, if you, star, are Petropolis, your city,/Your brother, Petropolis, is dying."

In traditional symbolism, a star offers guidance. But this is not that kind of star. At the beginning of the poem, the star seems to be likened to a "wandering fire": "At a fearful height a wandering fire." It is not clear whether this "wandering fire" is a star: "But does a star twinkle like this?" "Bluždajuščij ogon'" is more accurately translated as "will-'o-the-wisp ("ignis fatuus"). "Will-'o-the-wisps" frequently appear in superstitions and legends; a pale light appearing at night over swamps or cemeteries, it causes travelers to lose their way, or else is a death omen.[32] When the star itself is equated with the will-'o-the-wisp (line 3: "Oh transparent star, will-'o-the-wisp. . .") the theme of death is strongly, and frighteningly, felt. In addition, the adjective "prozračnyj" itself evokes death. "Prozračnyj" (transparent) is used in line 3 and this adjective is repeated in line 13 "Prozračnaja vesna nad černoju Nevoj/Slomalas', vosk bessmert'ja taet. . ." (Transparent spring over the

black Neva/Has shattered, the wax of immortality melts). Even within this
poem there is an obvious enough connection between "transparent" and
death: "Transparent star. . ./Your brother, Petropolis, is dying"; but in
addition to this, the "transparent spring" (l. 13) is an obvious self-
quotation. It recalls two poems in which Petersburg and death are interconnected:

Mne xolodno. Prozračnaja vesna
V zelenyj pux Petropol' odevaet,
No, kak meduza, nevskaja volna
Mne otvraščen'e legkoe vnušaet.
Po naberežnoj severnoj reki
Avtomobilej mčatsja svetljaki,
Letjat strekozy i žuki stal'nye,
Mercajut zvezd bulavki zolotye,
No nikakie zvezdy ne ub'jut
Morskoj volny tjaželyj izumrud.
                    (1916)

V Petropole prozračnom my umrem,
Gde vlastvuet nad nami Prozerpina,
My v každom vzdoxe smertnyj vozdux p'em,
I každyj čas nam smertnaja godina.
Boginja morja, groznaja Afina,
Snimi mogučij kamennyj šelom.
V Petropole prozračnom my umrem,
Gde carstvueš' ne ty, a Prozerpina.
                    (1916)

I'm cold. Transparent spring
Dresses Petropolis in green fluff,
But, like a medusa, the Neva wave
Inspires a slight disgust in me.
Along the quay of the northern river
The fireflies of automobiles rush along,
Dragonflies and steel beetles speed,
The gold pins of stars twinkle,
But no stars will kill
The heavy emerald of the sea wave.
                    (1916)

In transparent Petropolis we will die
Where Proserpina rules over us.
In every breath we drink deathly air,

And every hour is our time of death.
Goddess of the sea, terrible Athena,
Take off your mighty stone helmet.
In transparent Petropolis we will die,
Where Prosepina, not you, reigns.
                                        (1916)

In "Mne xolodno." the connection between "transparent" and death
does not emerge immediately. Initially, "transparent spring" together
with "green down" suggest that spring is just beginning to appear. The
trees are still almost bare, hence spring is "transparent." And because
winter is not completely over, the speaker is still cold. In an earlier
poem, to which this one ("Mne xolodno") alludes, the cold experienced by
the speaker is a kind of artistic impotence: "Ja vzdragivaju ot xoloda--
/Mne xočet'sja onemet'!" (I am trembling from the cold--/I want to grow
dumb; 1912). In "Mne xolodno," the cold is less profound. The first two
lines, then, merely describe the appearance of spring. In line 3, however, the poem shifts to a more threatening level. The Neva wave disgusts
the speaker as does a medusa. The medusa has definite associations with
Petersburg, specifically, with the Admiralty: "Serdito lepjatsja kapriznye
meduzy . . ." (Capricious medusas cling angrily; Admiraltejstvo, 1913).
As Nilsson has shown,[33] the medusas in the poem have two possible references. On the one hand, they are part of the poem's "sea imagery"; at
the same time "the 'meduzy' could refer to the facial masks over many windows of the Admiralty building." This holds true in "Mne xolodno," too,
where the medusas are associated with the Neva and by extension with the
Admiralty. The medusas, formerly (in "Admiraltejstvo") connected with the
Neva in a positive way are here joined with negative aspects of the Neva.
Both are now negative: the Neva and the medusas induce disgust.

The last three lines of the poem reemphasize the negative possibilities of the Neva. Line 8 "Mercajut zvezd bulavki zolotye" (The gold pins
of stars twinkle) refers back to the same earlier poem, "Ja vzdragivaju
ot xoloda—": Čto, esli, nad modnoj lavkoju/ Mercajuščaja vsegda,/ Mne
v serdce dlinnoj bulavkoju/ Opustitsja drug zvezda? (What, if, over the
modish shop/ Always twinkling,/ Into my heart like a long pin/ The star
suddenly sinks.) But if the stars in "Ja vzdraguvaju ot xoloda" are capable of exerting power over the speaker ("A v nebe tancuet zoloto—/
Prikazyvaet mne pet'." [And gold dances in the sky. . ./ Orders me to
sing]) and are threatening and destructive, here, in "Mne xolodno," they
are impotent: even these stars cannot quell the disgust inspired by the
Neva. The Neva itself is dangerous. This aspect of the Neva has a long
history in Russian literature—the Neva in "The Bronze Horseman," <u>Crime</u>
<u>and</u> <u>Punishment</u>, <u>Petersburg</u>.

It is in "V Petropole prozračnom my umrem" (In transparent Petropolis
we will die) that the connection between "prozračnyj" and death becomes explicit. This makes the "transparent spring" of "Mne xolodno" more ominous
and the cold experienced by the speaker becomes, it is clear, not only a
physical state, but an emotional, psychological one as well. In "V
Petropole prozračnom," the Neva again figures, though less prominently.
"Boginja morja, groznaja Afina,/Snimi mogučij kamennyj šelom" (Goddess of
the sea, terrible Athena,/Take of your mighty stone helmet): this refers
to a statue by Terebenev—Pallas-Athena, sculptured in stone and wearing
a helmet sits in the main vestibule of the Admiralty. It is for this
reason that Athena is here called "goddess of the sea." It is not she, a
goddess noted for her mercifulness and generosity, the goddess of wisdom,

who reigns, but Prosperine, queen of the underworld.

"At a fearful height a wandering fire" has references to yet another poem of Mandel'štam's, "Admiraltejstvo." Again, the references are explicit. In "Admiraltejstvo" we have "prozračnyj ciferblat," "fregat ili akropol' . . . vode i nebu brat," "lad'ja vozdušnaja" (transparent clock-face, frigate or acropolis . . . brother of water and sky, air ship). These details reemerge in "Na strašnoj vysote": "prozračnaja zvezda," "vode i nebu brat," "čudoviščnyj korabl' . . . nesetsja" (transparent star, brother of water and sky, a monstrous ship . . . is speeding). The Admiralty, which in "Admiraltejstvo" is in part a symbol of creation, is transformed in "Na strašnoj vysote" into an emblem of Petersburg undergoing destruction, death.

The last-mentioned phrase, "čudoviščnyj korabl' nesetsja" alludes, at the same time, to another poem of Mandel'štam's, also from 1913, about Petersburg, "Petergburgskie strofy" (Petersburg Stanzas): "Čudoviščna, kak bronesec v doke,/Rossija otdyxaet tjaželo" (Monstrous, like a battleship in the dock,/Russia breathes heavily). "Petersburgskie strofy" is a kind of montage of themes from history and literature connected with Petersburg. "The Overcoat" ("šinel'," l. 4), Onegin (l. 14), the Decembrist revolt (l. 15), Evgenij from "The Bronze Horseman" (l. 23), all from Petersburg's past, are interwoven into a complex whole and placed into a contemporary setting. The most pervasive device in this poem is anachronism (about which Mandel'štam wrote in relation to Blok's poetics in "Barsuč'ja nora" ["Badger Hole"]):

No veršina istoričeskoj poètiki Bloka, toržestvo evropejskogo
mifa, kotoryj svobodno dvižetsja v tradicionnyx formax--èto

"Šagi Komandora". Zdes' plasty vremeni legli drug na druga
v zanovo vspaxannom poètičeskom soznanii, i
zerna starogo sjužeta dali obil'nye vsxody (Tixij,
Černyj, kak sova, motor . . . iz strany blažennoj,
neznakomoj, dal'nej, slyšno pen'e petuxa.) [n.b. "motor"
in "Šagi Komandora" and "motorov verenica" in
"Peterburgskie strofy."]

                      ("Barsuč'ja nora," 1922, II, 315)

But the height of Blok's historical poetics, the triumph of the
European myth, which moves freely in traditional forms, which
does not fear anachronism and contemporaneity—this is "The
Steps of the Commander." Here, strata of time lie down on each
other in a newly plowed-up poetic consciousness, and the kernels
of the old subject yielded abundant shoots ("A silent, black,
like an owl, motor car . . . From a blessed, unknown, distant
country the cock's crow is heard.) [n.b. "motor car" in "The
Steps of the Commander" and "line of motor cars" in "Petersburg
Stanzas."]

    "Peterburgskie strofy" opens with a glaringly negative image: "Nad

želtiznoj pravitelstvennyx zdanij" (Over the yellowness of the government

buildings). The negative connotation of yellow associated with Petersburg

goes back to Dostoevskij, Annenskij and Blok.[34] Mandel'štam ties yellow

as a negative color with Petersburg in other places too (n.b. the colors

of the imperial standard were black and yellow):

        Tol'ko tam, gde tverd' svetla,
        Černo-želtyj loskut zlitsja,
        Slovno v vozduxe struitsja
        Zelč' dvuglavogo orla.

                ("Dvorcovaja ploščad'," 1917)

        Only there, where the firmament is bright,
        The black-yellow rag rages,
        As if in the air streamed
        The bile of the double-headed eagle.

              ("Palace Square," 1917)

Nikto ne znal v ètot želtyj zimnij den', čto ona prinimaet
novoroždennuju krasnuju Rossiju, čto každoe ubijstvo bylo roždeniem. . . .
Ves' Peterburg, grjaznyj, želtyj, s domami-jaščikami . . . prišel čerez

dvenadcat' let k Dvorcovoj ploščadi. . . .

("Krovavaja misterija 9-go janvarja," III, 131,
132)

On that yellow winter day no one knew that she was accepting a new-
born, red Russia, that each murder was a birth. . . . All of Petersburg, dirty, yellow, with its box-houses . . . came twenty years
later to the Palace Square.

("The Bloody Miracle-play of 9 January")

Ved' i deržus' ja odnim Peterburgom—koncertnym, želtym, zloveščim
naxoxlennym, zimnim.

(Egipetskaja marka, II, 62)

And I also can hold out only because of Petersburg—with its concerts,
yellow, sinister, sullen, wintery.

(The Egyptian Stamp)

In "Na strašnoj vysote bluždajuščij ogon'" the star, Petersburg's

brother, is "green." In Russian poetry one may find green stars which

are positive or green stars which are negative.[35] In Mandel'štam's poem,

the star is green at least partly because green relates back to the posi-

tive image of the Admiralty; in "Admiraltejstvo" it is surrounded by green:

"Pyl'nyj topol'," "zaputalsja v listve," "v temnoj zeleni fregat ili

akropol'" (dusty poplar, lost in the foliage, in the dark green a frigate

or acropolis).

The last stanza suggests that the fate of Petersburg is being de-

cided: "Vosk bessmert'ja taet" (the wax of immortality is melting). Wax

is traditionally used for divination; in Russian poetry the best-known ex-

amples are "Svetlana" and Evgenij Onegin, and in Mandel'štam's own poetry:

"Sklonjajas' and voskom, devuška gljadit" (Bending over the wax, a girl

peers; "Tristia," 1918). In "Na strašnoj vysote" the wax is melting in

preparation for its use in fortune-telling. The destiny of Petersburg

has yet to be settled. But, as suggested in this poem, the future is

Revolution / 69

filled with pessimism, for Petropolis is dying. The city is called Petropolis because Mandel'štam does not mean St. Petersburg of the given historical moment. "Petropol'" was Deržavin's and Puškin's name for Petersburg. Mandel'štam sees not a city as such which is in danger, but a whole
cultural tradition which is threatened, dying. Perhaps, too, the extensive
network of allusions in "Na strašnoj vysote bluždajuščij ogon'" to other
poems of Mandel'štam's dealing with Petersburg--poems which examine the
city from a multitude of perspectives--emphasize the fact that it is
Petersburg as a fact of Mandel'štam's own poetic biography which he sees
dying.

It is important to state that although the environment was hostile,
Mandel'štam nevertheless rejected, at least at this time, the possibility
of emigrating. Because he was Jewish, his life in the south was even more
difficult. Mandel'štam alludes to this in his sketch "Men'ševiki v
Gruzii" (The Menševiks in Georgia, 1923):

> S ètim paroxodom priexali krymskie bežency. Rodina Ifigenii
> iznemogala pod soldatskoj pjatoj. I mne prišlos' gladet' na
> ljubimye, suxie, polynnye xolmy Feodosii, na kimmerijskoe
> xolmogor'e iz tjuremnogo okna i guljat' po vyžžennomu dvoriku,
> gde sbilis' v kuču perepugannye evrei, a kramol'nye oficery iskali
> všej na gimnasterkax, slušaja dikij rev soldat, privetstvujuščix u
> morja svoego načal'nika.

> (II, 235)

> Crimean refugees arrived with this steamer. Iphigenia's
> homeland was growing exhausted under the soldier's heel. And I had
> to look at my favorite, dry, wormwood hills of Feodosia, at the
> Cimmerian hilly region, from a prison window, and to walk around
> the scorched yard where frightened Jews huddled, and seditious offi-
> cers searched for lice on their field shirts, listening to the wild
> roar of soldiers welcoming their commander near the sea.

His attitude toward a certain segment of whites is expressed in a poem dated 1920 and written while he was in Koktebel':

> Gde noč' brosaet jakorja
> V gluxix sozvezd'jax Zodiaka,
> Suxie list'ja oktjabrja,
> Gluxie vskormlenniki mraka,
> Kuda letite vy? Začem
> Ot dreva žizni vy otpali?
> Vam cužd i stranen Vifleem
> I jaslej vy ne uvidali.
>
> Dlja vas potomstva net--uvy!
> Bespolaja vladeet vami zloba,
> Bezdetnymi sojdete vy
> V svoi povaplennye groby
> I na poroge tišiny
> Sredi bespamjatstva prirody
> Ne vam ne vam obrečeny,
> A zvezdam večnye narody.
>
> Where night drops anchor
> In the dense constellations of the Zodiac,
> Dry leaves of October,
> Deaf nurslings of gloom,
> Where are you flying? Why
> Have you fallen away from the tree of life?
> Bethlehem is foreign and strange to you,
> And you haven't seen the crèche.
>
> For you there is no posterity, alas!
> A sexless spite rules you,
> Childless you will descend
> Into your whited sepulchres
> And on the threshhold of silence
> Amidst the unconsciousness of nature
> Not to you, not to you are fated
> The eternal peoples, but to the stars.

The editors who printed this poem appended the following remarks: "the poem sheds much light on Mandel'štam's attitude toward the October revolution and on the religious foundations of his views. It is close to the religious verse of the early 1920's in which a condemnation of the sterility of October underlies a eulogy to the fullness of the Christian revelation. Here Mandel'štam speaks plainly and answers Blok, who hoped in 1918 that the Revolution was with God and not against God."[36] We, however, find far more convincing the interpretation which Omry Ronen puts forth: "The editors claim that M. addressed it to the Bolsheviks ('Dry leaves of October'). However, it is more likely that the 'dry leaves' of the poem, torn off the Tree of Life (cf. Bal'mont's 'Proščanie s drevom': 'Èto drevo v vekax nazyvalos' Rossija,/I na stvol ego ostryj natočen topor' [Farewell to the tree": 'This tree has been called Russia through the ages,/ And the sharp ax is whetted on its trunk.]) by the winds of October, are the fleeing Whites, between whose counter-intelligence and M. there was no love lost in 1920. . . . In M. himself, a Wrangel newspaper evoked the image of the Russian autumn: 'Grjaznaja, na seroj drevesnoj bumage, vsegda poxožaja na korrekturu, gazetka "Osvaga" budila vpečatlenie russkoj oseni . . .' ('Barmy zakona') [The dirty little newspaper 'Osvag,' on gray pulpy paper like proof-sheets, always stirred up an impression of Russian autumn" ("The Royal Mantle of the Law")]).

    "The messianic symbolism of the poem ('Vifleem', 'jasli' [Bethlehem, crèche]), which the editors . . . interpret as a challenge to the godless Bolsheviks, is actually such a commonplace in the poetry of the Russian Revolution (Blok, Belyj, Esenin, Kljuev) that one is almost embarrassed to have to point this out. Kuzmin employed the same set of symbols in 'Roždenie' (The Birth, Peterburgskij sbornik, 1922): "Bez muk mladenec byl rožden,/A my roždaemsja v mučen'jax,/No drognet veščij nebosklon, /Uznav o novyx pesnopen'jax.//Ne sladkij glas, a jaryj krik/Prorežet tlennuju utrobu./Slepoj zarodyš ne privyk,/Čto put' ego—podoben grobu. . . ."[37] (The infant was born without pangs,/ And we are being born in torment,/But the prophetic horizon will flicker,/ Having learned of the new psalms.// Not a sweet voice, but a furious shout/ Will cut through the decaying womb./ The blind fetus hasn't grown used to the fact/ That its path is like the grave. . . .)

It is quite likely that Nadežda Mandel'štam is referring to "Gde noč' brosaet jakorja" when she writes: "In the Crimea in 1919 O.M. wrote two poems which he did not want to keep and they were lost with his friend Lenja L. I saw this person once in Moscow and he said that the poems were intact. This happened around 1922. But both the poems and Lenja vanished. I remember only a line or two from these poems. But, apparently, they will never surface."[38] Probably, Mandel'štam did not take the poems with him because the Wrangelites would have known to whom the poems referred. By 1922, Mandel'štam had changed his views on emigration and considered the possibility himself ("Pered ot"ezdom podaem zajavlenie v litovskuju missiju" [Before the departure we'll put in an application to the Lithuanian mission.] III, 199). To publish the poem in 1922 (the year "Akter i rabočij" [Actor and Worker] was published--probably the other of the two poems alluded to by Nadežda Mandel'štam) would have been in bad taste, since the Whites were completely defeated by that time.

Nadežda Mandel'štam's words as well as Ėmilij Mindlin's remarks (quoted below) suggest that "Akter i rabočij" was written well before 1922, when it was first published:

> Zdes', na tverdoj ploščadke jaxt-kluba,
> Gde vysokaja mačta i spasatel'nyj krug,
> U Južnogo morja, pod sen'ju Juga
> Derevjannyj paxučij stroilsja srub!
>
> Ėto igra vozdvigaet zdes' steny!
> Razve rabotat' ne značit igrat'?
> Po svežim doskam širokoj sceny
> Kakaja radost' vpervye šagat'!

Akter-korabel'ščik na palube mira!
I dom aktera stoit na volnax!
Nikogda, nikogda ne bojalas' lira
Tjaželogo molota v bratskix rukax!

Čto skazal xudožnik, skazal i rabotnik:
—Voistinu, pravda u nas odna!
Edinym duxom živ i plotnik,
I poèt, vkusivšij svjatogo vina!

A vam spasibo! I dni, i noči
My stroili vmeste, i naš dom gotov!
Pod maskoj surovosti skryvaet rabočij
Vysokuju nežnost' grjaduščix vekov!

Veselye stružki paxnut morem,
Korabl' osnaščen—v dobryj put'!
Plyvite že vmeste k grjaduščim zorjam,
Akter i rabočij, vam nel'zja otdoxnut'!

Here on the stable platform of the yacht club,
Where there is a tall mast and a life saver,
Near the Southern sea, under the protection of the South
A wooden pungent framework is being built!

The play erects the walls here!
To work—doesn't it mean: to play?
Along the fresh boards of the wide stage
What a joy it is to stride for the first time!

Actor-shipwright on the deck of the world!
And the actor's house stands on waves!
Never, never did the lyre fear
The heavy hammer in brotherly hands!

What the artist said, the worker said too:
"Indeed, we have the same truth!"
The same spirit gives life to both the carpenter
And the poet, who partook of the holy wine!

And to you, thanks! For days and nights
We built together, and our house is ready!
Under the mask of sternness the worker hides
The lofty tenderness of coming ages!

The gay shavings smell of the sea,
The ship is rigged—a good journey!
Sail together to the coming dawns,
Actor and worker, you may not rest!

Mindlin writes: "'Actor and Worker' was the last poem written by him in Theodosia. A group of actors under the leadership of Amurovskij opened a cafe-cabaret on a tennis court near the sea. A poem was ordered from Mandel'štam for the celebration. For his mood at that period the choice of themes was remarkable. It was almost audacious to write, when Wrangel was at his height, such poetry intended for public performance. . . . And nonetheless he wrote. The verses were read by one of the actors from the stage of the recently opened cafe-cabaret on the tennis court in a Theodosia filled with Wrangelites shortly before Mandel'štam's arrest."[39]

Chapter IV

REFLECTIONS ON CULTURE

Mandel'štam has several poems which can be grouped together under
the general heading "departure from the theater/opera: "Letajut
Val'kirii, pojut smyčki" (The Valkyries fly, bows sing, 1913), "Ja ne
uvižu znamenitoj 'Fedry'" (I won't see the famous "Phèdre," 1915), "Kogda
v temnoj noči zamiraet" (When in dark night dies, 1918?), "Čut' mercaet
prizračnaja scena" (The phantasmal stage scarcely glimmers, 1920), "V
Peterburge my sojdemsja snova" (We will meet again in Petersburg, 1920).
We will discuss three of them in some detail, making only cursory reference to the other two.

Kogda v temnoj noči zamiraet
Lixoradočnyj forum Moskvy,
I teatrov širokie zevy
Vozrasčajut tolpu ploščadjam,

Protekaet po ulicam pyšnym
Oživlen'e nočnyx proxoron,
L'jutsja mračno-veselye tolpy
Iz kakix-to božestvennyx nedr.

Èto solnce nočnoe xoronit
Vozbuždennaja igrami čern',
Vozvraščajas' s polnočnogo pira
Pod gluxie udary kopyt.

I kak novyj vstaet Gerkulanum,
Spjaščij gorod v sijan'i luny,
I ubogogo rynka lačugi,
I mogučij doričeskij stvol.

When in the dark night
The feverish forum of Moscow dies down,
And the broad jaws of the theaters
Return the crowd to the squares,

Along the magnificant streets flows
The animation of a night burial,

Gloomily gay crowds pour
Out of some divine depths.

It's the night sun
That the rabble, excited by the games, buries,
Returning from a midnight feast
To the muffled blows of hooves.

And like a new Herculaneum
The sleeping city arises in the glow of the moon,
And the shanties of the squalid market,
And the mighty Doric column.

In "Kogda v temnoj noči zamiraet" the action takes place in Moscow.

The theater alluded to in the first stanza is the Bol'šoj theater; this is

made clear from Mandel'štam's 1923 essay "Xolodnoe leto" (Cold Summer):

Četverka konej Bol'šogo teatra . . . Tolstye doričeskie kolonny
. . . Ploščad' opery--asfal'tovoe ozero, s solomennymi vspyškami
tramvaev--uže v tri časa utra razbužennoe cokan'em skromnyx gorodskix
konej . . .
Uznaju tebja, ploščad' Bol'šoj Opery--ty pupovina gorodov Evropy
--i v Moskve--ne lučše i ne xuže svoix sester.
Kogda iz pyl'nogo uročišča Metropolja--mirovoj gostinicy--gde
pod stekljannym šatrom ja bluždal v koridorax ulic unutrennego goroda--
izredka ostanavlivajas' pered zerkal'noj zasadoj, ili otdyxaja na
spokojnoj lužajke s pletenoj bambukovoj mebel'jo-- ja vyxožu na
ploščad', ešče slepoj, glotaja solnečnyj svet: mne udarjaet v glaza
veličavaja jav' Revoljucii i bol'šaja arija dlja sil'nogo golosa
pokryvaet gudki avtomobil'nyx siren.

(II, 167)

The team of four horses of the Bol'soj theater . . . Stout
doric columns . . . The opera square -- an asphalt lake with straw-
colored flashes of street-cars -- already at 3:00 A.M. awakened by
the clatter of modest city horses. . . .

I recognize you, square of the Bol'šaja Opera -- you are the hub
of the cities of Europe -- and in Moscow -- are no better and no
worse than your sisters.

When from the dusty plot of the Metropole -- an international
hotel -- where I wandered under the glass tent in the corridors of
the streets of the inner city -- now and then stopping in front of
the mirrored ambush, or resting in a quiet glade with wicker bamboo
furniture -- I go out into the square, still blind, swallowing the

sunlight: the great reality of the Revolution strikes my eyes and a great aria for a strong voice covers the tooting of the automobile sirens.

The "feverish forum" in the first stanza of this poem is given metonymically through the "Doric trunk" in the last stanza. The crowds leaving the theater, given this setting, are described by the narrator on two time levels simultaneously: the rabble excited by the games (vozbuždennaja igrami čern') suggests the Roman plebes leaving the circus, as well as Muscovites of the current time leaving the theater. The crowds are described by the compound adjective "mračno-veselyj" (gloomily gay, l. 7): gloomy because they have left the world of art, happy because that is where they have been. As the performance is coming to a close ("forum zamiraet"), the forum is called "feverish"—the fever being one of artistic creativity; cf., for example, the "nightingale fever" ("solov'inaja gorjačka") in "Čto pojut časy-kuznečik" (What does the grasshopper clock sing, 1917).[1] But when the performance is over, the opposite is true: Moscow is called a "new Herculaneum," that is, a dead city. Thus, in the context of this poem, the image of the night sun which is being buried (ll. 9-10: "Ėto solnce nočnoe xoronit/Vozbuždennaja igrami cern'"') can be understood as a metaphor for a world of art, seen in the theater, as if interred when the performance is over. The sun, a source of light and life, when buried plunges Moscow into darkness and death ("spjaščij gorod," "novyj Gerkulanum"). (We will return to the image of the "night sun" in our discussion of "V Peterburge my sojdemsja snova".)

"Kogda v temnoj noči zamiraet" closes with the "hovels of the squalid market" juxtaposed to the "mighty Doric trunk" which, as we said, recalls the forum of line 2; it is therefore a metonymic metaphor for art.

The "real" world is spectral in comparison with the world of art. This theme is varied by Mandel'štam in two poems from 1920: "Čut' mercaet prizračnaja scena" and "V Peterburge my sojdemsja snova" (The phantasmal stage scarcely glimmers, We will meet again in Petersburg).

I

Čut' mercaet prizračnaja scena,
Xory slabye tenej,
Zaxlestnula selkom Mel'pomena
Okna xraminy svoej.
Černym taborom stojat karety,
Na dvore moroz treščit,
Vse kosmato-- ljudi i predmety,
I gorjačij sneg xrustit.

Ponemnogu čeljad' razbiraet
Šub medvež'ix voroxa.
V sumatoxe babočka letaet,
Rozu kutajut v mexa.
Modnoj pestrjadi kružki i moški,
Teatral'nyj legkij žar,
A na ulice migajut ploški
I tjaželyj valit par.

Kučera izmajalis' ot krika,
I xrapit i dyšit t'ma.
Ničego, golubka Évridika,
Čto u nas studenaja zima.
Slašče pen'ja ital'janskoj reči
Dlja menja rodnoj jazyk,
Ibo v nem tainstvenno lepečet
Čužezemnyx arf rodnik.

Paxnet dymom bednaja ovčina,
Ot sugroba ulica černa.
Iz blažennogo pevučego pritina
K nam letit bessmertnaja vesna,
Čtoby večno arija zvučala:
-Ty verneš'sja na zelenye luga,
I živaja lastočka upala
Na gorjačie snega.

V Peterburge my sojdemsja snova,
Slovno solnce my poxoronili v nem,
I blaženennoe, bessmyslennoe slovo
V pervyj raz proiznesem.
V černom barxate sovetskoj noči,
V barxate vsemirnoj pustoty,
Vse pojut blažennyx žen rodnye oči,
Vse cvetut bessmertnye cvety.

Dikoj koškoj gorbitsja stolica,
Na mostu patrul' stoit,
Tol'ko zloj motor vo mgle promčitsja
I kukuškoj prokričit.
Mne ne nado propuska nočnogo,
Časovyx ja ne bojus':
Za blaženennoe bessmyslennoe slovo
Ja v noči sovetskoj pomoljus'.

Slyšu legkij teatral'nyj šorox
I devičeskoe "ax" –
I bessmertnyx roz ogromnyj vorox
U Kipridy na rukax.
U kostra my greemsja ot skuki,
Možet byt' veka projdut,
I blažennyx žen rodnye ruki
Legkij pepel soberut.

Gde-to grjadki krasnye partera,
Pyšno vzbity šifon'erki lož;
Zavodnaja kukla oficera;
Ne dlja černyx duš i nizmennyx svjatoš. . .
Čto ž, gasi, požaluj, naši sveči
V černom barxate vsemirnoj pustoty,
Vse pojut blažennyx žen krutye pleči,
A nočnogo solnca ne zametiš' ty.

The phantasmal stage scarcely glimmers,
Faint choruses of shades,
Melpomene has curtained with silk
The windows of her temple.
Coaches stand like a black gypsy camp,
Outside frost cracks,
Everything is shaggy-people and things,
And hot snow crunches.

Little by little servants sort out
The heaps of bearskin coats.
In the turmoil a butterfly flies,
A rose is muffled up in furs.
Little circles and knots of stylish colored fabric,
The light heat of the theater,
On the street oil lamps blink,
And heavy steam pours out.

The drivers are exhausted from shouting,
And the darkness snorts and breaths.
It's all right, Euridice, my dear,
That we have freezing cold winter.
Sweeter than the singing of Italian speech
For me is my native language,
For in it mysteriously bubbles
The spring of foreign harps.

The poor sheepskin smells of smoke,
The street is black from the snowdrift,
From the blessed, singing cozy shelter
Immortal spring flies toward us,
In order that the aria may sound:
--You will return to the green meadows,
And the living swallow fell
Onto the hot snows.

II

We will meet again in Petersburg,
As if we had buried the sun there,
And the blessed senseless word
We will utter for the first time.
In the black velvet of the Soviet night,
In the velvet of universal emptiness
The dear eyes of blessed women still sing,
Immortal flowers still bloom.

The capital arches like a wild cat,
A patrol stands on the bridge,
Only a fierce motor tears by in the gloom now and then,
And cries out like a cuckoo.
I don't need a night pass,
I don't fear sentries:
For the blessed senseless word
I will pray in the Soviet night.

I hear a light theater rustle,
And a girl's "ah"--
And a huge bunch of immortal roses
In Cypris' arms.

At the bonfire we are warming ourselves out of boredom,
Perhaps ages will pass,
And the dear hands of the blessed women
Will gather the light ashes.

Somewhere are the red flowerbeds of the parterre,
The chiffoniers of the loges are luxuriously fluffed up;
The clockwork doll of an officer;
Not for black souls and base hypocrites . . .
Well, blow out our candles
In the black velvet of universal emptiness,
The rounded shoulders of the blessed women are still singing,
And you won't notice the night sun.

These poems have certain elements in common. One investigator[2] has pointed to their strophic similarity and called them "twin poems." Each contains 32 lines which form four 8-line stanzas, rhyming AbAbCdCd. The meter for both poems is trochaic. However, in "Čut' mercaet prizračnaja scena" there is a fairly regular alternation of 5- and 4-foot trochaic lines (with only three 6-foot lines), whereas in "V Peterburge my sojdemsja snova" this pattern is consistently observed only in one stanza, the third. The two poems share several thematic elements: night, cold, opera, Orpheus.

The theme of "Čut' mercaet prizračnaja scena" is the transition from an elevated world (of art) to the world of reality. In "Ja ne uvižu znamenitoj 'Fedry'" (I won't see the famous "Phèdre," 1915), Mandel'štam used the theater as a metaphor for the world of art separated by a curtain from the real world:

> Teatr Rasina! Moščnaja zavesa
> Nas otdeljaet ot drugogo mira;
> Glubokimi morščinami volnuja,
> Mež nim i nami zanaves ležit.

> Theater of Racine! A mighty curtain
> Separates us from another world;

> Exciting with its deep creases,
> The curtain lies between it and us.

Inside, an opera is being performed: line 2: "xory slabye tenej," line 21: "pen'e ital'janskoj reči," line 29 "čtoby . . . arija zvučala" (1. 2 faint choruses of shades, 1. 21 singing of Italian speech, 1. 29 in order that the aria may sound). The opera is Gluck's "Orfeo et Euridice" which was performed in Petersburg in 1919 and 1920.[3] According to Nadežda Mandel'štam, in Voronež "O.M. often wrote the introductory remarks for concerts, in particular for Gluck's 'Orfeo et Euridice.' It made him happy that when he walked along the street his story about dear Euridice [golubka–Evridika] was spread from all loudspeakers."[4] The story of Orpheus and Euridice, as told by Ovid (Met. X) and Virgil (Georgics, 4), is tragic: Orpheus cannot restrain himself from looking back at Euridice, and she is thus lost to him forever. Gluck's version of the legend, though, is different; the story has a happy ending: "Pour adapter cette Fable à notre scene on a été obligé de changer la catastrophe, et d'y ajouter l'épisode de l'Amour qui reunit les Epoux."[5]

What is possible inside the theater, the artist in control of his "reality," reworking a tragic myth, may not be possible outside. The basic juxtaposition is between the opera, being performed within, and the winter night which is outside. The opposition is pronounced: "černyj tabor," "moroz," "vse kosmato," "gorjačij sneg," "par," "t'ma," "studenaja zima," "bednaja ovčina," "sugrob," "černaja ulica," "gorjačie snega" (black gypsy camp, frost, everything is shaggy, hot snow, steam, darkness, freezing cold winter, poor sheepskin, snowdrift, black street, hot snows); vs. "babočka," "roza," "žar," "blažennyj pevučij pritin,"

"bessmertnaja vesna," "zelenye luga" (butterfly, rose, heat, blessed
singing shelter, immortal spring, green meadows). The essence of this
contrast is perhaps seen most clearly in the phrases "studenaja zima,"
"zelenye luga" (freezing cold winter, green meadows). Outside, life seemingly returns to a primeval, even primitive, existence: "Everything is
shaggy -- people and things. In Zamjatin's "The Cave" ("Peščera") similar
imagery is used to convey this mood:

> One thing is clear: it's winter. And you must clench your
> teeth more firmly so they don't chatter; And you must split
> your wood with a stone axe; and every night you must carry
> your bonfire from cave to cave, deeper and deeper. And you
> must wrap more and more shaggy animal hides around you. . . .
> And wrapped in hides, blankets, rags, the cave people went
> from cave to cave.[6]

Inside, life is gay, untouched by the cold of winter. A girl is
referred to as a "butterfly" (1. 11) or a rose (1. 12; cf. Puškin, "O
deva-roza, ja v okovax" [O, maiden-rose, I am in chains] 1824). These
are obviously worn-out metaphors, yet they succinctly convey the opposition of spring-like warmth within opposed to the frigid cold outside.

The poem ends on an ambiguous note. Orpheus, probably, speaks to
Euridice in line 30: "Ty verneš'sja na zelenye luga" (You will return
to the green meadows). The "green meadows" refer to the world outside
of Hades, to spring. But immediately after this positive statement
comes "I živaja lastočka upala/Na gorjačie snega" (And the living swallow
fell onto hot snow). The swallow here, on one level, can be understood
as the bird which is a harbinger of spring. Immortal spring is what
exists inside the theater ("bessmertnaja vesna"). But spring, with all

that this metaphor implies, has not yet come to the world outside the theater. The swallow falls onto the snow, which is so cold that it seems to burn.

The image of the swallow in this poem has further levels of meaning as well. As Taranovsky has shown,[7] the swallow in such poems as "Čto pojut časy kuznečik" (What is the grasshopper-clock singing, 1917), "Kogda Psixeja-žizn' spuskaetsja k tenjam" (When Psyche-life descends to the shades, 1920), "Ja slovo pozabyl, čto ja xotel skazat'" (I forgot that I wanted to say, 1920) is an image which can be correlated with poetic creation. In "Čut' mercaet prizračnaja scena" we feel that the swallow can also be understood as part of the semantic field of poetry, art, beauty.[8] Moreover, we should note the parallelism between the following lines: "Ničego, golubka Èvridika,/Čto u nas studenaja zima" and "-Ty vernes'sja na zelenye luga,/I živaja lastočka upala/Na gorjačie snega" (It's all right, Euridice, my dear,/That it's freezing cold winter; You will return to the green meadows,/And the living swallow fell/Onto the hot snows). In both instances the cold, destructive in its potential, is contrasted with art. A quotation from "O prirode slova" (On the Nature of the Word, 1922) makes clear that "golubka Èvridika" is a metaphor for art and beauty (or even more specifically, for European art brought to Russia):

> Gumilev nazval Annenskogo velikim evropejskim poètom. Mne kažetsja, kogda evropejcy ego uznajut, smirenno vospitav svoi pokolenija na izučenii russkogo jazyka, podobno tomu, kak prežnie vospityvalis' na drevnix jazykax i klassičeskoj poèzii, oni ispugajutsja derzosti ètogo carstvennogo xiščnika, po- xitivšego u nix golubku Èvridiku dlja russkix snegov, sorvavšego s nežnost'ju, kak podobaet

russkomu poètu, zverinuju škuru na vse ešče
zjabnuvsego Ovidija.
                              (II, 294)

Gumilev called Annenskij a great European poet.
It seems to me that when the Europeans
learn about him, having humbly educated their
generations on the study of Russian,
just as previous ones were educated on
ancient languages and classical poetry, they
will be frightened of the daring of this
kingly plunderer who abducted the dove Euridice from them
for Russian snows, who tore the classical
shawl from Phèdre's shoulders, and who
tenderly placed, as befits a Russian poet,
the animal hide on the still freezing Ovid.

"Čut' mercaet prizračnaja scena" moves, therefore, from the slightly op-

timistic "Ničego, golubka Èvridika,/Čto u nas studenaja zima" (It's all

right Euridice, my dove,/That it's freezing cold winter) to the decidedly

ambiguous "--Ty verneš'sja . . ./ I živaja lastočka upala. . ." (You will

return . . ./ And the living swallow fell). The suggestion is clear that

"art" and "reality" are mutually exclusive categories. Art is viable only

in a sheltered, artificial atmosphere.

In "V Peterburge my sojdemsja snova" we are again confronted with a

cold night and an opera performance coming to an end. The second stanza

presents a frightening picture of contemporary Petersburg, 1920). Axmatova

has described the winter of 1920 in her memoirs:

All of the old Petersburg signs were still in place, but behind
them, except for dust, darkness, and yawning emptiness, there was
nothing. Typhoid, hunger, executions, darkness in the apartments,
damp logs, people emaciated to unrecognizability. At the bazaar it
was possible to gather a large bouquet of field flowers. The famous
wooden paving blocks of Peterburg were rotting. From the basement
windows of 'Kraft' it still smelled of chocolate. All the cemeteries
were destroyed. The city had not simply changed, but had completely
turned into its opposite.[9]

According to Šklovskij, the winter of 1920 was a severe one: "Let's return to 1920. We were living in winter. It was cold. . . . The cold filled the days. We sewed shoes out of pieces of material. We lit kerosine in bottles plugged with rags. This was instead of lamps."[10] The presence of a patrol and sentries in the second stanza show that the Red Terror was in effect.[11] Extraordinary measures were taken to deal with the threats to Bol'ševik power: "The All-Russian Extraordinary Commission sees no other measures for combatting counterrevolutionaries, spies, profiteers. . . and other parasites except ruthless anihilation at the place of the crime."[12] Petersburg itself is thus like a wild cat, threatening, poised to leap. A car, also animated, speeds through the gloom (to an interrogation?) and cries out like a cuckoo. Such a cry conveys either a feeling of terror, as in Zadonščina ("Zegzicy kukujut, trupa čelovečeskogo čajuči [Cuckoos cuckoo, hoping for a human corpse]), or, more usually mournfulness, as in Slovo o polku Igoreve (The Tale of Igor's Campaign) ("Jaroslavyn" glas"sja slyšit", zegziceju neznaema rano kyčet'" [Jaroslavna's voice is heard, like a desolate cuckoo she cries early in the morning]), or in Mandel'štam's own poetry ("I plačet kukuška na kamennoj bašne svoej" [And the cuckoo weeps on its stone tower; "Kogda gorodskaja vyxodit na stogny luna," When the city moon comes out onto the squares 1920], "Byli oči ostree točimoj kosy--/Po zegzice v zenice i po kaple rosy . . ." [Eyes were sharper than a whetted scythe--/A cuckoo and a drop of dew in each pupil, 1937]).

On such a night the speaker, almost challengingly, will pray for a "beatific senseless word." What kind of word is this? The word "blažennyj" is the Russian equivalent of Greek "makarios," Latin "beatus."[13] The adjective "blažennyj" has been used before by Mandel'štam

--in relation to art: "Ja polučil blažennoe nasledstvo--/Čužix pevcov
bluzdajuščie sny" (I received a blessed heritage,/ The wandering dreams
of other singers; "Ja ne slyxal rasskazov Ossiana," I haven't heard
Ossian's stories, 1914); the opera house: "Iz blažennogo pevučego
pritina/K nam letit bessmertnaja vesna" (From the blessed singing cosy
shelter/Immortal spring flies; "Čut mercaet prizračnaja scena," The phantasmal stage scarcely glimmers, 1920); poetry: "Triždy blažen, kto vvedet
v pesen' imja" (Thrice blessed is the one who introduces a name into a
song, "Našedšij podkovu," He Who Found a Horseshoe, 1923); love: "Ja
naučilsja vam, blažennye slova--/Lenor, Solominka, Ligeja, Serafita" (I
have learned you, blessed words, Lenore, Solominka, Ligeia, Seraphita,
"Solominka," 1916). He uses this word in relation to all that is important to him.

The word "bessmyslennoe" is more difficult to explain. It is not
likely that the speaker will pray for a word totally devoid of meaning,
a "'trans-sense word' meaning nothing."[14] Rather, we suggest that
"bessmyslennyj" might be best interpreted as "aimless"; Mandel'štam called
for such an "aimless," non-utilitarian word numerous times:

> V poèzii nužen klassicism, v poèzii nužen èllinizm, v poèzii nužno
> povyšennoe čuvstvo obraznosti, mašinnyj ritm, gorodskoj kollektivism,
> krest'janskij fol'klor . . . Bednaja poèzija šaraxaetsja pod
> množestvom navedennyx na nee revol'vernyx dul neukosnitel'nyx
> trebovanij. Kakoj dolžna byt' poèzija? Da, možet, ona sovsem ne
> dolžna, nikomu ona ne dolžna, kreditory u nee vse fal'šivye!
>
> (II, 270)

> Vsjačeskij utilitarizm est' smertel'nyj grex protiv èllinističeskoj
> prirody, protiv russkogo jazyka, i soveršenno bezrazlično, budet li
> èto tendencija k telegrafnomu ili stenografičeskomu šifru radi
> èkonomii i uproščennoj celesoobraznosti, ili že utilitarizm bolee
> vysokogo porjadka, prinosjaščij jazyk v žertvu mističeskoj intuicii,

antroposofii i kakomu by to ni bylo vsepožirajuščemu i golodnomu do slov myšleniju.

(II, 288)

Classicism is needed in poetry, Hellenism is needed in poetry, in poetry there is needed a heightened feeling of imagery, machine rhythm, urban collectivism, peasant folklore . . . Poor poetry dashes aside under the multitude of revolver muzzles of strict demands aimed at it. What is poetry obliged to be like? Well, perhaps it is not in the least obliged; it is obliged to no one; its creditors are all false!

Any kind of utilitarianism is a mortal sin against the Hellenistic nature, against the Russian language, and it does not matter whether this is a tendency towards a telegraphic or stenographic code for the sake of economy or simplified expediency, or whether it is utilitarianism of a higher order, sacrificing language to a mystical intuition, anthoposophy, or whatever kind of all-devouring and word-hungry thinking.

It is this kind of a poetic word that he prays for.

The image of the sun first mentioned in stanza one occurs throughout Mandel'štam's work, and there is no common denominator, no invariant meaning which we can abstract for it. In "Voz'mi na radost' iz moix ladonej/Nemnogo solnca i nemnogo meda" (Take from my palms for your joy/ A little sun and a little honey, 1920) the sun is the age-old "symbol of light and warmth."[15] In another poem, also from 1920, the container of the Eucharist is likened to the sun ("Vot daronosica, kak solnce zolotoe"). Peculiar to Mandel'štam is the sun as a metaphor for the poet's cultural heritage; this is found in "Vernis' v smesitel'noe lono" (Return to the incestuous womb, 1920):

Vernis' v smesitel'noe lone,
Otkuda, Lija, ty prišla,
Za to, čto solncu Iliona
Ty želtyj sumrak predpočla.

> Return to the incestuous womb.
> From where, Leah, you came,
> For having preferred to the sun of Ilium
> The yellow dusk.

In this poem Mandel'štam expresses his acceptance of the Hellenistic-
Christian tradition and rejects the Judaic element.[16] The former is conveyed in the image of the "sun of Ilium" (a metonymy for Hellas, Hellenism[17]), while the latter is referred to as "yellow dusk" cf. "černoželtyj
svet" (black-yellow light) in "Sredi svjaščennikov levitom molodym" (Among
the priests a young Levite, 1917). A similar sun appears in two other
poems of Mandel'štam's. In "Kassandre" (To Cassandra, 1917), the sun
seems clearly to refer to Puškin:

> Kasatka, milaja Kassandra,
> Ty stoneš', ty goriš'--začem
> Stojalo solnce Aleksandra
> Sto let nazad, sijalo vsem?

> My little swallow, dear Cassandra,
> You moan, you burn: why
> Did the sun of Alexander stand
> A hundred years ago, shine to all?

(In regard to this it is worth citing Kraevskij's well-known obituary of
Puškin: "The sun of our poetry set! Puškin passed away in the prime of
his life, in the middle of his great career."[18]) In "Sestry--tjažest' i
nežnost'--odinakovy vaši primety" (Sisters--heaviness and tenderness--
your marks are the same, 1920) the image of the sun in line 4 ("I
včerašnee solnce na černyx nosilkax nesut" [And yesterday's sun is carried
out on a black stretcher]) is again part of the semantic field of cultural
heritage.

It is such a sun, we feel, which appears in "V Peterburge my sojdemsja snova." It is a sun which is as if buried in Petersburg

("slovno solnce my poxoronili v nem"). Both the images of the buried sun

and the "night sun" (l. 32: "A nočnogo solnca ne zametiš' ty") appear in

Mandel'štam's essay "Puškin and Skrjabin," of which only fragments are pre-

served. (Significantly, although this essay seems to have been written

c. 1915, the editors of Mandel'štam's prose suggest that it was completed

and submitted for publication in 1919 or 1920 [II, 607], that is, at about

the time of "V Peterburge my sojdemsja snova" [which is dated 25 Nov. 1920

in Tristija, p. 47].)

     Puškin i Skrjabin—dva prevraščenija odnogo solnca, dva
prevraščenija odnogo serdca. Dvaždy smert' xudožnika sobirala
russkij narod i zažigala nad nim solnce. Oni javili primer sobornoj,
russkoj končiny, umerli polnoj smert'ju, kak živut polnoj žizn'ju,
ix ličnost', umiraja, rasširalas' do simvola celogo naroda, i solnce-
serdce umirajuščego ostanovilos' naveki v zenite stradanija i
slavy. . . .
     Puškina xoronili noč'ju. Xoronili tajno. Mramornyj Isaakij—
velikolepnyj sarkofag—tak i ne doždalsja solnečnogo tela poèta.
Noč'ju položili solnce v grob, i v janvarskuju stužu proskripeli
poloz'ja sanej, uvozivšix dlja otpevanija prax poèta
     Ja vspominaju kartinu puškinskix poxoron, čtoby vyzvat' v
vašej pamjati obraz nočnogo solnca, obraz poslednej grečeskoj
tragedii sozdannoj Èvripidom—videnie nesčastnoj Fedry.

     Puškin and Skrjabian are two transformations of the same sun,
two transformations of the same heart. The death of an artist
twice convoked the Russian people and lit the sun over it. They
gave an example of a public, Russian death; they died a full death,
as one lives a full life; their personality, dying, broadened to a
symbol of an entire people, and the sun-heart of the dying one
stopped forever at the zenith of suffering and glory. . . .

     Puškin's burial was at night. His burial was secret. The
marble St. Isaac's cathedral, a magnificent sarcophagus, was waiting in vain for the solar body of the poet. The sun was placed in
the grave at night, and in the severe cold of January the sledge
runners crunched along, carrying away the poet's ashes for the
funeral service.

     I am recalling this picture of Puškin's funeral so as to evoke
the image of the night sun in your memory, the image of the last

Greek tragedy created by Euripides -- the vision of unhappy Phèdre.

(II, 355-356; note too, that ostensibly [I, 454] for reasons of censorship Mandel'štam, in the 1928 edition of his poems, changed the adjective "sovetskij" to "janvarskij" (Soviet, January) in the poem under discussion, ll. 5, 16. But "January night " ("janvarskaja noč'") reinforces the connection with this essay: "v janvarskuju stužu" (in the severe cold of January). "Puškin i Skrjabin" was to have appeared in Mandel'štam's collection O poèzii, 1928 [II, 607]. Thus, even if extra-aesthetic considerations did dictate this change, it is significant that Mandel'štam chose the adjective "janvarskij," and not, say, "dekabr'skij," or "nojabr'skij" (December, November), especially given that the poem is dated 25 November in Tristija.[19])

With this context, we can say that the sun which is buried in Petersburg represents its cultural heritage. To meet where this sun is buried suggests that tribute will be paid to it; respect for a past tradition is being expressed here. But with the sun buried, the world becomes dark and cold; hence, "in the black velvet of the January night." Black, of course, is traditionally associated with death and destruction, and it often acquires this meaning in Mandel'štam's poetry: "I s beskonečnoj čelobitnoj/O spravedlivosti ljudskoj/Černeet na skam'e granitnoj/ Samoubijca molodoj" (And with an endless petition/About human justice/ On the granite bench/The young suicide appears black; "V allee kolokol'čik mednyj," A brass bell in the lane, 1913); "Černym barxatom zavešannaja plaxa" (The executioner's block is draped with black velvet; "Venicejskoj žizni mračnoj i besplodnoj," Venice's barren, gloomy life, 1920); "I černyj parus vozvratitsja/Ottuda posle poxoron" (And the black sail will return from there after the funeral; "Ešče daleko asfodelej," Still far away the asphodels', 1917); etc.

The image of the "velvet" night is interesting. One usually

thinks of velvet as being a luxurious, even sensuous, fabric. But most
likely, the connection between "black velvet" and death from the above-
cited poem where the executioner's block is draped with black velvet
carries through here.

Even in the midst of the cold, cosmic void ("V barxate vsemirnoj
pustoty") there exist "blessed women." The same epithet which is applied
to the "word" is used to characterize them: "blažennyx žen rodnye oči,"
"blažennyx žen rodnye ruki," "blažennyx žen krutye pleči." (dear eyes of
the blessed women, dear hands of the blessed women, curved shoulders of
the blessed women). The adjective "blažennyj" is, of course, found
throughout Russian religious literature ("blažennyj Boris," "blažennaja
Feodosija"). The most obvious connotation is that someone who is blessed
is spiritually and ethically elevated, ready to suffer and undergo persecution. In the first stanza we read "Vse pojut blažennyx žen rodnye oči"
(The dear eyes of the blessed women still sing). "Rodnoj" suggests that
the women are both close and dear to the speaker.

In this poem the "blessed women" have several roles. But on one
level it is clear that they have a connection with art; specifically,
with the opera which is being performed. Perhaps they are part of the
chorus. This is clear from lines 25-26 of the 1928 version of the poem:
"Gde-to xory sladkie Orfeja/I rodnye temnye zrački" (Somewhere there are
the sweet choruses of Orpheus/And dear dark pupils); this obviously
parallels "Vse pojut blažennyx žen rodnye oči" (The dear eyes of the
blessed women still sing). Moreover, that the blessed women stand in a
close relation to art is clear from line 8, a syntactic replica of line 7
("Vse pojut . . . oči," "Vse cvetut . . . cvety" [Still sing . . . eyes,

still bloom . . . flowers]). The immortal flowers which bloom can be
understood as a metaphor for art. Just as the eyes which sing acquire an
added dimension thanks to the repetition of this image in the last stanza,
so too do the flowers become more sharply delineated; "bessmertnye cvety"
(immortal flowers) reappear in lines 19-20 "I bessmertnyx roz ogromnyj
vorox/U Kipridy na rukax" (And a huge bunch of immortal roses/In Cypris'
arms). (Note too another "flower" metaphor connected with the theater,
line 27: "I na grjadki kresel s galerei" [And on to the flower beds of
stalls from the galleries]). Both images function on one level as part of
the opera performance. In one instance, we have the chorus, in the other,
the scene is shifted to the end of the performance where an actress is being presented a bouquet of "immortal roses." The rose here has metaphoric
value as well; it is associated with poetry, beauty in general. This can
be deduced from another poem of Mandel'štam's which has the line "Vremja
vspaxano plugom, i roza zemleju byla" (Time is plowed up with a plow and
the rose was earth; "Sestry—tjažest' i nežnost'—odinakovy vaši primety"
Sisters—heaviness and tenderness—your marks are the same, 1920). Mandel'štam elucidated this complicated image for us in his essay "Slovo i
kul'tura" (The Word and Culture, 1920):

> Poèzija—plug, vzryvajuščij vremja tak, čto glubinnye sloi
> vremeni, ego černozem okazyvajutsja sverxu. No byvajut takie èpoxi,
> kogda čelovečestvo, ne dovol'stvujas' segodnjašnem dnem, toskuja po
> glubinnym slojam vremeni, kak paxar', žaždet celiny vremen. . . .
>   Itak, ni odnogo poèta ešče ne bylo. My svobodny ot gruza
> vospominanij. Zato skol'ko redkostnyx predčuvstvij: Puškin, Ovidij,
> Gomer. Kogda ljubovnik v tišine putaetsja v nežnyx imenax i vdrug
> vspominaet, čto èto uže bylo: i slova i volosy, i petux, kotoryj
> prokričal za oknom, kričal uže v Ovidievyx tristijax, glubokaja
> radost' povtoren'ja oxvatyvaet ego, golovokružitel'naja radost':

Slovno temnuju vodu, ja p'ju pomutivšijsja
   vozdux,
Vremja vspaxano plugom i roza zemleju
   byla.

Tak i poèt ne boitsja povtorenij i legko p'janeet klassičeskim
vinom.

(II, 266-267)

Poetry is a plow which blows up time in such a way that the deep
layers of time, its black earth, come to the surface. But there are
epochs when humanity, not content with today, longing for the deep
strata of time, like a plowman, craves the virgin soil of time . . .

Thus, there still has not been a single poet. We are free from
the burden of recollections. But how many rare presentiments there
are: Puškin, Ovid, Homer. When in the quiet a lover mixes up tender
names and suddenly recalls that all this had already been: the words,
and the hair, and the rooster that crowed outside the window was already crowing in Ovid's tristias, a deep joy of repetition seizes
him, a giddy joy:

Like dark water I drink the turbid air,

Time is plowed up with a plow and the rose
   was earth.

The poet too does not fear repetitions and is easily intoxicated by classical wine.

We should mention, too, the connection between Cypris and roses
("I bessmertnyx roz ogromnyj vorox/U Kipridy na rukax" [And a huge bunch
of immortal roses/ In Cypris' arms]). Cypris, one of the names for
Aphrodite, is the Greek goddess of love and beauty. On the one hand, as
we said, she can represent here a beautiful actress as such, who is given
a bouquet of flowers. But, interestingly, there is a long tradition of
associating Cypris with roses; for example, in the Iliad (XXIII, 184-
187), in Euripides' Medea. Russian pseudo-classical poetry continued
this tradition; e.g. Batjuškov's "Radost'," "K Žukovskomu" (Joy, To
Žukovsky). Puškin, also, used this imagery. In the poem which we shall

quote, the rose, associated with Cypris, becomes a symbol of eternal
beauty:

> Est' roza divnaja: ona
> Pred izumlennoju Kiferoj
> Cvetet, rumjana i pyšna,
> Blagoslovennaja Veneroj.
>
> Votšče Kiferu i Pafos
> Mertvit dyxanie moroza,
> Blestit meždu minutnyx roz
> Neuvjadaemaja roza . . .
>
> There is a marvelous rose:
> Before the amazed Cythera
> It blooms, red and magnificant,
> Blessed by Venus.
>
> In vain does the frost's breath
> Deaden Cythera and Paphos,
> Among the momentary roses
> Shines the everlasting rose . . .

And again, possibly, in "Krivcovu" (To Krivcov, to which we will return
later): "U pafosskija caricy/Svežij vyprosim venok [roz?]" (We will request a fresh wreath [of roses?]/From the queen of Paphos). Thus, it is
for this reason, too, that Mandel'štam chose to have Cypris hold a "huge
bunch of immortal roses in her arms."

Altogether, then, the complex of interrelated images—dear eyes,
immortal flowers, Cypris, roses, curved (shapely) shoulders—implies
both love and beauty.

The third stanza makes it clear that some kind of performance has
come to a close. Similarly, lines 27-28 of the 1928 version develop this
theme: "I na grjadki kresel s galerei/Padajut afiški-golubki" (And on to
the garden beds of stalls/ Playbill-doves fall). The performance within,

as in "Čut' mercaet prizračnaja scena," is contrasted with life outside.

An earlier poem of Mandel'štam's also presents an opera performance coming to a close:

> Letajut Val'kirii, pojut smyčki.
> Gromozkaja opera k koncu idet.
> S tjaželymi šubami gajduki
> Na mramornyx lestnicax ždut gospod.
>
> Už zanaves nagluxo upast' gotov;
> Ešče rukoplешčet v rajke glupec;
> Izvozčiki pljašut vokrug kostrov.
> Karetu takogo-to! Raz"ezd. Konec.
>
> (1913)
>
> The Valkyries are flying, the bows sing,
> The cumbersome opera is approaching the end.
> With heavy coats footmen
> Await their masters on marble staircases.
>
> The curtain is ready to fall tightly.
> A fool still applauds in the gallery.
> The coachmen dance around bonfires.
> So-and-so's carriage! Departure. The end.

The bonfire in "V Peterburge my sojdemsja snova" is of a different sort. It is part of the atmosphere of revolutionary Petersburg; cf. the following excerpt from Axmatova's memoirs:

> I met Mandel'štam especially often in 1917-18. Mandel'štam came for me and we would go by cab over the unbelievable pits of the revolutionary winter, amidst the famous bonfires which burned almost until May, while we listened to the rifle reports coming from an unknown place.[20]

Now, the blessed women will perform another task; they will "gather the light ashes" ("I blažennyx žen rodnye ruki/Legkij pepel soberut."). The primary subtext for this is Puškin's "Krivcovu" (To Krivcov):

Ne pugaj nas, milyj drug,
Groba blizkim novosel'em:
Pravo, nam takim bezdel'em
Zanimat'sja nedosug.
Pust' ostyloj žizni čašu
Tjanet medlenno drugoj;
My ž utratim junost' našu
Vmeste s žizn'ju dorogoj;
Každyj u svoej grobnicy
My prisjadem na porog;
U pafosskija caricy
Svežij vyprosim venok,
Lišnij mig u vernoj leni,
Krugovoj nal'em sosud--
I tolpoju naši teni
K tixoj Lete ubegut.
Smertnyj mig naš budet svetel;
I podrugi šalunov
Soberut ix legkij pepel
V urny prazdnye pirov.

Do not frighten us, dear friend,
With the grave's imminent housewarming:
Truly, we don't have time to devote
To such idleness.
Let the cup of life grown cold
Be slowly imbibed by another;
We will lose our youth
Together with our dear life;
Each at his own tomb
We will briefly sit down on the threshold;
We will request a fresh wreath
From the queen of Paphos,
An extra moment from faithful idleness;
We will fill the round vessel --
And in a throng our shades
Will run off to quiet Lethe.
Our last moment will be bright.
And the friends of the mischief makers
Will gather their light ashes
Into the feasts' empty urns.

Puškin's poem is a joyful affirmation of life and beauty even in the face

of death's inevitability; and after death his ashes will be gathered and

buried. So, too, do Mandel'štam's "blessed women" gather the ashes in

order to bury them. Their task is a sacred one, so for this reason as well they are "blessed." Thus, just as the sun, in part, is Puškin, so too are the ashes his, and, as well, Russia's spiritual heritage. Perhaps the suggestion is that not only is the old culture "burning," but the poets themselves. But their ashes will at some future time be gathered and venerated.

The last four lines of the third stanza ("U kostra . . ./Legkij legkij pepel soberut," At the bonfire . . ./They will gather our light ashes) may contain another literary allusion:

> Tak gori, i jar, i svetel,
> Ja Že--legkoju rukoj
> Razmetu tvoj legkij pepel
> Po ravnine snegovoj.
>
> (Blok, "Na snežnom kostre")[21]
>
> So burn, and raging and bright
> I, with a light hand
> Will sweep away your light ashes
> Along the snowy ravine.

The symbolism of Blok's poem is not, I feel, present in Mandel'štam's; the function of this literary allusion is different. In a way it serves to reinforce the Puškin subtext. Nilsson's observation, although made in a different context, is pertinent to our discussion:

> What we encounter here, then, is a play with allusions. . . . The purpose is not difficult to grasp: they conjure up poets who by their life or works are connected with Petersburg. A historical atmosphere and background are evoked, tradition as a living part of the present.[22]

The last stanza returns us to the theater. It is in the theater, of course, that the candles are burning; for example:

Ja ne uvižu znamenitoj "Fedry",
V starinnom mnogojarusnom teatre,
S prokopčennoj vysokoj galerei,
Pri svete oplyvajuščix svečej.

(1915)

Dlja načala ona [Komissarževskaja] vykinula vsju teatral'nuju
mišuru: i žar svečej, i krasnye grjadki kresel [cf. "grjadki
krasnye partera," "grjadki kresel"], i atlasnye gnezda lož.

(II, 138)

I will not see the famous <u>Phèdre</u>
In the ancient many-tiered theater,
From a high smoky gallery,
By guttering candlelight.

To start with, she [Komissarževskaja] threw out all the
theatrical trumpery: the heat of the candles, the red garden
beds of the orchestra seats [cf. "the red garden beds of the
parterre," "the garden beds of orchestra seats"] and the
satin nests of the loges.

To blow out the candles thus signals that the performance is over. But
the metaphoric meaning here is quite different. With the candles extinguished, the world is plunged into darkness. The sentence "Čto ž,
gasi, požaluj, naši sveči" on the one hand has no specific addressee,
but in its resigned tonality is closer to "pust' gasnut' . . .": "Well,
let them blow out our candles." What follows is an expression of the
poet's optimism. Even if the candles are blown out, the "curved
[shapely] shoulders of the blessed women are still singing." The adverb
"vse" here may almost acquire the meaning of an adversative conjunction:
"Well, let them . . ., <u>nonetheless</u> the curved shoulders of the blessed
women are singing." The second person singular pronoun, "ty," in the
last line relates back to the second person singular of the preceding
imperative, "gasi." The person who blows out the candles "will not

notice the night sun." It is a night sun because it continues to shine even in the black velvet of the January night"; and it is a night sun because it was buried in the night (cf. "Noč'ju položili solnce v grob" [The sun was put in the grave at night], II, 355). The last line of the poem is expanded in the meaning by the first two: "V Peterburge my sojdemsja snova,/Slovno solnce my poxoronili v nem/ . . . /A nočnogo solnca ne zametiš' ty" (We will meet again in Petersburg/ As if we had buried the sun there/ . . . /And you won't notice the night sun): you who will blow out the candles will not notice the sun, but nonetheless it is preserved, and we will notice it. Again, the visual element is stressed: the "blessed women," who preserve, have "dear eyes"; but the unspecified "you" won't (even) notice.

The sentence "Čto ž, gasi, požaluj, naši sveči" (Well, blow out our candles) can be interpreted so that it conveys more frightening implications. The candle is a commonplace metaphor for life, in literature (one of the best-known examples occurring in Anna Karenina), and in proverbs. Mandel'štam had used it already in his own poetry:

> I dumal ja: vitijstvovat' ne nado.
> My ne proroki, daže ne predteči,
> Ne ljubim raja, ne boimsja ada,
> I v polden' matovyj gorim, kak sveči.
>
>   ("Ljuteranin," 1912)

> And I thought: there's no need to orate.
> We are not prophets, not even precursors,
> We do not love heaven, nor fear hell,
> And in the matte noon we burn like candles.
>
>   (The Lutheran)

Thus, if we interpret candle as life in "V Peterburge my sojdamsja snova," then the person who extinguishes the candle (the unspecified "ty") becomes an enemy force.[23] And, lastly, the candles reinforce the buried sun metaphor. The sun, the culture, is buried. The candle, the individual poet, a "small sun," is extinguished. But just as the sun's burial is in a sense temporary, so too with the poets who will some day be venerated.

If the poem's message is potentially pessimistic as regards the speaker's fate ("soberyt [naš] legkij pepel," "gasi . . . naši sveči" [they will gather the (our) light ashes, blow out . . . our candles]), it is nonetheless optimistic in what it prophesies for Russia's cultural heritage, which is seen as something that can and will be preserved. On this level the thrust of the poem is more optimistic than "Čut' mercaet prizračnaja scena," which, as we have tried to show, ends on a decidedly ambivalent note.

Chapter V

THE AGE

In "Vek" (1923), Mandel'štam saw historical events bringing about
the end of one age and the beginning of a new one:

      Vek moj, zver' moj, kto sumeet
      Zagljanut' v tvoi zrački
      I svoeju krov'ju skleit
      Dvux stoletij pozvonki?
      Krov'-stroitel'nica xleščet
      Gorlom iz zemnyx veščej,
      Zaxrebetnik liš' trepeščet
      Na poroge novyx dnej.

      Tvar', pokuda žizn' xvataet,
      Donesti xrebet dolžna,
      I nevidimym igraet
      Pozvonočnikom volna.
      Slovno nežnyj xrjašč rebenka-
      Vek mladenčeskoj zemli,
      Snova v žertvu, kak jagnenka,
      Temja žizni prinesli.

      Čtoby vyrvat' vek iz plena,
      Čtoby novyj mir načat',
      Uzlovatyx dnej kolena
      Nužno flejtoju svjazat'.
      Èto vek volnu kolyšit
      Čelovečeskoj toskoj,
      I v trave gadjuka dyšit
      Meroj veka zolotoj.

      I ešče nabuxnut počki,
      Bryznet zeleni pobeg,
      No razbit tvoj pozvonočnik,
      Moj prekrasnyj žalkij vek.
      I s bessmyslennoj ulybkoj
      Vspjat' gljadiš', žestok i slab,
      Slovno zver', kogda-to gibkij,
      Na sledy svoix že lap.

      My age, my beast, who will be able
      To look into your pupils
      And with his own blood glue together
      The vertebrae of two centuries?

Blood-the-builder gushes
From the throat of earthly things,
Only a parasite trembles
On the threshold of new days.

A creature, as long as it has enough life,
Must carry its backbone,
And a wave plays
With the invisible backbone.
Like a baby's tender cartilege,
Oh age of infant earth,
Once again the sinciput of life, like a lamb,
Has been sacrificed.

In order to pull the age out of captivity,
In order to begin a new world,
The elbows of nodular days
Must be bound with a flute.
It's the age that rocks the wave
With human anguish,
And in the grass a viper breathes
The golden measure of the age.

Buds will again swell,
A sprout of green will spurt,
But your backbone is broken,
My beautiful, pitiful age.
And with a senseless smile
You look backward, cruel and weak,
Like a beast, once supple,
At the tracks of your own paws.

"Vek" begins with an implicit equation ("Vek moj, zver' moj") that
the age is a beast. The age is addressed in the vocative (l. 1 "Vek moj,
zver' moj," My age, my beast l. 14 "Vek mladenčeskoj zemli," O age of infant earth l. 28 "Moj prekrasnyj žalkij vek," My beautiful, pitiful age)
as if it were a sentient being. It is given the physical attributes of
some kind of animal (l. 2 "zrački," l. 4 "pozvonki," l. 10 "xrebet," l. 32
"lapy" [pupils, vertebrae, backbone, paws]), and is modified by various
personifying epithets (l. 28: "žalkij," l. 29: "bessmyslennaja [ulybka
veka]," 1.30: "žestokij," "slabyj," l.31 "gibkij" [pitiful, senseless,
cruel, weak, supple]). The age is also characterized from the point of

view of nature (l. 19: "uzlovatyx dnej kolena," ll. 25-26: "počki

nabuxnut," "pobeg zeleni bryznet" [elbows of nodular days, buds will

swell, sprout of green]). In other works from the early 1920s,

Mandel'štam personified the age in various guises: "V žilax našego

stoletija tečet tjaželaja krov' črezvyčajno otdalennyx monumental'nyx

kul'tur" (In the veins of our century flows the heavy blood of extra-

ordinarily distant, monumental cultures, II, 325); "Predystoričeskie gody,

kogda žizn' žaždet edinstva i strojnosti, kogda vyprjamljaetsja

pozvonočnik veka" (The prehistoric years when life thirsts for unity,

when the backbone of the age is becoming straight, II, 125; also II, 83,

320, 324). In "Našedšij podkovu," the age is likened to a hungry beast:

> Odni
>   na monetax izobražajut l'va,
> Drugie—
>   golovu;
> Raznoobraznye mednye, zolotye, i bronzovye lepeški
> S odinakovoj počest'ju ležat v zemle.
> Vek, probuja ix peregryzt', ottisnul na nix svoi zuby.

> Some
>   depict a lion on coins,
> Others—
>   a head;
> Various copper, gold, and bronze crackers
> With identical honor lie in the earth.
> The age, trying to gnaw through them, printed its teeth
>   on them.

The age is personified again in "1 janvarja 1924" (1 January 1924):

> Dva sonnyx jabloka u veka-vlastelina
> I glinjanyj prekrasnyj rot,
> No k mlejuščej ruke starejuščego syna
> On, umiraja, pripadet.

>   (1924, my italics)

The age-sovereign has two sleepy apple-eyes
And a beautiful clay mouth,
But to his aging son's hand, which is growing numb,
He, dying, will press himself.

and in "Net, nikogda ničej ja ne byl sovremennik" (No, never was I anyone's contemporary):

I v žarkoj komnate, v kibitke i v palatke
Vek umiraet— a potom
Dva sonnyx jabloka na rogovoj oblatke
Sijajut peristnym ognem.

(1924)

And in a hot room, in a covered wagon, and in a tent
The age is dying -- and afterwards
Two sleepy apples on a cornea
Shine with pinnate fire.

The recurring motif of the dying age suggests Mandel'štam's
familiarity with the then widespread idea of culture as an organism
which goes through a predictable course of birth, growth, maturity, and
death. This concept has been expressed by a wide range of thinkers. An
early exponent was Herder in his <u>Ideen</u> <u>zur</u> <u>Philosophie</u> <u>der</u> <u>Geschichte</u> <u>der</u>
<u>Menscheit</u>: "Es fält in die Augen, dass das menschliche Leben, sofern es
Vegetation ist, auch ads Schiksal der Pflanzen habe. [. . . . .] Unsre
Lebensalter sind die Lebensalter der Pflanze: wir gehen auf wachsen,
blühen, blühen ab und sterben."[1] More recently, Oswald Spengler used
this biological metaphor as the basis of his metaphysics, stating that
every culture completes its own unique cycle of development: "Haben die
für alles Organische grundlegenden Begriffe Geburt, Tod, Jugend, Alter,
Lebensdauer in diesem Kreise vielleicht einen strengen Sinn, den noch
niemand erschlossen hat?" "Kommen wir zur Einsicht dass das 19. und 20.

Jahrhundert, vermeintlich der Gipfel einer geradlinig anstreigenden
Weltgeschichte, als Phänomen tatsächlich in jeder bis zum Ende gereiften
Kultur nachzuweisen ist . . ."[2] In "Vek," Mandel'štam states that his era
is young, that it is not given a chance to grow old, but is sacrificed.

In order to understand the dying age, someone must look into its
pupils. Pupils are here used as a synecdoche for eyes; metaphorically,
the eye traditionally suggests a mirror of the soul, a window into a person's being. The person who looks into the eyes of the age-beast should
also be able to glue together with his blood[3] the vertabrae of two centuries. The vertabrae must be glued together because the backbone is
broken: "No razbit tvoj pozvonočnik,/Moj prekrasnyj žalkij vek" (But
your backbone is broken, my beautiful, pitiful age). Who precisely will
do both these things is left unstated in the first stanza, but stanza
three strongly suggests that it is the job of the poet. Opposed to the
positive suggestion of a person performing these deeds is the negative opposition in line 7: "Zaxrebetnik liš' trepeščet . . ." (Only a parasite
trembles). Literally, a "zaxrebetnik" is a kind of parasite that lives on
the backs and necks of animals. Figuratively, it may refer to a person,
usually with the idea of a social parasite, more colloquially, sponger.
Coupled here with the verb "trembles," it connotes the idea of cowardice.
It is a well-chosen word, underpinning the image of the century personified, adding to the biological metaphor. Structurally, it gives cohesion
to the first and second stanzas by revealing its etymology in line 10:
"donesti xrebet dolžna" (must carry its backbone). The speaker in "1
janvarja 1924" at one point expresses fear at confronting the beginning
of the new age: "I nekuda bežat' ot veka-vlastelina . . ./Mne xočetsja

bežat' ot moego poroga./Kuda? Na ulice temno . . ." (There's nowhere to
run from the age-sovereign . . ./I want to run from my threshold./Where?
It's dark in the street). In that poem, however, the initial fear is over-
come.

"Zaxrebetnik" is semantically opposed to "kto" (who) in stanza one,
as well as to "tvar'" (creature) in stanza two. The creature that must
carry its backbone in the first instance is probably the age-beast which
is dying. But "tvar'" signifies any living being; consequently, man as
such can be intended here. The image of the wave playing upon the invisible backbone in this stanza has complex associations. Synecdochically,
a wave can stand for water as such -- for example, the sea. In this sense
we might understand "volna" as a metaphor for life, the wave being connected with the action of the age. The idea seems to be that life amuses
itself at the expense of men, or at the expense of the age. As we have
said, the backbone can be either man's or the age's. In either case, it
is broken, and the man or age to which it belongs does not have long to
live. The wave might also be interpreted as the movement of history. A
game that is played with the backbone of (dead) animals is "babki"
(knucklebones). The first time that Mandel'štam used this was in his
1916 poem "Na rozval'njax, uložennyx solomoj" (On a sledge piled with
straw): "A v Ugliče igrajut deti v babki" (But in Uglič children are playing babki). A seemingly innocent children's game is being played at a
place where the Carevič is to be cruelly murdered. The frightening overtones suggested by the 1916 poem can easily be incorporated into "Vek."
"Našedšij podkovu," like "Vek," written in 1923, helps further to expand
the implications of the game of "babki." "Našedšij podkovu" combines the

imagery from "Na rozval'njax, uložennyx solomoj" and "Vek": "Deti igrajut
v babki pozvonkami umeršix životnyx./Xrupkoe letoisčislenie našej èry
podxodit k koncu" (Children are playing knucklebones with the vertebrae
of dead animals./The fragile chronology of our era is coming to an end).
The second line ("Xrupkoe letoisčislenie [The fragile chronology]), coming as a seeming non sequitur, in fact suggests a connection between the
game of babki, associated with death, and time coming to an end, the end
of an era. This connection is still further strengthened when we note
the seventh line in stanza two of "Vek": "Slovno nežnyj xrjašč rebenka"
(Like a baby's tender cartilege). The epithet "nežnyj" (tender) is often
associated with death in Mandel'štam's poetry.[4] The juxtaposition of
"vertabrae of dead animals" with "fragile chronology," and "invisible
spine" with "baby's tender cartilege" helps to elucidate this difficult
imagery.

In the second half of the stanza a lamb is added to the complementary
images of "infant earth," "baby's cartilege," "sinciput of life." The age,
like the child and the lamb, is sacrificed. A child and the lamb are young,
perhaps helpless; the age is young too (two centuries old). Mandel'štam had
earlier used the lamb in his vision of a Golden Age: "Poka jagnjata i voly/
Na tučnyx pastbiščax vodilis'" (While the lambs and oxen/ Were in the fertile pastures "Zverinec"). A lamb and a child are prominent in the Golden
Age depicted in the book of Isaiah (11:6,8). In Virgil's Fourth Eclogue,
which portrays a Golden Age, a child is of crucial importance: it is the
birth of the mysterious child (centuries of commentators have yet to identify him conclusively) that presages the beginning of the Golden Age:

The Virgin comes back to dwell with us, and the rule of Saturn
is restored. The Firstborn of the New Age is already on his way from
high heaven down to earth. With him, the Iron Race shall end and
Golden Man inherit all the world.[5]

Even without this, one may suppose that the sacrifice of a child in the
context of this poem is an ominous sign. But if we consider Mandel'štam's
fascination with the myth of the Golden Age, we may perhaps give added significance to the sacrifice. If the birth of an infant presages the advent
of the Golden Age, then the sacrifice of a child may signify the fact that
the prophecy will not be realized. More simply, the second half of this
stanza may mean that life is being sacrificed; life as such, the sacrifices
which went into the revolution. This is alluded to in the first stanza:
"Krov'-stroitel'nica xleščet/Gorlom iz zemnyx veščej" (Blood the builder
gushes from the throat of earthly things).

The third stanza begins with a clear parallelism between the first
two lines: "Čtoby vyrvat' vek iz plena,/Čtoby novyj mir načat'": to tear
the age out of captivity is the same as to start a new world. The idea is
clearly expressed through the image of the captured beast that this age is
now without freedom. Mandel'štam had earlier expressed the idea that the
revolution had the possibility of constraining man's freedom: "Kogda
oktjabr'skij nam gotovil vremenščik/Jarmo nasilija i zloby" (When October's
favorite was preparing/A yoke of violence and spite for us). In order to
end this lack of freedom it is necessary to "bind the elbows of nodular
days." "Koleno" is an elbow or joint on a plant. Therefore, the idea expressed here is similar to what is stated in the first stanza, "na poroge
novyx dnej" (on the threshold of new days)—the time is one of a junction,
a turn to something new and different. The epithet "uzlovatyj" means

"nodular, with nodes," the node being the point where a leaf or bud diverges from the stem to which it is attached. This junction of days is capable of giving birth to life. In order that all of this may be realized, the flute must be used. The flute has complex associations in literature as a whole and in Mandel'štam's work in particular. In Greek art the flute was the emblem of Dionysus and of the muse Euterpe, who was for many the muse of lyric poetry. As regards Dionysus, his significance goes far beyond associations with wine and orgiastic ecstasy. He was called Auloneus, god of the flute. Euripides, for example, in The Bacchae, describes Dionysus' mission in the following way:

> These are his gifts:
> dancing in the sacred band
> and laughing as the flute plays
> and putting an end to cares
> whenever the grape-cluster's gleam
> comes in the feast of the gods, and in the ivy-
> bearing festivities the mixing -
> bowl casts sleep over men.[6]

In Sophocles' Antigone, the passion of the music of Dionysus is portrayed as a great cosmic force that vibrates through the heavens and the stars: "thou whom the fire-breathing stars follow in the dance, thou harkener of voices in the night."[7] Equally important, especially in the context of the lines "Uzlovatyx dnej kolena/Nužno flejtoju svjazat'" (The elbows of nodular days/Must be bound with a flute), is the fact that Dionysus was recognized by many as a deity of vegetation in general. He was early seen as an earth deity whose life worked in the warm sap of the soil. Walter Pater wrote: "As Apollo inspires and rules over all the music of the strings, so Dionysus inspires and rules over all the music of the reed, the water plant in which the ideas of water and vegetable life are brought close together, natural property, therefore, of the spirit of life in the green sap."[8] Thus, the flute, through Euterpe, is emblematic specifically of lyric poetry, and through Dionysus—of music and of Dionysus' role as a life-giving, life-affirming principle.

The flute is important in two other poems of Mandel'štam's. "Kuvšin" (Pitcher, 1937) describes a black and red Grecian pitcher. Several elements are used to evoke an ancient Greek pastoral scene. The dancing goats are suggestive of Dionysus, who was often conceived of as a goat, and of Pan, who is represented in art as partly goat-like in form. Wine is obviously connected with Bacchus, one of the names of Dionysus. Most important, perhaps, is the music of the flute, emblem of Dionysus, which helps the fruits to ripen; the images of Dionysus as a god of vegetation and as an inspirer to music are here united. In "Flejty grečeskoj tèta i jota" (Theta and iota of a Greek flute, 1937), the flute theme again figures prominently. Theta and iota are probably, as Terras suggests,[9] musical notes; more specifically, notes from the Phrygian scale, which was regularly associated with the flute (II, 358). The flutist, as a creator, emerges in stanza three:

> A flejtist ne uznaet pokoja—
> Emu kažetsja, čto on odin,
> Čto kogda-to on more rodnoe
> Iz sirenevyx vylepil glin.

> But the flutist will know no peace —
> It seems to him that he is alone,
> That he once modelled his dear sea
> Out of lilac clay.

"More" (sea) is an image frequently used by Mandel'štam to suggest life.

In the penultimate stanza, creation implies the poet's own work; his
poetry has become a plague to him: "I kogda ja napolnilsja morem,/Morom
stala mne mera moja" (And when I was filled with the sea/My measure became a plague to me).[10] It is clear that for Mandel'štam the flute is
associated with several interconnected motifs; it figures as an emblem of
art and at times as a life-affirming principle. A hopeful, optimistic
possibility is generated in the first half of this stanza; the suggestion
is made that artistic creation can somehow liberate the age. Art may
perhaps be capable of bringing about a new world, joining the old age and
the new. The question asked in the first stanza, "kto sumeet/Zagljanut'
v tvoi zrački/I svoeju krov'ju skleit/Dvux stoletij pozvonki?" (who will
be able/To look into your pupils/And with his own blood glue together/
The vertebrae of two centuries?) is thus tentatively answered: it is the
artist, the creator, who can do all these things. (Cf. "1 janvarja 1924"
answers the question, "who will be able?": "liš' tot pojmet tebja/V kom
bespomoščnaja ulybka čeloveka,/Kotoryj poterjal sebja" [only he will understand you/Who has the helpless smile of a man/Who has lost himself]--
the poet.) The semantic opposition which we saw in the first stanza
(kto [who]--zaxrebetnik [parasite]) has its parallel in the third stanza:
flejta (flute)--gadjuka (viper). The viper is manifestly negative. The
image of the snake in the grass as a harbinger of tragedy has many antecedents: Ovid, Metamorphoses, X:8-10: "The outcome of the wedding was
worse than the beginning; for while the bride was strolling through the
grass with a group of maids in attendance, she fell dead, smitten in the
ankle by a serpent's tooth"; X:23-24: "The cause of my journey is my
wife, into whose body a trodden serpent shot his poison and so snatched

away her budding years"[11]; Virgil, _Eclogues,_ III:92-93: "You lads there, gathering flowering and strawberries from the earthy beds, take to your heels. There's a clammy snake lurking in the grass."[12] In the fourth eclogue (24-25) the return to peace and innocence is to be preceded by the disappearance of the snake. The viper in "Vek" breathes the "golden measure of the age," that is, man. Two quotations from Mandel'štam's prose make this clear. In "Gumanizm i sovremennost'" (Humanism and the Present, 1923), we read: "No est' drugaja social'naja arxitektura, ee masštabom, ee meroj tože javljaetsja čelovek" (But there is another social architecture; its scale, its measure is also man); and in "[Žjul' Romèn]": "Odnako, opasnost' èta minovala Žjulja Romèna: xudožestvennoe čut'e podskazalo emu pravil'nyj put': zdorovaja rasa truda. Dux Uitmena vozrodilsja v jasnyx i otčetlivyx latinskix formulax. 'Kto-nibud'', 'odin iz mnogix'--stal meroj veščej, zolotoj meroj veka, istočnikom ritma i sily" ([Jules Romains] However, this danger passed Jules Romains: his artistic feeling prompted the correct path to him: the healthy race of labor. The spirit of Whitman was revived in clear and precise Latin formular. 'Someone,' 'one of many'--became the measure of things, the golden measure of the age, the source of rhythm and strength). Both of these ultimately go back to the words of Protogoras: "Man is the measure of all things, of things that are that they are, and of things that are not that they are not."[13]

The last stanza continues the pattern of optimism followed immediately by pessimism. The first two lines suggest the possibility of a renewal of life: "I ešče nabuxnut počki,/Bryznet zeleni pobeg . . ." (Buds will swell again,/A sprout of green will burst). Mandel'štam, in

Šum vremeni (The Noise of Time), used similar biological imagery in describing the end of an age:

> Čto možet byt' sil'nee, čto možet byt' organičnee:
> ja ves' mir predstavljal xozjajstvom, čelovečeskim
> xozjajstvom—i umolkšie sto let nazad veretena
> anglijskoj domašnej promyšlennosti ešče zvučali
> v zvonkom osennem vozduxe! Da, ja slyšal s
> živost'ju nastoržennogo dalekoj molotilkoj v
> pole sluxa, kak nabuxaet i tjaželeet ne jačmen'
> v kolos'jax, ne severnoe jabloko, a mir, kapit-
> alističeskij mir nabuxaet, čtoby upast'! (II, 126)

> What could be stronger, what could be more organic: I per-
> ceived the whole world as an economy, a human economy — and
> the spindles of English home industry which fell silent a
> hundred years ago were still sounding in the ringing autumn
> air! Yes, I heard with the liveliness of an ear which was
> caught by a distant threshing machine's sound in the field,
> the swelling and increasing heaviness not of barley in ears,
> not of the northern apple, but of the world, the capitalist
> world swelling in order to fall!

Time will continue to move, and spring will come again, but this age is dying and will not survive long. The image of a hurt, wounded animal as the personification of an entire era is extensively developed in "Našedšij podkovu." In that poem history is viewed in terms of enormous epochs which are now part of the past. "A steed covered with lather lies in the dust and snorts" refers to the death of Czarist Russia. "Vek" and "Našedšij podkovu," both published in 1923, employ similar imagery to evoke the end of an era. In "Krovavaja misterija 9-go janvarja," (The Bloody Mystery Play of January 9) written in 1922, Mandel'štam was expli-cit in equating the beast with pre-revolutionary Russia:

Xarakterno, čto nikto ne slyšal signal'nyx rožkov pered strel'boj.
Vse otčety govorjat, čto ix proslyšali, čto streljali kak by bez
predupreždenija. Nikto ne slyšal, kak prozvučal v moroznom janvar-
skom vozduxe poslednij rožok imperatorskoj Rossii--rožok ee agonii,
ee predsmertnyj ston. Imperatorskaja Rossija umerla kak zver'--
nikto ne slyšal ee poslednego xripa. (III, 130)

It is characteristic that no one heard the signal horns before the
firing. All accounts say that they were heard by hearsay, that the
firing was as though without warning. No one heard the last horn of
Imperial Russia sound in the frosty January air -- the horn of its
death agony, its dying groan. Imperial Russia died like a beast --
no one heard its last wheeze.

In Voronež Mandel'štam again used this imagery; but now the age was crueler,

more predatory: "Mne na pleči kidaetsja vek-volkodav,/No ne volk ja po

krovi svoej . . ." (The wolfhound-age throws itself onto my shoulders,/

But I'm not a wolf by blood).

The last four lines reiterate the hopelessness of the situation.

The age looks back at the path it has travelled--a two-hundred year path

which thus began approximately with the era initiated by Peter the Great,

an era now ending. It is important to point out that Mandel'štam's atti-

tude toward this age, as expressed in "Vek," is by no means unambiguous.

First, the age is a "zver'" (beast). While this word may be rendered in

English by the semantically neutral "animal" (as "pušnoj zver'," "fur-

bearing animal"), one's first reaction would be to view this word as se-

mantically negative, connoting the overtones of "wild," "predatory"

("xiščnyj zver'"). Without the context of the whole poem, one would

probably be justified in seeing the first two lines of the poem as

frightening--the image of the age as a beast into whose eyes someone must

look. However, in the course of the poem, our initial perception is

somehow changed; the beast is, after all, wounded, dying. It is, we are

116 / Osip Mandel'štam and His Age

told, young. In the complex simile in the second stanza, the age is
likened to a child, a lamb. We are told that the beast is captured, that
its backbone is broken. All this information tempers our initial reaction to the word "zver'." The last stanza restates the opening simile:
"[Ty=vek] gljadiš' . . . slovno zver'" (You=age) look backwards . . .
like a beast. Therefore, the epithets which are applied to "vek" can
equally well be applied to "zver'"; the epithets are decidedly mixed.
"Prekrasnyj" (beautiful) is clearly positive; yet it is practically ne-
gated when it comes in contact with the immediately following "žalkij"
(pitiful). These two coordinate adjectives may perhaps be interpreted
as standing in a temporal relationship to each other: once beautiful, now
pitiful. The adjectival phrase "s bessmyslennoj ulybkoj" (with a senseless smile) is emotionally charged and has the effect of arousing our
pity for this beast. It underscores the epithet "pitiful." It is immediately followed by a series of three more modifiers: "žestokij"
(cruel), "slabyj" (weak), "kogda-to gibkij" (once supple). "Cruel" is
juxtaposed to "weak" through the coordinate conjunction "i" (and) as if
these two states stood in some possible logical relation to each other.
One would rather expect to see the conjunction "xot'" (in the sense of
"xotja," although). When these two modifiers are viewed in relation to
the phrase "kogda-to gibkij," the implication seems to be that when this
beast was supple -- that is, before its back was broken -- it might have
been even crueler. All this is to say that Mandel'štam's characterization
of the age's death, using this complexly developed simile, is by no means
one-sidedly mournful. In "Vek," Mandel'štam says that the age suffered
at the expense of history: "I nevidimym igraet/Pozvonočnikom volna"

(And a wave plays upon the invisible spine). But it perpetrated its own cruelties as well: "Èto vek volnu kolyšit/Čelovečeskoj toskoj" (It's the age that rocks the wave with human anguish). Moreover, the parallelism between lines 5 and 7 in the third stanza ("vek volnu kolyšit" [age rocks the wave] + instrumental case, "gadjuka dyšit" [viper breathes] + instrumental case) suggest a close relationship between the age and the viper.

Mandel'štam thus had mixed reactions to the passing of his age. It is revealing to compare his feelings with those of the Proletarian poet N. I. Kolokolov, whose poem is quoted below. Mandel'štam's poem may be conscious polemics against Kolokolov's; even if this is not so, the poem is historically interesting as representing a totally different view:

> Staromu miru
>
> Zver' umirajuščij, bessil'nyj, temnyj zver'!
> Naprasno smotriš' ty tak mstitel'no i diko
> Na tex, kto, ne ščadja sebja v bor'be velikoj,
> Otkryl v grjaduščee blistajuščuju dver'!
>
> Byloe ne vernut'. Krovavyj, mutnyj vzgljad
> Pogasnet navsegda pod dunoven'em buri.
> Najden borcami put' k nemerknuščej lazuri.
>   Znamena zor' plenitel'no gorjat.
>
>   Naprasno ždeš' spasenija sebe:
>   Ne izbežat' besslavnogo udela
>   Tebe, sražennomu v bor'be.
>   Truba suda poslednego propela.
>
> Ujdi, ujdi v zabven'ja zluju noč'!
> Ne vozbudiš' otnyne sožalenij
> Ty, na puti neščetnyx prestuplenij
> Vsë svetloe otbrasyvavšij proč'!
>
> Prokljatyj zver'! Ty sliškom obagren
> Čužoju krov'ju--čistoj i nevinnoj.
> Pozornyx del užasen spisok dlinnyj,
> I dlja tebja bezžalosten zakon.

Pogibneš' ty pod kryl'jami zari,
I o tebe navek pogibnet pamjat.
Ugrjumyj zver', ty vidiš' èto plamja?
                    Umri![14]

To the Old World

Dying beast, impotent, dark beast!
Vainly do you look so vengfully and wildly
At those who, not sparing themselves in the great struggle,
Opened a shining door to the future!

The past can't be returned. The bloody, dulled glance
Will be forever extinguished by the storm's breath.
The path to the unfading azure is found by the fighters.
    Dawns' banners burn fascinatingly.

        Vainly do you await your salvation:
        You, crushed in the struggle
        Cannot avoid an infamous fate.
        The trumpet of the last judgement has sung.

Go, go into the evil night of oblivion!
Henceforth you will not arouse pity, you
Who cast off all that is bright
On the path of innumerable crimes!

Damned beast! You are too stained
With others' blood -- pure and guiltless.
The long list of infamous crimes is terrible,
And for you the law is pitiless.

You will perish under the wings of dawn
And memory of you will perish forever
Morose beast, do you see this flame?
                    Die!

Chapter VI

A NEW INTERVENTION

In 1923 there appeared in the collection L̈et (Sbornik stixov
[Flight, Collection of Poetry] ed. N. N. Aseev, Moscow), a poem by
Mandel'štam which begins "Vojna. Opjat' raznogolosica" (War. Again there
is dissonance). It contains eighty-four lines, and thus is Mandel'štam's
second longest work (after "Našedšij podkovu," also 1923). However, it
is difficult to say whether Mandel'štam conceived of this poem as a
single unit. The section which begins "Veter nam utešen'e prines" (The
wind brought us comfort), first appeared separately, in 1922, and was republished several times thereafter as a single poem. The section "Kak
tel'ce malen'koe krylyškom" (Like a little body with a small wing) also
appeared as a separate poem after its initial appearance in L̈et (e.g.,
in Stixotvorenija [Poems], 1928), as did "A nebo buduščim beremenno" (But
the sky is pregnant with the future, Novyj mir 1929, no. 4). The entire
work, as it appeared in L̈et, consists of six parts. The first two parts
are separated from each other by stars, and the next section is headed by
the number one; then follows two, after which there is a gap in the number-
ing, so that three is not present. One can only speculate about why the
segments are so numbered. Perhaps it is simply a printer's error. Or,
perhaps Mandel'štam had planned to expand this work at some later date.
This, had he chosen to do so, he could have done without infringing the
unity of the work. For, "Vojna. Opjat' raznogolosica" is not a poèma,
but is closer in nature to a lyrical cycle of poems (as for example Blok's
"Snežnaja maska" [Snow Mask]).

The anthology in which "Vojna. Opjat' raznogolosica" appeared was published sometime after July 1923; only some of the poems appearing in it are dated, and the latest one is M. Pasynok's "O letčike s barabanom" (About a Pilot with a Drum), 4 July 1923. The anthology contains poems by Aseev, Bezymenskij, Gorodeckij, Majakovskij, Tixonov, Mandel'štam, and others. Most of the poems relate somehow to the Soviet air force, especially the need to protect the country from foreign intervention. In 1923 it was felt that there was a strong possibility of a new intervention, because in May of that year Lord George Curzon, the British foreign secretary (1919-1924), delivered an ultimatum to the Soviet government. It was interpreted as containing threats of a new intervention against the USSR, demanded monetary compensation, and so on. The ultimatum was accompanied by new anti-Soviet activity. Announcements appeared in the international press about the deployment of British troops to Poland and Rumania and about the British fleet's being dispatched to the Baltic Sea and the Dardanelles. In the Soviet press the British ultimatum was given wide coverage. For example, a headline from Pravda, 12 May 1923, reads: "The English government sent a gunboat into the White Sea following the ultimatum." Similarly, a headline from Pravda of 16 May 1923: "Curzon wants war. Curzon provokes war" (their italics). It was also at about this time that articles began appearing in Pravda on the need to build a Soviet air force, because the Soviet Union faced a grave threat of attack by air. Thus we read in an article ("We Must Conquer the Air," Pravda, 25 May 1923): "We must conquer the air in order to be able to defend ourselves against an enemy who will come to us primarily by air." Another typical article ("The Weapon of the Future," Pravda, 3 July 1923) describes the immense destructive potential of air power: "Aside from directly destructive actions, aviation also has as one of its tasks a devilish play on the nerves of the home front -- with the aim of terrifying and demoralizing the population, and at the same time striking at the root the enemy army's power of resistence." Of interest, too, is the article "Wars of the Future" (P. Sadyker, Krasnaja nov', 1922, no. 2): "General Mitchell predicts the future war to be an air war especially, with the help of enormous aviational masses. He regards the tactical unit to be a group of one hundred planes. . . . With the merciless, inhuman use of aviation, where are the limits to the destruction wreaked by it? Airplanes can, by dropping tanks of asphyxiating gas, poison entire regions, destroying everything living there." We can find references to the fledgling state of the Soviet air force in comparison with what other countries had in other places too:

> "How will the Bolsheviks wage war? With old rifles? And an air-force? A certain well-known Communist told me they have -- well, what do you think; how many planes?"
>
> "Two hundred?"
>
> "Two hundred ? Not two hundred, but thirty-two!
>
> And France has eighty thousand battle planes."[1]

Some of the poems in Lët deal explicitly with the threat of a new intervention. In order to show the context in which Mandel'štam's poem appeared it will be helpful to quote briefly from this anthology.

> Ran'še vojny velis' prosto--
> Medlenen byl sobytij xod:
> Natašcit byvalo pušek do sta
> I vedetsja osada iz goda v god.

A teper': nav'jučat na kryl'ja
Dinamitu desjat' pudov,
Gljadiš'--i stolicu vzryli
Bezo vsjakix osobyx trudov.
Čtoby nosa ne prjatat' v zemlju,
Ožidaja "nebesnyj plod"
Graždane! Ne vsem li
Nado stroit' vozdušnyj flot?
Vyše vsjakix pomyslov pročix
Podymajsja, naš krasnyj letčik,
Čtoby svet v glazax ne pomerk,
Zabirajsja štoporom vverx.

                    (N. Aseev, "Beregite oblaka," p. 4)

Earlier, wars were conducted simply --
The course of events was slow.
One would pile up a hundred cannons
And the siege goes on from year to year.
But now: they load up onto wings
A half ton of dynamite,
You look -- and they've plowed up the capital
Without any especial difficulties.
In order not to hide your nose in the earth
While awaiting the "heavenly fruit"
Citizens! Don't we all
Have to build an air force?
Ascend higher than any other intentions,
Our red pilot,
Lest the light in our eyes be extinguished,
Climb upwards in a spin.

                    N. Aseev, "Guard the Clouds"

V bleske voennyx zarnic
Pust' kružatsja zamorskie xiščniki.
I na našem sovetskom ptičnike
Slyšen klev iz jaic.
. . . .
My ne budem v grjaduščej groze
Vraž'e kopirovat' robko.
. . . .
My kuem vozdušnye meči.
Nam k licu-l' raznogolosica?
Von, rukava i mozgi zasučiv,
Konstruktory krasnye vozjatsja.
Von, rodnye stroit motory
Moskovskij metallist.

                    (I. Kataev, "Lebedinoe gnezdo. Sovetskim
                    aviozavodam" pp. 20 ff.)

In the brightness of military lightning
Let the overseas predators whirl.
And at our Soviet hen-house
The pecking from eggs can be heard.

...In the coming storm we will not
Timidly copy the enemy.

...We are forging air swords.
Does the discord suit us?
There, having rolled up their sleeves and brains
The red constructors are busy.
There, the Moscow metal worker
Is building our own motors.

      I. Kataev, "Swan's Nest. To Soviet
      Aviation Factories"

Čto značit,
     čto g-n Kerzon
razrazilsja
     grozoju not?
Èto značit,
     čtob tiše
         lez on,
krepi
   vozdušnyj
      flot!

Čto značit,
     čto g-n Foš
Pol'šej parady korčit?
Èto značit—
     točitsja nož.
S neba smotri zorče!
Čto značit,
     čto fašistko tuporyl'e
            osmelilos'
               našego tronut'?
Èto znacit,
     gotov' kryl'ja!
Krepi
   SSSR oboronu!

     (V. Majakovskij, "Èto/značit/vot čto!",
     pp. 26 ff.[2])

What does it mean
   that Mr. Curzon
Has burst into
   a storm of notes?

```
It means
      that to make him
            crawl quieter
Strengthen
      the air
            force!

What does it mean
      that Mr. Foesch
Arranges parades in Poland?
It means—
      a knife is being sharpened.
Look at the sky more vigilently!
What does it mean
      that the dumb Fascist mugs
            dared
                  to touch ours?

It means
      prepare the wings!
Strengthen
      the USSR's defenses!
```

We will include as well the text of "Vojna. Opjat' raznogolosica" as it appeared in <u>Lët</u>, since our discussion will deal primarily with this version of the poem.

```
 1 Vojna. Opjat' raznogolosica
   Na drevnix ploskogor'jax mira,
   I lopast'ju propeller losnitsja,
   Kak kost' točenaja tapira.
 5 Kryla i smerti uravnenie,
   S algebraičeskix pirušek
   Sletev, on pomnit izmerenie
   Drugix èbenovyx igrušek,
   Vraginju-noč', rassadnik vražeskij
10 Suščestv korotkix lastonogix
   I moloduju silu tjažesti:
   Tak načinalas' vlast' nemnogix . . .
   Itak, gotov'tes' žit' vo vremeni,
   Gde net ni volka, ni tapira,
15 A nebo buduščim beremenno,
   Pšenicej sytogo èfira.
   A to segodnja pobediteli
   Kladbišča leta obxodili,
   Lomali kryl'ja strekozinye
20 I molotočkami kaznili.
            * * *
```

Veter nam utešen'e prines,
I v lazuri počujali my
Assirijskie kryl'ja strekoz,
Perebory kolenčatoj t'my.
25 I voennoj grozoj potemnel
Nižnij sloj pomračennyx nebes,
Šestirukix letajuščix tel
Sljudjanoj perepončatyj les.
Est' v lazuri slepoj ugolok,
30 I v blažennye poldni vsegda,
Kak sgustivšejsja noči namek,
Rokovaja trepeščet zvezda.
I s trudom probivajas' vpered
V češue iskalečennyx kryl,
35 Pod vysokuju ruku beret
Pobeždennuju tverd' Azrail.

I

Davajte slušat' groma propoved',
Kak vnuki Sebast'jana Baxa,
I na vostoke i na zapade
40 Organnye nastavim kryl'ja!
Davajte, brosim buri jabloko
Na stol pirujuščim zemljanam
I na stekljannom bljude oblako
Postavim jastv poseredine.
45 Davajte vse pokroem zanovo
Kamčatnoj skatert'ju prostranstva
Peregovarivajas', radujas',
Drug drugu podavaja brašna.

II

Kak tel'ce malen'koe krylyškom
50 Po solncu vskljan' perevernulas',
I zažigatel'noe steklyško
Na èmpirei zagorelos'.
Kak komarinaja bezdelica
V zenite nyla i zvenela
55 I pod surdinku pen'em žuželic
V lazuri mučilas' zanoza:
Ne zabyvaj menja, kazni menja,
No daj mne imja, daj mne imja:
Mne budet legče s nim – pojmi menja,
60 V beremennoj glubokoj sini.

IV

Na krugovom, na mirnom sud'bišče
Zareju krov' oledenitsja.
V beremennom glubokom buduščem
Žužžit bol'šaja medunica.
65 A vam, v bezvremen'i letajuščim
Pod xlyst vojny za vlast' nemnogix –

Xotja by čest' mlekopitajuščix,
Xotja by sovest' lastonogix.
I tem pečal'nee, tem gorše nam,
70 Čto ljudi-pticy xuže zverja,
I čto stervjatnikam i koršunam
My ponevole bol'še verim.

V

Kak šapka xoloda al'pijskogo,
Iz godu v god, v žaru i leto,
75 Na lbu vysokom čelovečestva
Vojny xolodnye ladoni.
A ty, glubokoe i sytoe,
Zabremenevšee lazur'ju,
Kak česuja mnogoočitoe,
80 I al'fa i omega buri, –
Tebe, čužoe i bezbrovoe,
Iz pokolen'ja v pokolen'e
Vsegda vysokoe i novoe
Peredaetsja udivlen'e.

War. Again there is dissonance
On the ancient plateaus of the world,
And the propeller's blade shines
Like a tapir's carved bone.
The equation of wing and death,
Having flown away from the algebraic feasts,
It remembers the dimension
Of other ebony toys,
Enemy-night, the hostile breeding ground
Of short pinniped creatures,
And the young force of gravity.
So would begin the power of the few . . .
And so get ready to live in the time
Where there is neither a wolf nor a tapir,
But the sky is pregnant with the future,
With the wheat of the sated ether.
In fact, today the conquerors
Were making the rounds of the cemeteries of flight,
Breaking the dragonfly wings,
Executing with small hammers.

* * *

The wind brought us comfort,
And in the azure we sensed
The Assyrian wings of dragonflies,
Sequences of elbow-shaped darkness.
And with a martial thunderstorm
The lower stratum of the clouded heavens grew dark,

A micaceous webbed forest
Of six-handed flying bodies.
There is a blind spot in the azure
And always at blessed noons,
Like a hint of thickened night,
A fatal star flickers.
And struggling forward with difficulty
In the scales of crippled wings --
Azrael takes the conquered firmament
Under his protection.

I

Let's listen to the sermon of the thunder,
Like Sebastian Bach's grandchildren,
And in the east and in the west
Let's place organ wings!
Let's throw the apple of the storm
Onto the feasting earthings' table
And on the glass plate
Let's set a cloud in the middle of the victuals.
Let's cover everything anew
With the damask tablecloth of space,
Exchanging remarks, rejoicing,
Giving each other viands.

II

Like a little body, using its small wing,
It turned over with its convex surface along the sun
And the kindling lense
Blazed toward the empyrean.
Like a mosquito trifle
It rang and whined at the zenith
And secretly, singing like a carabid,
The splinter suffered in the azure:
Don't forget me, punish me,
But give me a name, give me a name;
It will be easier for me with it--understand me,
In the pregnant deep blue.

IV

At the mutually guaranteed peace court
Blood will freeze into a dawn.
In the pregnant, deep future
The large worker bee buzzes.
And you who are flying in hard times
To war's whip, for the power of a few--
If you had only the honor of mammals,
If you could have only the conscience of pinnipeds.

And it's all the sadder, all the more bitter for us,
That people-birds are worse than a beast,
And that carrion crows and kites
We unwillingly believe more.

V

Like a cap of alpine cold,
Year in, year out, in the heat and summer,
On mankind's lofty brow
Are war's cold palms.
And you, deep and sated,
Pregnant with the azure,
Many-eyed like scales,
Both the alpha and the omega of the storm,--
To you, alien, eyebrowless,
From generation to generation
An always lofty and new
Surprise is transmitted.

Mandel'štam's poem, appearing in an anthology of poetry concerned mainly with the Soviet air force and the newly revived threat of foreign intervention, may, a priori, be expected to contain allusions to both of these historical facts. At the same time, various parts of this long poem, especially insofar as they appeared separately, divorced from the context provided by Lët, are less concretized, more abstract. Imagery which can be deciphered in terms of the given historical situation may be seen to have an added dimension.

Before beginning our analysis of this poem, it will be helpful if we examine its composition. Basically, "Vojna. Opjat' raznogolosica" consists of descriptive and rhetorical segments. Lines 1-12 are essentially descriptive in nature, focusing on a single airplane; lines 21-36 describe many airplanes, and lines 49-56 focus again on one plane. Line 12, "Itak, gotov'tes'" (And so prepare) signals, through the second person imperative, a shift to a rhetorical section, which embraces lines 13-20.

Line 37, "Davajte . . . slušat'"(Let's listen) is again rhetorical; this
time, though, the hortative is used throughout ("davajte pokroem,"
"davajte slušat'," "[davajte] nastavim," "davajte brosim," "[davajte]
postavim" [let's cover, listen, place, throw, set]), the speaker thus including himself in the object of the exhortation. In these two sections
it is not immediately apparent who is being addressed. We suggest (and
will attempt to prove below) that the addressee in both instances is a
group whom we may perhaps call "citizens of the universe." Lines 57-60
are rhetorically directed to an impersonal addressee, and lines 73-84 are
addressed to the sky (respectively "Ne zabyvaj menja" [don't forget me],
"A ty, glubokoe i sytoe [nebo]" [And you, deep and sated (sky)]). Lines
61-72 are directed towards the interventionist pilots. Thus, the poem
moves from descriptive to rhetorical elements: descriptive (11. 1-12),
rhetorical (11. 13-20), descriptive (11. 21-36), rhetorical (11. 37-48),
descriptive (11. 49-56), rhetorical (11. 57-60, 61-72, 73-84).

The poem begins with two veiled references to an earlier poem by
Mandel'štam, "Zverinec" (1916), which, as we have seen, is explicitly concerned with war, in this instance World War I. "Drevnie ploskogor'ja"
(ancient plateaus) recalls the phrase "gornye strany" (mountainous lands,
1. 4) which, in the context of "Zverinec," referred to Arcadia and suggested a primeval Golden Age. We are not obliged to interpret "ancient
plateaus" as a classical reference, but clearly the inference to be drawn
is that war is intruding itself into a land which had previously been at
peace. The metaphor "raznogolosica vojny" (dissonance of war) has its
parallel in the phrase from "Zverinec" "kozlinyj golos" (reedy voice).
"Reedy voice" had clearly negative implications, suggesting the dissonant

nature of war's music. Similarly, "raznogolosica," which literally refers to musical dissonance, carries such a suggestion. In this context,
its figurative meaning -- clashing opinions -- is present too.

The word "raznogolosica" does not always have highly charged negative connotations in Mandel'štam's work. For example, in "Bax" (Bach)
(1913) the lines "Raznogolosica kakaja/V traktirax bujnyx i cerkvax"
(What dissonance/In turbulent taverns and churches) probably refer simply
to actual facts in Bach's life. In 1706 his employers complained that he
had harmonized the chorales so freely that the congregation could not sing
to his accompaniment. Also, there were many hostelries around Leipzig
where very popular concerts of secular music were given.[3] Thus, in this
poem "raznogolosica" suggests the bouyant, positive effect of Bach's music.
In the 1916 poem "V raznogolosice devičeskogo xora" (In the dissonance
of a girls' chorus) the word "raznogolosica" probably refers to the mixture
of architectural styles found in Uspenskij Sobor in Moscow: a Russian
version of a Byzantine cathedral (the Uspenskij Sobor at Vladimir-on-the-
Kliazma) built by an Italian architect (Rodolfo Fioraventi). Here, too,
there is no negative implication. But in the poem under consideration it
is clear that "raznogolosica" can only be negative.

In the third line we see contrasted with the ancient (peaceful) plateaus of the world the modern, twentieth century propeller, a metonymy for
the airplane. War in line one is bound to the negative auditory metaphor
"raznogolosica." But we should not disregard the auditory qualities of
plane. The sound of a plane is, after all, the first thing that we notice
as it approaches; it is one of the components of the "dissonance" in line
1 (Section II pays more attention to the plane's sound.) Blok, in the

first chapter of "Vozmezdie" (Retribution), presented the airplane as a harbinger of disaster and paid special attention to its threatening sound:

> I neustannyj rev mašiny,
> Kujuščej gibel' den' i noč' . . . .
> Čto ž, čelovek? Za revom stali,
> V ogne, v poroxovom dymu,
> Kakie ognennye dali
> Otkrylis' vzoru tvoemu?
> O čem––mašin nemolčnyj skrežet?
> Začem––propeller, voja, režet
> Tuman xolodnyj––i pustoj?

> And the tireless roar of the machine
> Forging destruction day and night. . . .
> What, then, man? Beyond the roar of steel,
> In flame, in gun-powder dust,
> What flaming distances
> Have opened to your glance?
> About what is the incessant gnashing of machines?
> Why does the propeller, howling, slice
> The fog, cold and empty?

In "Aviator" (1912), Blok used auditory as well as visual imagery in describing the airplane:

> Ego vinty pojut, kak struny. . . .
> Už v vyšine nepostižimoj
> Sijaet dvigatelja med'. . .
> Tam, ele slyšnyj i nezrimyj,
> Propeller prodolžaet pet'. . .

> Its propellers sing like strings. . . .
> In the unfathomable heights
> The copper of the motor shines. . .
> There, barely audible and visible
> The propeller continues to sing. . .

The airplane's propeller in Mandel'štam's poem "shines like a tapir's carved bone." A more usual comparison would be "like a carved

132 / Osip Mandel'štam and His Age

ivory bone." The propeller is the equation ("uravnenie") of wing and
death. The mathematical term ("equation") evokes the phrase
"algebraičeskie piruški" (algebraic feasts; algebra itself being used to
solve equations). "Algebraičeskie piruški" with the signal words
"uravnenie," "izmerenie" (equation, dimension) can perhaps be understood
as a metaphor for the scientific investigations which enabled planes to
fly. The "algebraičeskie piruški" thus focus on the earliest successes
with airplanes. The "algebraic feasts (triumphs)" are presented here in
conjunction with the negative potential of the airplane ("kryla i smerti
uravnenie" [equation of wing and death]) and this will be kept in mind
when we examine line 42, "pirujuščie zemljane" (feasting earthlings).

The phrase "izmerenie/Drugix ěbenovyx igrušek" (the dimension of
other ebony toys) again refers to the earliest stages in the evolution of
airplanes. "Igruški," a toy or plaything, is obviously used ironically
here (as "utešenie" [comfort] is in l. 21); these "ebony toys" are probably
the first planes that were built, which were constructed out of wood.

The plane, which has been equated with death, remembers night.
Night can be positive as well as negative in Mandel'štam's work and we
will examine these possibilities later, in conjunction with the line "Kak
sgustivšejsja noči namek/Rokovaja trepeščet zvezda" (Like a hint of
thickened night,/A fatal star flickers). Here night is clearly a hostile
force. It is called an enemy ("vraginja"; cf. Mandel'štam's translation
of Max Barthel: "Ešče carujet noč'-dikarka/i polyxaet v serdce ten'"
Night the savage still reigns/And a shadow blazes in the heart.[4]). This
appelative then appears as a modifier ("vražeskij") describing "rassadnik,"
another thing that the plane remembers. A "rassadnik" is a place where

seedlings are grown, or figuratively, a breeding ground in general; here
we have a breeding ground of "short pinnipeds." Pinnipeds, mammals which
have not yet made the transition from a marine to a land environment, suggest animals at the earliest stage of evolution. The airplane, a particularly modern phenomenon, is juxtaposed with ancient life. Blok made a
similar comparison: "Čto-to drevnee est' v povorote/Mertvyx kryl'ev,
podognutyx vniz" (There is something ancient in the turning/Of dead wings
bent under; "V neuverennom, zybkom polete" [In uncertain, shaky flight],
1910). The entire image can be understood as a metaphor for enemy soldiers
which, seen from the height of an airplane, look like pinnipeds. Lastly,
we read, "on pomnit . . . moloduju silu tjažesti" (it remembers . . . the
young force of gravity). This again stresses the newness of the experience and thus refers to the early stages of aviation.

The adverb "tak" (so) in the line "Tak načinalas' vlast' nemnogix"
(So began the power of the few) may be understood as summarizing, recapi-
tulating the above lines: it was with the first flights of military airplanes that the power of the few began. The rhyme "lastonogix"/"nemnogix"
(pinniped/few) cements this association between the few and the primitive;
"the few" emerge as a hostile, highly threatening force. At the end of
the poem, "the few" will be more specifically identified, ll. 65-66: "A
vam . . . letajuščim/ . . . za vlast' nemnogix" (And you . . . flying/
. . . for the power of a few). The fliers are obviously pilots in the
service of hostile governments.

The implication is that aviation is the key to power, and that those
who control it have available immense destructive potential. The first
eleven lines of the poem, therefore, focus on one airplane flying now,

with a clear reference to the early stages of aviation.

Line 12 begins with "itak" (and so), which suggests the deduction that we may draw from all of the above information. If the period described is so highly hostile, we should prepare to live in a time which is the antithesis to it, a time where there is "neither wolf nor tapir." The wolf is unambiguous as a symbol of something predatory, threatening. Mandel'štam used it as such in other poems: "V kustax igrušečnye volki/ Glazami strašnymi gladjat" ("Susal'nym zolotom gorjat" [Toy wolves in the bushes/Gaze with terrible eyes; Burning with tinsel] 1908); "My smerti ždem, kak skazočnogo volka" ("Ot legkoj žizni my sošli s uma" [We wait for death like for a fairy-tale wolf; We went insane from easy living] 1913); "Ne k vam vlečetsja dux v godiny tjažkix bed,/Sjuda vlačitsja po stupen'- jam/Širokopasmurnym nesčast'ja volčij sled,/Emu voveki ne izmenim" ("Ljublju pod svodami sedyja tišiny" [The spirit in not drawn to you in the times of severe misfortune,/Here along the wide gloomy steps/The wolf track of misfortune drags itself along,/We will never betray it; Under the vaults of gray silence I love] 1921). The tapir is to be understood here as the antipode of the wolf, a defenseless animal. The phrase "where there is neither a wolf nor a tapir" suggests the absence of either preda- tor or victim.[5] It is reminiscent of the Golden Ages of Virgil ("The ox will not be frightened of the lion, for all his might"[6]), Isaiah ("The wolf and the lamb shall feed together" [LXV, 25]).

The time when there will be neither wolf nor tapir is in the future: "And so get ready to live in the time/Where . . . the sky is pregnant with the future,/With wheat of the sated ether." Wheat is another attribute of the Golden Age: "Anon the earth, untilled, brought forth her stores of grain, and the fields, though unfallowed grew white with the heavy, bearded wheat."[7] The ether had earlier been equated by Mandel'štam with peace: "Otveržennoe slovo 'mir'/V načale oskorblennoj èry;/. . . vozdux gornyx stran—èfir;/Èfir, kotorym ne sumeli,/Ne zaxoteli my dysat'" (The rejected word 'peace'/In the beginning of the offended era;/. . . air of mountainous lands—ether;/Ether which we could not/Did not want to breathe; "Zverinec"). In "Zverinec" ether becomes associated with a Golden Age in the past which disappeared with the rise of war and strife. Here ether is presented as a hope for the future. Another positive metaphor, wheat, is used as part of this complex image. In a poem from 1921 ("Ljublju pod svodami sedyja tišiny" [Under the vaults of gray silence I love]), the church, its spiritual heritage, is described through metaphors which ultimately go back to the New Testament:

> Sobory večnye Sofii i Petra,
> Ambary vozduxa i sveta,
> Zernoxranilišča vselenskogo dobra
> I rigi Novogo Zaveta.
> . . . .
> Zane svoboden rab, preodolevšij strax,
> I soxranilos' svyše mery
> V proxladnyx žitnicax, v glubokix zakromax
> Zerno glubokoj, polnoj very.
>
>   (my italics; cf. Matthew 13:24, 31, 33

> Eternal cathedrals of Peter and Sophia
> Granaries of air and light,
> Storehouses of ecumenical good,
> And threshing barns of the New Testament.
>
> . . . Because the slave who overcame fear is free,
> And over the measure there has been preserved
> In cool granaries, in deep corn-bins
> A grain of deep, full faith.
>
>   (cf. Matthew 13:24, 13:31, 13:33)

In "Kak rastet xlebov opara" (How the leavened dough rises, 1922) dough is used as a metaphor of the word:

> Kak rastet xlebov opara,
> Po načalu xoroša,
> I besnuetsja ot žaru
> Domovitaja duša,--
>
> Vremja--carstvennyj podpasok--
> Lovit slovo-kolobok.
>
> I svoe naxodit mesto
> Čerstvyj pasynok vekov--
> Usyxajuščij dovesok
> Prežde vynutyx xlebov.

> How the leaven of the loaves grows,
> From the very beginning it's good-looking,
> The housewifely soul
> Raves from the heat--
>
> Time -- kingly herdsboy --
> Tries to catch the word -- small-round loaf.
>
> And the stale stepson of the ages
> Finds his place --
> The drying out makeweight
> For loaves pulled out before.

In "Našedšij podkovu" (1923) wheat is used as a simile for poetry: "To, čto ja sejčas govorju, govorju ne ja,/A vyryto iz zemli podobno zernam okameneloj pšenicy," (What I am now saying, I am not saying./But it is dug out of the ground like grains of petrified wheat). But the most important subtext for "nebo . . . beremenno . . . pšenicej sytogo èfira" (the sky is pregnant . . . with the wheat of the sated ether) is to be found in "Slovo i kul'tura" (The Word and Culture, 1921).

> Govorjat, čto pričina revoljucii--golod v mežduplanetnyx prostranstvax. Nužno rassypat' pšenicu po èfiru.
> Klassičeskaja poèzija--poèzija revoljucii. (II, 269)

It is said that the cause of revolution is hunger in inter-
planetary spaces. It is necessary to scatter wheat throughout the
ether.

Classical poetry is the poetry of revolution.

Among other things, in this essay Mandel'štam is polemicizing with
those who wanted to reject the art of the past in favor of a revolutionary
art which would be more accessible to the proletariat. The Proletariat
poets most consistently expounded this view:

> My vo vlasti mjatežnogo, strastnogo xmelja;
> Pust' kričat nam: "Vy palači krasoty",
> Vo imja našego Zavtra—sožžem Rafaèlja,
> Razrušim muzei, rastopčem iskusstva cvety.
>
> My sbrosili tjažest' nasled'ja gnetuščego,
> Obeskrovlennoj mudrosti my otvergli ximery;
> Devuški v svetlom carstve Grjaduscego
> Budut prekrasnej Milosskoj Venery . . . [8]

> We are in the power of a rebellious passionate drunkenness.
> Let them shout at us: 'You are executioners of beauty,'
> In the name of our tomorrow — we will burn Raphael,
> Will destroy museums, will trample on the flowers of art.
>
> We have thrown off the burden of an oppressing legacy,
> We have spurned the chimeras of lifeless wisdom;
> Girls in the bright kingdom of the Future
> Will be more beautiful than Venus de Milo.

In "Slovo i kul'tura," as in other essays, Mandel'štam is insisting on the
necessity of preserving, cherishing the past. Thus, on one level, classical poetry is equated with wheat as something which satisfies hunger; it
must be scattered through the ether to end revolution/hunger. But at the
same time — the sentence "it is necessary to scatter wheat throughout
ether" has broader ramifications. Mandel'stam is alluding to the metaphysics of G. I. Gurdžiev:

What is war? It is the result of planetary influences. Somewhere
up there two or three planets have approached too near to each other;
tension results . . . For them it lasts, perhaps, a second or two.
But here, on earth, people begin to slaughter one another, and they
go on slaughtering maybe for several years . . . They fail to realize to what an extent they are mere pawns in the game. They think
they signify something; they think they can move about as they like;
they think they can decide to do this or that. But in reality all
their movements, all their actions, are the result of planetary influences. And they themselves signify literally nothing. The moon
plays a big part in this. . . . [T]he evolution of humanity beyond a
certain point . . . would be fatal for the moon. The moon at
present feeds on organic life, on humanity. Humanity is a part of
organic life; this means that humanity is food for the moon. . . .
Likewise also the moon can be satisfied at one period with the food
which is given her by organic life of a certain quality, but after-
ward the time comes when she ceases to be satisfied with the food,
cannot grow on it, and begins to get hungry. Organic life must be
able to satisfy this hunger, otherwise it does not fulfill its function, does not answer its purpose. This means that in order to
answer its purpose organic life must evolve and stand on the level
of the needs of the planets, the earth and the moon.[9]

Thus, the image of scattering wheat along the ether is part of Mandel'-
štam's poetic vision of a future Golden Age devoid of war and strife.[10]

Finally, as is clear from the entire context, the wheat in this
poem must be interpreted not only as classical poetry, or even as poetry
per se, but also as the word which satisfies man's spiritual hunger.
Throughout "Slovo i kul'tura" Mandel'štam writes in these terms:

Da, staryj mir--"ne ot mira sego", no on živ bolee čem kogda-
libo. Kul'tura stala cerkov'ju. Proizošlo otdelenie cerkvi-
kul'tury ot gosudarstva. Svetskaja žizn' nas bol'še ne kasaetsja,
u nas ne eda, a trapeza, ne komnata, a kel'ja, ne odežda, a
odejanie. Nakonec my obreli vnutrennjuju svobodu, nastojaščee
vnutrennee vesel'e. Vodu v glinjanyx kuvšinax p'em kak vino. i
solncu bol'še nravitsja v monastyrskoj stolovoj, čem v restorane.
Jabloki, xleb, kartofel'--otnyne utoljajut ne tol'ko fizičeskij,
no i duxovnyj golod. Xristianin, a teper' vsjakij kul'turnyj
čelovek--xristianin, ne znaet tol'ko fizičeskogo goloda, tol'ko
duxovnoj pišči. Dlja nego i slovo plot' i prostoj xleb--vesel'e
i tajna.

V žizni slova nastupila geroičeskaja èra. Slovo--plot' i
xleb. Ono razdeljaet učast' xleba i ploti: stradanie.

(II, 265, 267)

Yes, the old world is "not of this world," but it is more
alive than ever. Culture has become a church. The separation of
the church/culture from the government has taken place. Secular
life no longer concerns us; we do not have a meal, but a refectory
meal; not a room but a cell; not clothes, but garb. At last we have
found inner freedom, real inner joy. We drink water in clay
pitchers, like wine, and the sun likes to be in a monastery dining hall
more than in a restaurant. Apples, bread, potatoes henceforth
satisfy not only physical but spiritual hunger as well. A Christian,
and now any cultured man is a Christian, does not know merely physical hunger, merely spiritual food. For him the word is also flesh
and simple bread is joy and mystery.

A heroic era has come in the life of the word. The word is
flesh and bread. It shares the fate of bread and flesh -- suffering.

Mandel'štam's Golden Age of the future is without war or aggression;

it is one where poetry can flourish. The possibility of this occurring in

the future is predicated on what has happened recently, that is, the

events described in lines 17-20. "A to" (l. 17) may perhaps best be in-

terpreted as "in fact," "in reality." The phrase "kladbišča leta" makes

most sense if read it as "kladbišča lëta" ("cemeteries of flight," not

"of summer"). It should be noted again that this poem first appeared in

the collection Lët). Mandel'štam is referring here to the Allies' destruc-

tion of Germany's air force. In "Segodnjašnij Berlin" (Today's Berlin,

first published 31 January 1923[11]), Majakovskij described this as follows:

Already on the train you come across degrading scenes, when some
Frenchman who's gone too far pushes a standing German woman away
from the window. --you see, he felt like looking at the view! And
not a single protest -- far from it: these are the all-powerful
conquerors. At your entrance into Berlin you are struck by the
cemetery stillness [kladbiščenskaja tiš']. (Comparatively.) This
is primarily the result of the Verailles housekeeping. For example, near Berlin is the so-called 'cemetery of airplanes'

[kladbišče aeroplanov] -- these are brand-new planes which are
scattered about, rusting and rotting: the Frenchmen went about
with hammers and smashed the brand-new motors!

(Majakovskij is referring to the fact that, according to the provisions
of the Treaty of Versailles, the German air force was to be destroyed.)
Thus, Mandel'štam is implying that if we do not prepare to live in a time
when there is neither wolf nor tapir this might well happen again.

Lines 13-20, therefore, build a set of positive expectations.
Mandel'štam holds out hope for a future golden age and there seems to be
a causative connection between the future and the present. "And so, get
ready to live in the time where there is neither a wolf nor a tapir, but
[where] the sky is pregnant with the future. In fact today the conquerors were breaking the dragonfly wings."

The next section of this poem ("Veter nam utešen'e prines" [The
wind brought us comfort]) appears at first to continue the mood of rising
expectations. There is nothing initially to suggest that the wind (1. 21)
is anything but good. In some of Mandel'štam's early poems, the wind of
poetic inspiration is not uncommon ("Smutno dyšaščimi list'jami" [Vaguely
breathing leaves], 1911; "Otčego duša tak pevuča" [Why is my soul so
melodious?], 1911). The word "lazur'"(azure, 1. 22), moreover, suggesting that the sky is serene and cloudless, is usually a positive image.
For the symbolists, "lazur'" was a very important word, often semantically
positive. For Blok, especially, azure has consistently (in "Stixi o
Prekrasnoj Dame" [Verses about the Beautiful Lady]) positive associations.
In particular, this section of Mandel'štam's poem, which seems to hint
initially at growing hopes, is remarkably reminiscent of the second poem
in Blok's "Stixi o Prekrasnoj Dame":

Veter <u>prines</u> izdaleka
Pesni vesennej <u>namek</u>,
Gde-to svetlo i gluboko
<u>Neba</u> otktylsja kločok.

V <u>è</u>toj bezdonnoj <u>lazuri</u>,
<u>V</u> sumerkax blizkoj vesny
Plakali zimnie buri,
Rejali <u>zvezdnye</u> sny.

Robko, temno i gluboko
Plakali struny moi.
<u>Veter prines</u> izdaleka
Zvučnye pesni tvoi.

                    (my italics)

<u>The</u> <u>wind</u> <u>brought</u> from afar,
The hint of a spring song,
Somewhere bright and deep
A patch of <u>sky</u> has opened.

<u>In</u> this bottomless <u>azure</u>,
In the dawn of an imminent spring,
The winter storms cried,
<u>Starry</u> dreams fluttered.

Timidly, darkly and deeply
My strings cried.
<u>The</u> <u>wind</u> <u>brought</u> from afar
Your sonorous songs.

Blok's poem presents a mood of expectations; the poet is waiting for Her
to descend. Mandel'štam's "Veter nam utešen'e prines" could be viewed as
an ironic rejoinder to Blok's optimistic hopes. Blok's positive "namek
vesennej pesni" (the hint of a spring song) should be compared to Mandel'-
štam's "namek sgustivšejsja noči" (a hint of thickened night) which, as we
will see, is highly negative. In Blok's azure there are "starry dreams";
in Mandel'štam's are sensed Assyrian wings and darkness. Blok's wind
brings hints of the Beautiful Lady and hopes of a harmonious life; Mandel'-
štam's brings Azrail. The azure, usually such a positive image, is here
invaded by planes carrying death and destruction.

The wings which are sensed in the azure (the Assyrian wings of dragon flies) have already been associated with death, "kryla i smerti uravnenie" (the equation of wing and death). In "Devjatnadcatyj vek" (The Nineteenth Century, 1920), which closes with a quotation from "Veter nam uteŝen'e prines," Mandel'ŝtam talks of wings which betray their original purpose and weigh heavy rather than make light:

> K devjatnadcatomu veku primenimy slova Bodlera ob al'batrose:
> "Ŝatrom gigantskix kryl on prigneten k zemle."
>
> Naĉalo stoletija eŝĉe probovalo borot'sja s tjagoj zemli, sudorožnym pryžkami, meŝkovatymi i gruznymi polupoletami, konec stoletija pokoilsja uže nepodvižno, prikrytyj ogromnoj palatkoj nepomernyx kryl. Pokoj otĉajan'ja. Kryl'ja davjat, protivoreĉat svoemu estestvennomu naznaĉeniju.
>
> Gigantskie kryl'ja devjatnadcatogo veka, èto ego poznavatel'nye sily. (II, 318)

> Baudelaire's words about the albatross are applicable to the nineteenth century: By its tent of giant wings it is pressed to the earth.
>
> The beginning of the century still tried to battle with the earth's pull, with spasmodic jumps, awkward and heavy semi-flights; the end of the century lay motionless, covered with an immense tent of excessive wings. The rest of despair. The wings oppress, contradict their natural function.
>
> The gigantic wings of the nineteenth century are its cognitive powers.

Dragonflies' wings are tough membranes ("sljudanoj pereponĉatyj les" [a micaceous webbed forest]) covered by an elaborate system of veins; they are reminiscent of the lined wings found on Assyrian human-headed bulls. In "Devjatnadcatyj vek" (Nineteenth Century) we have another gloss of the epithet "Assyrian":

No vkus k istoričeskim perevoploščenijam i vseponimaniju ne
postojannyj i prexodjaščij i naše stoletie načinaetsja pod znakom
veličestvennoj neterpimosti, isključitel'nosti i soznatel'nogo
neponimanija drugix mirov. V žilax našego stoletija tečet
tjaželaja krov' črezvyčajno otdalennyx monumental'nyx kul'tur, byt'
možet egipetskoj i assirijskoj:

> Veter nam utešen'e prines,
> I v lazuri počujali my
> Assirijskie kryl'ja strekoz,
> Perebory kolenčatoj t'my.

(II, 325)

But a taste for historical reincarnations and total understanding is
not constant, is transient, and our century begins under the sign of
grand intolerance, exclusiveness, and conscious incomprehension of
other worlds. In the veins of our century flows the heavy blood of
extraordinarily distant, monumental cultures, perhaps Egyptian and
Assyrian:

> The wind brought us comfort,
> And in the azure we sensed
> The Assyrian wings of dragonflies
> Sequences of elbow-shaped darkness.

In "Gumanizm i sovremennost'" (Humanism and the Present, 1923) Mandel'-
štam again used the word "Assyrian":

Byvajut èpoxi, kotorye govorjat, čto im net dela do čeloveka,
čto ego nužno ispol'zovat', kak kirpič, kak cement, čto iz nego
nužno stroit', a ne dlja nego. Social'naja arxitektura izmerjaetsja
masštabom čeloveka. Inogda ona stanovitsja vraždebnoj čeloveku i
pitaet svoe veličie ego uniženiem i ničtožestvom.

Assirijskie plenniki kopošatsja, kak cypljata, pod nogami
ogromnogo carja, voiny, olicetvorjajuščie vraždebnuju čeloveku
mošč' gosudarstva, dlinnymi kop'jami ubivajut svjazannyx pigmeev
i egiptjane i egipetskie stroiteli obraščajutsja s čelovečeskoj
massoj, kak s materialom, kotorogo dolžno xvatit', kotoryj dolžen
byt' dostavlen v ljubom količestve. [. . . .] Esli podlinno
gumanističeskoe opravdanie ne ljažet v osnovu grjaduščej social'noj
arxitektury, ona razdavit čeloveka, kak Assirija i Vavilon.

(II, 394, 396)

There are epochs which say that they have nothing to do with
man, that he is to be used like a brick, like cement, that it is
necessary to build out of him and not for him. Social architecture
is measured by the scale of man. Sometimes it becomes hostile to
man and nourishes its greatness on his degradation and insignifi-
cance.

Assyrian prisoners swarm like chicks under the feet of an
immense king, warriors, personifying the might of a state hostile
to man, with long spears kill the bound up pygmies; and the Egyp-
tians and Egyptian builders handle the human mass like a material
which must suffice, which must be supplied in any quantity. . . .
If a genuinely humanistic justification is not placed at the founda-
tion of the coming social architecture, it will crush man, like
Assyria and Babylon.

Thus for Mandel'štam "Assyrian" connotes such concepts as ancient, monu-

mental, antihumanistic, crushing, and is clearly a highly negative epi-

thet.

The airplanes are called "dragonflies," as they had been in line

19: "kryl'ja strekozinye" (dragonfly wings). In Blok's poem "Kometa"

(The Comet, 1910), a comet is something shown as threatening the very

existence of our planet: "Ty nam groziš poslednim časom,/Iz sinej

večnosti zvezda!" (You threaten us with the final hour,/Star from blue

eternity!). The airplane, called a "stal'naja strekoza" (steel dragon-

fly), is seen as man's weak equivalent of nature's comet, and hence

emerges as something dangerous and threatening.[12]

The phrase "kolenčataja t'ma" (elbow-shaped darkness) relates to

the dragonflies, too. "Elbow-shaped" probably described the configura-

tion of the wings attached to the body. "T'ma" suggests the idea that

there are so many dragonflies that one cannot see; this meaning of "t'ma"

("darkness") emerges from the following two lines: "I voennoj grozoj

potemnel/Nižnij sloj pomračennyx nebes." (And with a martial thunder-

storm/The lower statum of the clouded heavens grew dark). The dragonfly

as the precursor of a storm is apparent here. Two texts support this

connection between the dragonfly and the storm; both are linked with

Tjutčev, and one reveals a metaphoric meaning of "storm." First is an

undated fragment of Mandel'štam's: ". . . Proobrazom istoričeskogo
sobytija v prirode služit groza. . . . Vsmotrimsja pristal'no vsled za
Tjutčevym, znatokom žizni, v roždenie grozy. Nikogda èto javlenie prirody
v poèzii Tjutčeva ne voznikaet, kak tol'ko . . ." (A storm is the prototype of a historical event in nature. . . . Let us carefully scrutinize,
following Tjutčev, an expert on life, the birth of a storm. This manifestation of nature never arises in Tjutčev's poetry, when . . .; the
fragment ends here, II, 287). The connection between Tjutčev and the
dragonfly is alluded to in a poem from 1932. In a Harvard seminar, Professor Kiril Taranovsky suggested an answer to the riddle asked by Mandel'-
štam in his poem "Dajte Tjutčevu strekozu--/Dogadajtes' počemu. . ." (Give
Tjutčev a dragonfly--/Guess why). Tjutčev used the word "dragonfly"
(strekoza) only once:

> V dušnom vozduxa molčan'e,
> Kak predčuvstvie grozy,
> Žarče roz blagouxan'e,
> Rezče golos strekozy.

> In the stuffy silence of the air,
> Like the presentiment of a thunderstorm,
> The fragrance of roses is more ardent,
> The dragonfly's voice is sharper.

Finally, in Mandel'štam's poem on the death of Belyj, the dragonfly has
one more association:

> Menja presledujut dve-tri slučajnux frazy--
> Ves' den' tveržu: pečal' moja žirna,
> O Bože, kak černy i sineglazy
> Strekozy smerti, kak lazur' černa!
> (10 janvarja 1934)[13]

I am pursued by two or three chance phrases.--
All day long I repeat: my sadness is abundant,
O God, how black, how blue-eyed
Are the dragonflies of death, how black the azure!

(10 January 1934)

Lines 27-28 further describe the sky. "Micaceous" of course is suggestive of the dragonflies' transparent, net-veined wings, and "perepončatyj," here meaning "membraneous," refers to their wings as well. The dragonflies' bodies are called "six-handed" because the dragonfly has six limbs on the forward part of its body in which it catches flying insects.

Lines 25-28, then, juxtapose the threat of war with a darkening sky swarming with flying insects. This is remarkably reminiscent of the "apocalyptic" sky[14] of "Koncert na vokzale" (Concert at the Railway Station, 1921) which swarmed with worms: "Nel'zja dyšat', i tverd' kišit červjami" (It's impossible to breathe and the sky is swarming with worms). The sky is hostile and frightening in these two poems, and such skies can be found throughout Mandel'štam's poetry: "Ja vižu mesjac bezdyxannyj/I nebo mertvennej xolsta" ("Slux čutkij parus naprjagaet" [I see a lifeless moon/And a sky deader than canvas; Hearing tenses its keen sail] 1910); "Nebo tuskloe s otsvetom strannym--/Mirovaja tumannaja bol'--" (Vozdux pasmurnyj vlažen i gulok" [A dull sky with a strange reflection--/Foggy world pain; The overcast air is humid and rumbling], 1911); "Ja vižu kamennoe nebo/Nad tuskloj pautinoj vod (Vest. russkogo stud. dviz., III, 1970, p. 116; [I see a stone sky/ Over the dull spiderweb of waters] 1909?); "Umyvalsja noč'ju na dvore--/Tverd' sijala grubymi zvezdami" (I washed at night in the courtyard--/The firmament shined with coarse stars, 1921).

In the following four lines the imagery becomes considerably more complex. "Est' v lazuri slepoj ugolok" (There is a blind corner in the azure) is ambiguous; the adjective can be understood as modifying either "azure" ("Est' v _lazuri_ _slepoj_ ugolok" [There is a corner in the blind azure]) or "corner" ("Est' v lazuri _slepoj_ _ugolok_" [In the azure there is a blind corner]). For the first possibility, similar images can be found in other poems of Mandel'štam's "O nebo, nebo, ty mne budes' snit'sja!/ Ne možet byt', čtob ty sovsem osleplo" (O sky, sky, I'll dream of you!/ It can't be that you have gone completely blind; 1911); "No žertvy ne xotjat slepye nebesa" (But the blind heavens do not a sacrifice, "Dekabrist," 1917); "A blizorukoe šaxskoe nebo--/Sleporoždennaja birjuza" ("Koljučaja reč' araratskoj doliny" [And the near-sighted sky of the Shah--/A tourquoise blind from birth; Thorny speech of the valley of Ararat] 1930). For the second possibility, the azure, a metonymy for the sky, has a blind spot in it.

Even when the sun is brightest ("I v blažennye poldni"), a star can be seen which hints at night's presence. Two themes important in Mandel'-štam's work as a whole emerge here: the theme of stars and the theme of night. As one investigator of Mandel'štam's poetry has shown, star imagery in Mandel'štam's work is highly complex: "An analysis of M.'s entire corpus shows that his astral imagery is ambivalent. . . ."[15] It is often associated with the semantic field "threatening, frightening, highly negative": "Čto, esli, nad modnoj lavkoju/Mercajuščaja vsegda,/ Mne v serdce dlinnoj bulavkoju/Opustitsja vdrug zvezda?" ("Ja vzdragivaju ot xoloda" [What if, over the modish shop/Always twinkling/

Into my heart like a long pin/The star suddenly sinks] 1912); "Ja
nenavižu svet/Odnoobraznyx zvezd" (I hate the light/Of monotonous stars,
1912); "Mercajut zvezd bulavki zolotye" (Mne xolodno. Prozračnaja vesna"
[The gold pins of the stars twinkle; I'm cold. Transparent spring] 1916;
"Nel'zja dyšat, i tverd' kišit červjami,/I ne odna zvezda ne govorit,"
("Koncert na vokzale" [It's impossible to breathe and the firmament swarms
with worms/And not one star speaks; Concert at the Railway Station] 1921);
"Umyvalsja noč'ju na dvore--/Tverd' sijala grubymi zvezdami" (I bathed at
night in the courtyard--/The firmament shined with coarse stars, 1921).
Not only is the star in this poem itself threatening ("rokovaja zvezda"),
but it evokes other things as well: it is a hint of night, which in this
poem has already been explicitly labeled as a hostile force, "vraginja-
noč'." Night for Mandel'štam can be a positive or a negative time. It
can be the time of poetic creation, the time when thoughts and feelings
mature. This kind of night can be found in "Rakovina" (Seashell, 1911),
"Otravlen xleb i vozdux vypit" (The bread is poisoned and the air drunk,
1913), "Grifel'naja oda" (State Ode, 1923). But in "Vojna. Opjat'
raznogolonica" night is an enemy. The star is thus indeed fatal. It is
present even in the brightness of day as a reminder of night which might
emerge at any time.

The last quatrain presents a grim picture. It is made clear what
kind of "consolation" the wind has brought: death, in the guise of
Azrael. In Jewish mysticism he is the embodiment of evil; in Islamic
lore, he is the angel of death, popularized in Russian poetry by Lermontov.

Section I of the poem begins now. It presents several signals

which are unmistakable within the context of Mandel'štam's work. First,
within the context of this poem, "groma propoved'" (sermon of thunder)
stands juxtaposed to "raznogolosica vojny" (dissonance of war), and
"organnye kryl'ja" (organ wings) to "strekozinye," "assirijskie kryl'ja"
(dragonfly, Assyrian wings). Further, the words "Bach," and "organ" are
inextricably bound with the themes of music and poetry; they stress the
concepts of organization, proof, logic.

In "Ja nenaviž̌u svet" (I hate the light, 1912), Mandel'štam presents
the poetic expression of a theme which was fully explored in his prose
"Utro akmeisma" (The Morning of Acmeism, published 1919). The formless-
ness of nature ("svet odnoobraznyx zvezd" [light of monotonous stars]) is
rejected, and man's conscious mastery of material, Gothic art, is affirmed:
"Zdravstvuj moj davnij bred—/Bašni strel'čatoj rost!" (How do you do, my
ancient delirium—/Height of the Gothic arched tower!). The organ is associated with Gothic art: "V tot večer ne gudel strel'čatyj les organa"
(That evening the Gothic arched forest of the organ did not drone, 1917);
and, of course, with Bach as well:

Zadolgo do Baxa i v to vremja, kogda ešče ne stroili bol'šix monumental'nyx organov, no liš' očen' skromnye embrional'nye proobrazy
buduščego čudišča . . . Alig'eri postroil v slovesnom prostranstve
beskonečnyj mogučij organ. . . .
(II, 412)

Long before Bach, and at a time when large monumental organs were
not yet being built, but only the very modest embryonic prototypes
of the future monster . . . Alighieri built in verbal space an in-
finite, powerful organ. . . .

Esli u vas ne zakružilas' golova ot ètogo čudesnogo pod"ema,
dostojnogo organnyx sredstv Sebast'jana Baxa, to poprobujte
ukazat', gde zdes' vtoroj, gde zdes' pervyj člen sravnenija . . ."
(II, 425-426)

If your head did not go around from this miraculous ascent, worthy
of the organ of Sebastian Bach, then try to show where the second,
where the first member of the simile is.

In "The Morning of Acmeism" Mandel'štam was explicit in stating what
Bach, Gothic, and so on, signified for him:

My vvodim gotiku v otnošenija slov, podobno tomu, kak
Sebast'jan Bax utverdil ee v muzyke. . . . Logika est' carstvo
neožidannosti. Myslit' logičeski, značit nepreryvno udivljat'sja.
My poljubili muzyku dokazatel'stva [cf. "Bax": "Oporu duxa v samom
dele/Ty v dokazatel'stve iskal?"] Logičeskaja svjaz' dlja nas ne
pesenka o čižike, a simfonija s organom i peniem. . . . Kak
ubeditel'na muzyka Baxa! Kakaja mošč' dokazatel'stva! Dokazyvat'
i dokazyvat' bez konca. . . .
                           (II, 363, 366)

We are introducing the Gothic into relationships of works as
Sebastian Bach established it in music. . . . Logic is the kingdom
of the unexpected. To think logically means to be continually
amazed. We have grown to love the music of proof [cf. "Bach":
"Did you really seek/a buttress for spirit in proof?"] For us a
logical connection is not a children's song, but a symphony with
organ and singing. . . . How convincing is Bach's music! What
power of proof! To prove and to prove without end. . . .

His poem "Bax" (1913) conveys a somewhat different, slightly ironic, understanding of Bach:

Vysokij sporščik, neuželi,
Igraja vnukam svoj xoral,
Oporu duxa v samom dele
Ty v dokazatel'stve iskal?

Čto zvuk? Šestnadcatye doli,
Organa mnogosložnyj krik,
Liš' vorkotnja tvoja, ne bole,
O nesgovorčivyj starik!

Elevated polemicist, did you really,
Playing your choral to your grandchildren,
Seek a buttress for spirit
In proof?

What is sound? Sixteenth notes,
The complex cry of an organ,
It's only your grumbling, no more,
O stubborn old man!

The first four lines of part I suggest, then, such ideas as music, especially the concept of reason in music, and harmony, proof and logic,
poetry. These are presented as antipodes to the images of war as discord
allied with chaos. The opposition is made unambiguous through the change
in epithets ("strekozinye," "assirijskie" vs. "organnye" [dragon fly,
assyrian vs. organ]), as well as by Mandel'štam's obvious self-quotation
("Davajte slušat' groma propoved/Kak vnuki Sebast'jana Baxa"--"Vysokij
sporščik, neuželi,/Igraja vnukam svoj xoral . . ./I ljuteranskij
propovednik . . ." [Let's listen to the sermon of the thunder,/Like Sebastian Bach's grandchildren -- Elevated quarreler, did you really,/
Playing your choral to your grandchildren . . ./And the Lutheran preach-
er . . .]). Art, organization, peace is opposed to war, chaos. Art having the power to save emerged in another poem from 1923, "Vek": "Čtoby
vyrvat' vek iz plena,/Čtoby novyj mir načat',/Uzlovatyx dnej kolena/
Nužno flejtoju svjazat'" (In order to pull the age out of captivity,/In
order to begin a new world,/The elbows of nodular days/Must be bound
with a flute).

Lines 41-42, in comparison, are somewhat more obscure in their
reference: "Davajte, brosim buri jabloko/Na stol pirujuščim zemljanam"
(Let's throw the apple of the storm/Onto the feasting earthlings' table).
The "apple of the storm" is undoubtedly a reference to the famous apple
of discord of Eris, herself the personification of discord. Eris was to
be present at the wedding of Peleus and Thetis. She caused a quarrel

among the goddesses concerning which of them was the most beautiful.
This led to the Judgment of Paris and thence to the Trojan War. In the
version given by Hyginus, Eris comes to the door and throws in an apple:

> Jove is said to have invited to the wedding of Peleus and
> Thetis all of the gods except Eris, or Discord. When she came
> later and was not admitted to the banquet, she threw an apple
> through the door, saying that the fairest should take it.[16]

In Mandel'štam's poem the myth is reworked; the feasting gods are replaced
by feasting earthpeople. The feast of line 42 is similar to the one which
is mentioned in line 6, the "algebraic feasts" frequented by the airplane.
Hence, for us to throw the apple of discord ("jabloko razdora"="dis-
cordia"="raznogolosica") onto their table would simply mean that we
should return the discord to the source from which it originated. The
image of the cloud in line 47 ("I na stekljannom bljude oblako/Postavim
jastv poseredine" [And on the glass plate/Let's set a cloud in the middle
of the victuals]) is extremely puzzling, and difficult to account for
satisfactorily, but makes most sense if interpreted as having positive
implications.[17]

The last four lines of section I are very optimistic. The tablecloth ("skatert'") is reminiscent of the imagery used in line 16, "wheat
of the sated ether (pšenica sytogo èfira) and is part of the positive semantic field. Moreover, there appears to be an obvious allusion to
Tjutčev in lines 45-46 "pokroem . . . kamčatnoj skatert'ju prostranstva"
(let's cover . . . with the damask tablecloth of space):

> Na mir tainstvennyj duxov,
> Nad ètoj bezdnoj bezymjannoj
> Pokrov nabrošen zlatokannyj
> Vysokoj voleju bogov.

Den'--sej blistatel'nyj pokrov--
Den', zemnorodnyx oživlen'e,
Duši boljašcej iscelen'e,
Drug čelovekov i bogov!

No merknet den'--nastala noč';
Prišla--i s mira rokovogo
Tkan' blagodatnuju pokrova,
Sorvav, otbrasyvaet proč' . . .
I bezdna nam obnažena
S svoimi straxami i mglami,
I net pregrad mež ej i nami--
Vot otčego nam noč' strašna!

          ("Den' i noč'.")

Onto the mysterious world of spirits,
Over this nameless abyss
A cover woven of gold has been thrown
By the exalted will of the gods.
Day is that brilliant cover --
Day, the animation of mortals,
Healing of the aching soul,
Friend of men and gods!

But day fades --night falls;
It came, and from the fateful world
Having torn off the beneficial cloth
Of the cover, throws it aside. . .
And the abyss is bared to us
With its fears and gloom,
And there is no barrier between it and us:
That is why night is dreadful to us!

          ("Day and Night")

The parallels between Mandel'štam's and Tjutčev's metaphors seem clear
enough. Day for Tjutčev is positive and shields man from the watery
black chaos of night. In Mandel'štam's poem it is suggested that the
"tablecloth" was removed and must be returned ("pokroem zanovo"). To
replace the cover is to protect ourselves from the threatening predatory
night.

Section I of this poem is heavily saturated with hortatives:
"Let's listen, let's place, let's throw, let's set, let's cover." The

speaker includes himself in the exhortation and is addressing more than one person (davajte). There seems to be a definite opposition between the addresser-addressees and another group, the "earthlings" (zemljane) of line 46. The question arises, if the addresser sees himself (as well as his addressees) as distinct from the "feasting earthlings," then to what group does he belong? We suggest that the opposition is between "earthlings" and "citizens of the universe." This suggestion becomes even more plausible when we realize that it was during the early twenties that the literary current known as "cosmism" reached its zenith. "Cosmism," in the words of one investigator, tried to "penetrate into the cosmos and there make its own kind of revolution."[18] Cosmism hyperbolically carried the revolution from the earth to the entire universe: "Požar vostanij, revoljucij/I mjatežej dostig do zvezd" (The conflagration of insurrections, revolutions/And revolts reached the stars).[19] Thus, the scene of the first act of Majakovskij's <u>Misterija-buff</u> is "vsja vselennaja" (the whole universe). The second variant of <u>Misterija-buff</u> (1920-21) concluded as follows:

> Ètot gimn naš pobednyj,
> vsja vselennaja, poj!
> S Internacionalom
> vosprjanul rod ljudskoj.
> > (This refrain is repeated three times.)

> This victory hymn of ours,
> whole universe, sing!
> With the International
> the human race is cheered up.

This theme is expressed in other poems of Majakovskij's:

```
Kovrom
      vselennuju vzvej.
Mol' iz vselennoj
                  vybej!
Veli
    letet'
          levej
vsej
    vselennskoj
                glybe!
```

("Molodaja gvardija," 1923)

Raise the universe like a carpet.
Beat the moth out of the universe!
Order the entire universal clod to fly more left!

("Young guard")


```
My idem!
Šturmuem dveri raja.
My idem.
Probili dver' drugim.
Vyše, naše znamja!
Serp,
ognem igraja,
obnimajsja s molotom radugoj dugi.

        V dveri èti!
        Star i mal!
        Vselen'sja, Tretij
        Internacional!
```

("III Internacional," 1920)

We are going!
We assult the doors of paradise.
We are going.
We struck through the door to others.
Higher, our banner!
Sickle,
Playing with fire,
Embrace the hammer with the rainbow of your arc.

        To these doors!
        Old and small!
        Universalize, Third
        International!

We can find this idea in Esenin's work, too:

> Ej, rossijane!
> Lovcy vselennoj,
> Nevodom zari začerpnuvšie nebo,--
> Trubite v truby.
>
> ("Preobraženie," 1917)

> Eh, Russians!
> Fishermen of the universe,
> Having scooped up the sky with the net of dawn, --
> Sound your trumpets.
>
> ("Transformation")

This theme was part of the spirit of the time. It was given its fullest
expression by the Proletarian poets (who of course did not inspire Mandel'-
štam):

> My zabryžžem, my zatopim ves' cvetami staryj mir,
> K solncu, zvezdam slyšen budet nas beskrajnyj,
>   /xmel'nyj pir . . .[20]

> We will start to splash, we will flood the entire
>   /old world with flowers,
> To the sun, stars our intoxicating limitless feast will be
>   /audible.

Budet vremja,--odnim nažimom my oborvem rabotu vo vsem mire, usmirim
mašiny. Vselennaja napolnitsja togda radostnym exo truda. . . .[21]

There will be a time, -- with a single onslaught we will cut short
work in the whole world, subdue machines. Then the universe will be
filled with the joyous echo of labor.

> Pen'ju trepetno vnimaja,
> Mudrost' Mira postigaju:

> Xor gudkov--Jazyk vselennoj,
> Gimn-Edinstva, gimn-Truda . . .[22]

> Anxiously listening to the singing,
> I grasp the Wisdom of the World:

```
The chorus of whistles is the Language of the universe,
The Hymn-of-Unity, hymn-of-Labor.


Krepkie ruki, xleb da voda,
S skarbom ubogim mešok neizmennyj,--
Vot on, tvorec mirovogo truda
I graždanin vsej vselennoj!. .

S ètim imen'em on versty idet . . .

Vot on--sozdatel' zemnogo truda--
I graždanin vsej vselennoj . . .23


Strong hands, bread and water,
The immutable sack with its wretched belongings --
Here he is, the creator of world labor
And a citizen of the entire universe! . . .

With this name he goes miles . . .

Here he is -- creator of earthly labor --
And a citizen of the entire universe.
```

Hence this section of Mandel'štam's poem can be understood as a variation on a then often expressed theme. His Golden Age of the future exists in a universe distinct from the earth. Here, the "sky is pregnant with the future, with the wheat of the sated ether"; food imagery continues to be used: "kamčatnaja skatert' prostranstva" (the damask tablecloth of space) "drug drugu [i.e. "my," "graždane vselennoj"] podavaja brašna" (giving each other [i.e. "we," "citizens of the universe] viands); we should point out that the first meaning given to "brašno" in Sreznevskij's dictionary is "farinaceous food" (cf. OR borošno, rye flour).[24] Hence it recalls "wheat of the sated ether." Opposed to this meatless feast, and seemingly occurring at the same time, is a second feast, the earthlings' feast ("pirujuščie zemljane"), destructive in its potential (especially as it recalls the "algebraic feasts" of 1. 6). We might even

suggest that the earthlings' feast is a metaphor for war. This metaphor
(feast, pir=war, battle) of course, can be found throughout Russian literature.[25]

Mandel'štam, therefore, seems to be expressing his own kind of internationalism, where humanity is seen a citizen of the universe, not of
the earth, or at least not of the earth as connected with war and strife.

The first two quatrains of section II each break into two parts.
In lines 49-50 we have a simile whose tenor is omitted: "Kak tel'ce
malen'koe krylyškom/Po solncu vskljan' [ona] perevernulas'" (Like a
little body with a small wing/It [Fem.] turned over full to the edges
along the sun). The tenor is not stated until line 56: "zanoza" (splinter). That "splinter" refers to an airplane can be deduced from the context of section II as a whole. In "Xolodnoe leto" (Cold Summer, 1923),
Mandel'štam made this identification explicit:

> Tot ne ljubit goroda, kto ne cenit ego rubišča,
> ego skromnyx i žalkix adresov, kto ne zadyxalsja
> na černyx lestnicax, putajas' v žestjankax pod
> mjaukan's košek, kto ne zagljadyvalsja v kat-
> oržnom dvore Vxutemasa na zanozu v lazuri, na
> živuju, životnuju prelest' aèroplana. . . .

(II, 168)

> That person does not like the city who does not value its
> tatters, its modest and pitiful addresses; who hasn't panted
> on backstairs, getting tangled up in tin cans to the meow of
> cats; who hasn't stared in admiration in the prison-like
> courtyard of Vxutemas [Higher State Art and Craft Shops] at
> a splinter in the azure, at the living, vital charm of an
> airplane. . . .

In the poem, the airplane/splinter is described as something very fragile

and frail. There is an abundance of diminutives and hypocoristic forms:
"tel'ce" ("telo": small, slim little body), "krylyško" (diminutive of
wing) "steklyško" (diminutive of glass). The airplane is presented through
a series of visual images. Jurij Terapiano questioned the meaning of these
lines: "A 'little body' could not turn 'along the sun full to the edges'.
According to Dal' only a glass can be filled even with the edges, i.e.
'vsklen' '."[26] The word "tel'ce" little body, as stated, refers to an airplane. What we see here is a plane with a convex window. ("Vskljan'" does
indeed suggest "full to the edges," but liquid so poured would then form a
convex surface which is used here to describe the pilot's window. Moreover Mandel'štam is making use of the etymological, or paronomastic, connection between "vskljan'," "skljanka," "steklo" [glass]. This is why
Mandel'štam used "vskljan'.") The convex window of the plane
("zažigatel'noe steklyško") is turned toward the sun, and the glass
shines and reflects the light back to the empyreans. In lines 53-56 the
plane is presented through insect imagery (cf. ll. 21-28). The airplane
sounds and whines like a mosquito, and complains quietly, like the singing of a beetle. Lines 49-56, therefore, show a plane turning, shining,
and making noise.

The complaints of the plane are voiced in lines 57-60. Sound
imagery plays a role here; the repetition of stressed "i" as well as
repetition of "mi," "im," "ni," "in" suggest, onomatopoetically, the
whining sound of an insect:

> Ne zabyvaj menja, kazni menja,
> No daj mne imja, daj mne imja:
> Mne budet legče s nim—pojmi menja,
> V beremennoj glubokoj sini.

Don't forget me, punish me,
But give me a name, give me a name,
It will be easier for me with it -- understand me,
In the pregnant, deep blue.

We surmise that this airplane is unhappy because it does not want to be a warplane; it longs to be something else: it wishes to be given a name. This name, as Taranovsky suggests,[27] is given in line 64, "worker bee" (medunica); we will return to this shortly.

On another level, the airplane may be understood as an analogue for the poet and his poetry. This possibility arises from several texts of Mandel'štam's. In a poem from 1922 we have the following stanza:

Ja ne znaju, s kakix por,
Èta pesen'ka načalas'--
Ne po nej li šuršit vor,
Komarinyj zvenit knjaz'? (cf. ll. 53-54: "Kom-
arinaja bezdelica . . . zvenela.")

I don't know when
This song began --
Doesn't the thief rustle to it,
The mosquito prince ring? (cf. ll. 53-54: "The
    mosquito trifle . . . rang.")

This poem touches upon both the theme of poetry and the possible fate of Mandel'štam's own poetry. Taranovsky has suggested that Mandel'štam's image of the "mosquito prince" derives from Deržavin's "Poxvala Komaru" (Praise to the Mosquito).[28] The mosquito is described there as an "inspirer to poetic creation," like the nightingale or lark. "Ja ne znaju, s kakix por" shows that there is a link between the mosquito, poetry and the poet. In Egipetskaja marka (The Egyptian Stamp) the mosquito is linked with Mandel'štam's oppressed hero, Parnok, and by extension with Mandel'štam himself:

Komarik zvenel:
. . .--Ja knjaz' nevezen'ja--kolležskij asessor iz
goroda Fiv . . . Vse takoj že--ničut' ne izmenilsja--
oj, strašno mne zdes'--izvinjajus'. . .
--Ja--bezdelica. Ja--ničego.

(II, 75; my italics)

The little mosquito rang: --I am the prince of bad luck -- a
collegiate assessor from the city of Thebes . . . All's the
same, not a bit changed -- oh, I am terrified here -- I
apologize . . . -- I am a trifle. I am nothing.

In Egipetskaja marka, the mosquito is oppressed, threatened, and in

danger. As we have seen, the mosquito is linked with poetry and the

poet. The words uttered in lines 57-60, the direct discourse of the

poet, relate to poetry. The key word here, twice repeated, is "name"

(imja). Beginning with his earliest works, Mandel'štam used the word

"imja" in connection with poetry and poetic creation; for example, in

the following early poem which combines motifs from Puškin's "Prophet"

and "The Poet":

Kak oblakom serdce odeto
I kamnem prikinulas' plot',
Poka naznačen'e poèta
Emu ne otkroet Gospod'.

Kakaja-to strast' naletela,
Kakaja-to tjažest' živa;
I prizraki trebujut tela,
I ploti pričastny slova.

Kak ženščiny, žaždut predmety,
Kak laski, zavetnyx imen,
No tajnye lovit primety
Poèt, v temnotu pogružen.

On ždet sokrovennogo znaka,
Na pesn', kak na podvig, gotov:

I dyšit tainstvennost' braka
V prostom sočetanii slov.

(VRSXD, No. 3 [1970], p. 117)

The heart is clothed as if in a cloud,
And flesh pretends to be a stone,
Until the poet's mission
Is revealed to him by God.

Some kind of passion flies down,
Some kind of heaviness is alive,
And phantoms demand a body,
And words are connected to flesh.

Like women, things crave
Endearment, sacred names,
But the poet tries to catch secret signs,
While sunk in darkness.

He waits for the concealed sign,
Ready for a song as for an exploit;
And the mystery of marriage breathes
In the simple uniting of words.

"Sacred names" become "dear names" in a poem dealing with poetic inspiration:

Otčego duša tak pevuča
I tak malo milyx imen,
I mgnovennyj ritm—tol'ko slučaj,
Neožidannyj Akvilon?

(1911)[29]

Why is my soul so melodious
And there are so few dear names,
And momentary rhythm -- only a chance,
The unexpected Aquilon?

"Imja" associated with poetry continues into later works; for example, "Nam ostaetsja tol'ko imja—/Čudesnyj zvuk na dolgij srok" ("Ne verja voskresen'ja čudu," Only the name remains for us—/A miraculous sound for a long time, Not believing the miracle of resurrection, 1916); "Ja v xorovod tenej, toptavšix nežnyj lug,/S pevučim imenem vmešalsja" (In the round dance of the shadows treading the tender meadow I took part/With a singing name, 1920); Triždy blažen, kto vvedet v pesn' imja" ("Našedšij podkovu," Thrice blessed is the one who introduces a name into a song — He Who Found a Horseshoe, 1923).

The whole of section II deals as well with the poet and poetry. When he implores, "Don't forget me . . . but give me a name" we suggest that he hopes his name, through his poetry, will live on after his death, immutable. "Ne zabyvaj menja"—the immutability that he seeks is achieved through artistic creation. Poets have expressed this hope often (e.g. Horace, III, 30; Ovid, Met., XV, 871 ff.; Puškin) and it can be found in Mandel'štam's own work beginning with his earliest poems: "Dano mne telo—čto mne delat' s nim" (A body is given to me — what shall I do with it, 1909), "Ajja-Sofija" (Hagia Sophia, 1912), "Est' cennostej nezyblemaja skala" (There is an unshakeable scale of values, 1914), "Ne verja voskresen'ja čudu" (Not believing in the miracle of resurrection, 1916), "Ešče daleko asfodelej" (Still distant the asphodels', 1917), "Ja ne znaju, s kakix por" (I don't know when, 1922), "Ja po lesenke pristavnoj" (I climbed the step ladder, 1922), "Našedšij podkovu" (He Who Found a Hourseshoe, 1923) and others. In "Kak tel'ce malen'koe krylyškom" he is asking that he not be forgotten. The last imperative is "understand me, in the pregnant deep blue" (v beremennoj glubokoj sini), that is to say, in the future (1. 15: "nebo buduščim beremenno," 1. 63: "v beremennom glubokom buduščem [the sky is pregnant with the future, in the pregnant, deep future]).

Section IV returns us to the theme of intervention. At first

Mandel'štam expresses hope for a future golden age: "In the 1923 poem 'And the sky is pregnant with the future,' a longing for an irretrievably lost golden age of humanity gives way to a vague hope for a future golden age [ll. 61-64 quoted]. There is no doubt that the buzzing bee is one of the servants of the goddess of fertility, one of the bees sucking the heavy rose."[30] We can juxtapose the "buzzing bee," part of the future golden age, with the singing of the carabid (n.b. anagram "žužžit bol'šaja medunica" -- "žuželica"). Bees have other positive associations in Mandel'štam's poetry: poets are like bees ("Na kamennyx otrogax Pierii" [On the stony spurs of Pieria], 1920), and kisses are like bees ("Voz'mi na radost' iz moix ladonej" [Joyfully take from my palms], 1920).

In line 65, Mandel'štam addresses the interventionist pilots: "A vam, v bezvremen'i letajuščim/Pod xlyst vojny za vlast' nemnogix" (And you who are flying in hard times/To war's whip, for the power of a few). They are flying "v bezvremen'i." The hard times, the time of adversity, is the present time. It contrasts with the future (l. 13), "Itak, gotov'tes' žit' vo vremeni,/Gde net ni volka, ni tapira (And so, get ready to live in the time /Where there is neither wolf nor tapir). The pilots are said to have less conscience than pinnipeds and are worse even than the most predatory of birds, carrion vultures and kites. War is personified; its cold palms, like a cap of Alpine snow (i.e. a snow- or cloud-cap on a mountain), stifle man.

The poem closes (ll. 77-84) with an extended apostrophe to the sky; it is given the following attributes: deep, sated, pregnant with the azure, many-eyed like scales, alpha and omega of the storm, alien, eyebrowless. Such a catalogue makes the sky's potential at best ambiguous.

This is what we have come to expect in the course of the poem. For on the one hand we have the sky pregnant with the future, with the wheat of the sated ether, obviously positive possibilities. (But only possibilities; for the sky, to realize this metaphor, is pregnant—it has yet to give birth.) But on the other hand, we know other things about the sky: the lower stratum has grown dark with a martial thunderstorm; Azrael has conquered the firmament. This last section of the poem recapitulates the ambivalent nature of the sky. The sky is first defined by a series of three epithets. The first, "glubokoe" (deep), within the context of this poem, has positive connotations: line 60: "beremennaja glubokaja sin'," line 63: "beremennoe glubokoe buduščee" (the pregnant deep blue, the pregnant deep future). "Sytoe" (sated), too, initially suggests the positive image of line 16, "pšenica sytogo ěfira" (wheat of the sated ether). Lastly, the modifier "beremennoe" (pregnant) especially as it has been further defined with a complement, "beremennoe buduščim" (pregnant with the future), has been associated with positive possibilities. But here we have "zabremenevšee lazur'ju" (pregnant with the azure). If we assume that a new azure is going to be born, then this is obviously hopeful. But earlier in the poem we have learned that the azure has been invaded (ll. 22-23), is wounded (l. 56), or (perhaps) has a blind spot (l. 29). Hence, how can we know what to expect from this sky pregnant with azure? Further, the sky is called "mnogoočitoe kak češuja" (many-eyed like scales). "Mnogoočityj" is a biblical word usually applied to cherubim.[31] Eyes are an expression of life and intelligence and may symbolize the all-seeing Godhead. A "many-eyed sky" suggests a sky which can see everything. But "many-eyed like scales" is not a pleasant image; cf. line 34 "v češue iskalečennyx

kryl" (in the scales of crippled wings) and especially a later poem of
Mandel'štam's:

Ne iskušaj čužix narečij, no postarajsja ix zabyt'--
Ved' vse ravno ty ne sumeeš' stekla zubami ukusit'!

Ved' umirajuščee telo i mysljaščij bessmertnyj rot
V poslednij raz pered razlukoj čužoe imja ne spaset.

O, kak mučitel'no daetsja čužogo klelota počet--
Za bezzakonnye vostorgi lixaja plata sterežet.

Čto esli Ariost i Tasso, obvorožajuščie nas,
Čudovišča s lazurnym mozgom i češuej iz vlažnyx glaz.

I v nakazan'e za gordyn'ju, neispravimyj zvukoljub,
Poluciš' uksusnuju gubku ty dlja izmenničeskix gub.

                    (1933; my italics)

Don't tempt foreign dialects, but try to forget them--
You see, all the same you won't be able to bite the
        glass with your teeth!

You see, the dying body and the thinking, immortal mouth
At the last moment before parting won't be saved by a
        foreign name.

Oh, how agonizingly one achieves the respect of a foreign
        [eagle's] scream --
An evil payment for your illegal ecstacies watches.

What if Ariosto and Tasso, charming us,
Are monsters with an azure brain and scales of moist eyes.

And as punishment for pride, incorrigible sound-lover,
You will receive a vinegar sponge for your traitorous lips.

The phrase "alpha and omega" is from the New Testament (Revelation
I:8). God is the speaker in this verse, which suggests that He is eternal: He was here before man and will be here after man; also, that God
in the beginning created the heavens and He will bring an end. The sky
is the alpha and omega of the storm; again, this is ambiguous, for to be
the beginning of the storm suggests destruction, while to be the end of

the storm suggests peace.

The last two epithets applied to the sky are ominous. "Čužoj" suggests that it is a strange, alien sky which is suspended over man, one from which we need not expect, a priori, good to come. Lastly, the personifying epithet "eyebrowless" is frightening, if not grotesque. It is only natural, therefore, that such a sky would, with all of these attributes, elicit surprise. We are surprised, after all, at what is unexpected or incomprehensible. Clearly, what Mandel'štam expresses in this poem is a hope for a future golden age, but with no certain expectation of its ultimate arrival.

Chapter VII

AN ENDURING VISION

Osip Mandel'štam's poem "Našedšij podkovu" (He who found a horseshoe) was first published in 1923 with the subtitle "Pindaričeskij
otryvok." Even in his most apparently obscure poems Mandel'štam never
attempts to trick his reader; he merely forces him to relate to the poem
in a somewhat new way. The concepts of "subtext" and "context" used in
relation to Mandel'štam's work presuppose that most, if not all, of a
given work can be accounted for; a safe working hypothesis is that little
in Mandel'štam is unmotivated.

Našedšij podkovu

[I]   Gljadim na les i govorim:
      Vot les korabel'nyj, mačtovyj,
      Rozovye sosny,
      Do samoj verxuški svobodnye ot moxnatoj noši,
      Im by poskripyvat' v burju,
      Odinokimi pinijami,
      V raz"jarennom bezlesnom vozduxe;
      Pod solenoju pjatoju vetra ustoit otves, prignannyj k
          pljašuščej palube.
      I moreplavatel'
      V neobuzdannoj žažde prostranstva,
      Vlača čerez vlažnye rytviny xrupkij pribor geometra,
      Sličit s pritjažen'em zemnogo lona
      Šeroxovatuju poverxnost' morej.

[II] A vydxaja zapax
      Smolistyx slez, prostupivšix skvoz' obšivku korablja,
      Ljubujas' na doski
      Zaklepannye, slažennye v pereborki
      Ne vifleemskim mirnym plotnikom, a drugim -
      Otcom putešestvij, drugom morexoda, -
      Govorim:
      I oni stojali na zemle,
      Neudobnoj, kak xrebet osla,
      Zabyvaja verxuškami o kornjax,
      Na znamenitom gornom krjaže,
      I šumeli pod presnym livnem,

Bezuspešno predlagaja nebu vymenjat' na ščepotku soli
Svoj blagorodnyj gruz.

[III] S čego načat'?
Vse treščit i kačaetsja.
Vozdux drožit ot sravnenij.
Ni odno slovo ne lučše drugogo,
Zemlja gudit metaforoj,
I legkie dvukolki,
V broskoj uprjaži gustyx ot natugi ptič'ix staj,
Razryvajutsja na časti,
Soperničaja s xrapjaščimi ljubimcami ristališč.

[IV] Triždy blažen, kto vvedet v pesn' imja;
Ukrašennaja nazvan'em pesn'
Dol'še živet sredi drugix -
Ona otmečena sredi podrug povjazkoj na lbu,
Isceljajuščej ot bespamjatstva, sliškom sil'nogo
          odurjajuščego zapaxa -
Bud' to blizost' mužčiny,
Ili zapax šersti sil'nogo zverja,
Ili prosto dux čobra, rastertogo meždu ladonej.

 [V] Vozdux byvaet temnym, kak voda, i vse živoe v nem plavaet,
          kak ryba,
Plavnikami rastalkivaja sferu,
Plotnuju, uprugugu, čut' nagretuju, -
Xrustal', v kotorom dvižutsja kolesa i šaraxajutsja
          lošadi,
Vlažnyj černozem Neery, každuju noč' raspaxannyj zanovo
Vilami, trezubcami, motygami, plugami.
Vozdux zamešen tak ze gusto, kak zemlja, -
Iz nego nel'zja vyjti, v nego trudno vojti.

[VI] Šorox probegaet po derev'jam zelenoj laptoj:
Deti igrajut v babki pozvonkami umeršix životnyx.
Xrupkoe letoisčislenie našej èry podxodit k koncu.
Spasibo za to, čto bylo:
Ja sam ošibsja, ja sbilsja, zaputalsja v sčete.
Èra zvenela, kak šar zolotoj,
Polaja, litaja, nikem ne podderživaemaja,
Na vsjakoe prikosnovenie otvečala "da" i "net".
Tak rebenok otvečaet:
"Ja dam tebe jabloko", ili: "Ja ne dam tebe jabloka".
I lico ego točnyj slepok s golosa, kotoryj proiznosit
          èti slova.

[VII] Zvuk ešče zvenit, xotja pričina zvuka isčezla.
Kon' ležit v pyli i xrapit v myle,
No krutoj povorot ego šei
Ešče soxranjaet vospominanie o bege s razbrosannymi
          nogami -

Kogda ix bylo ne četyre,
A po čislu kamnej dorogi,
Obnovljaemyx v četyre smeny
Po čislu ottalkivanij ot zemli pyšuščego žarom inoxodca.

[VIII] Tak,
Našedšij podkovu
Sduvaet s nee pyl'
I rastiraet ee šerst'ju, poka ona ne zablestit,
Togda
On vešaet ee na poroge,
Čtoby ona otdoxnula,
I bol'še už ej ne pridetsja vysekat' iskry iz kremnja.

[IX] Čelovečeskie guby,
                      kotorym bol'se nečego skazat',
Soxranjajut formu poslednego skazannogo slova,
I v ruke ostaetsja oščuščen'e tjažesti,
Xotja kuvšin
          napolovinu raspleskalsja,
              poka ego nesli domoj.
To, čto ja sejčas govorju, govorju ne ja,
A vyryto iz zemli, podobno zernam okameneloj pšenicy.
Odni
     na monetax izobrazajut l'va,
Drugie -
       golovu;
Raznoobraznye mednye, zolotye i bronzovye lepeški
S odinakovoj počest'ju ležat v zemle.
Vek, probuja ix peregryzt', ottisnul na nix svoi zuby.
Vremja srezaet menja, kak monetu,
I mne už nexvataet menja samogo.

                    (Stixotvorenija, M.-L., 1928)

HE WHO FOUND A HORSESHOE

[I] We look at a forest and say:
Here's a forest for ships, masts,
Rose-colored pines
Free of their shaggy burden to the very top,
They should creak in a storm,
Like lonely pines,
In the infuriated treeless air;
Under the salty heel of the wind the plumb will remain
   balanced, adjusted to the dancing deck.
And the seafarer
In an unbridled thirst for space,
Dragging through the damp ruts the delicate apparatus
   of a geometrician,

Will check the gravity of the earth's bosom
Against the rough surface of the seas.

[II] And inhaling the smell
Of the resinous tears which seeped through the ship's
    planking,
Admiring the boards
Riveted, put into bulkheads
Not by the peaceful carpenter of Bethlehem, but by the
    other one,
Father of voyages, friend of sea-farers, --
We say:
They too stood on the earth,
Uncomfortable as a donkey's spine,
Their tops forgetting about their roots,
On the famous mountain range,
And stirred under the saltless downpour,
Unsuccessfully offering the sky to exchange for a
    pinch of salt
Their noble load.

[III] What to begin with?
Everything cracks and rocks.
The air quivers from similes.
Not one word is better than another,
The earth hums with metaphor,
And light two-wheeled carts,
In a garish harness of flocks of birds dense from strain,
Break themselves to pieces
Vying with the snorting favorites of the hippodromes.

[IV] Thrice blessed is the one who will introduce a name into
    a song;
The song adorned with a name
Lives longer among others --
It is marked among its friends by a fillet on its forehead,
Which heals the loss of memory, the odor which is too
    strong and stultifying,
Whether it is the nearness of a man,
Or the smell of the fur of a strong beast,
Or simply the aroma of savory rubbed between the palms.

[V] The air is sometimes dark, like water, and everything
    alive in it swims like a fish,
With fins pushing apart the sphere,
Dense, elastic, slightly heated, --
A crystal, in which wheels move and horses shy,
The moist blackearth of Neaira, plowed anew every night
With pitchforks, tridents, hoes, plows;
The air is kneaded as thickly as earth, --
It is impossible to leave it, and difficult to enter it.

[VI]   A rustle runs along the trees like a green game
      with a ball
Children are playing knucklebones with the vertebrae
      of dead animals.
The fragile chronology of our era is coming to an end.
Thanks for what was:
I myself made a mistake, became confused, lost count.
The era rang like a golden globe.
Hollow, cast, supported by no one,
To each touch answered "yes" and "no."
So a child answers:
"I'll give you the apple," or, "I won't give you the
      apple."
And his face is an exact mold of the voice which says
      these words.

[VII]   The sound still rings, though the cause of the sound
      disappeared.
A steed covered with lather lies in the dust and snorts,
But the steep bend of its neck
Still preserves the memory of running with scattered
      legs --
When there were not four of them,
But as many as the stones of the road,
Being renewed in four shifts
According to the number of the blazing ambler's pushings-
      off from the earth.

[VIII]   So,
He who found a horseshoe
Blows the dust from it
And rubs it with fur until it shines,
Then
He hangs it over the threshold,
So it can rest,
And it will never again have to strike sparks from the
      flint.

[IX]   Human lips,
        which have nothing more to say,
Preserve the form of the last word said,
And a feeling of heaviness remains in the hand,
Although the clay pitcher
      half spilled
        while being carried home.
What I am now saying, I am not saying,
But it is dug out of the ground like grains of petrified
      wheat.
Some
      depict a lion on coins,
Others--
      a head.

> Various copper, gold and bronze crackers
> With identical honor lie in the earth.
> The age, trying to gnaw through them, printed its
>   teeth on them.
> Time cuts me, like a coin,
> And already I don't even have enough of myself.

Mandel'štam's interest in and knowledge of classical antiquity is well known. Assuming that he did not read Pindar in the original, Mandel'štam might have used any of several German, French, or Russian translations.[1] Of Pindar's complete works only forty-five odes survive, as well as numerous fragments, and it is with the ode that Pindar's name is primarily associated. As a genre, the ode tends to be used by poets as a means of conveying their reflections on historical events or developments. Most often the contents of an ode relate not only to the poet, but also to a larger audience which becomes the recipient of the poet's insights into these events. The ode presupposes an audience or an addressee, and a topic of more than personal importance.[2] Pindar is essentially responsible for these characteristics of the ode. In subtitling his poem "a Pindaric fragment" Mandel'štam might have been attempting to alert his audience, the potential "poetically literate reader" (poètičeski gramotnyj čitatel') to expect such subject matter. For as we will see "Našedšij podkovu" deals with history and poetry, and the poet's relation to both.

The construction of the Pindaric ode is similarly discernible in Mandel'štam's poem. Horace described the Pindaric ode as follows:

> As a river roars down a mountain, swollen
> by showers of rain, spilling over its banks,
> so Pindar rages and the deep of his voice
> pours ever onward.[3]

This seeming lack of restraint essentially stems from the apparent absence of a coherent structure. Pindar effects extraordinarily rapid transitions from one theme to another. Critics have spoken of his habit of "leaping" from subject to subject; of his "plunging," with no apparent bridge, from the past to the present. In dealing with myths, he will include only the most essential features, presupposing his audience's ability to supply the missing facts and see a coherent whole.[4] These are the things which first strike the reader of "Našedšij podkovu." Throughout the poem Mandel'štam passes from theme to theme with no seeming order; and to determine what the themes are requires a very close reading of the text, as well as the ability to make use of the subtexts. With both poets, the reader is expected to be able to take a hint. Omitting the obvious, the poets compel their audiences to pay attention to what might otherwise go unnoticed. In Pindar's odes as well as in Mandel'štam's "Našedšij podkovu" it is the very absence of clearly delimited transitions which helps to underscore the fact that what might at first appear to be widely disparate subjects are in fact closely related.

Mandel'štam and Pindar share an essentially similar view toward poetry's ability to remain timeless in a transitory, often disorderly world. It is the poem which is uniquely able to remain intact while all else changes, and hence to contact an unknown future recipient of an unexpected gift in which is preserved also a part of the poet. In Olympian X, for example, Pindar likens his ode to a child born to an old father who thus carries on his father's name.[5] This basic idea occurs throughout Pindar's odes.[6]

Mandel'štam's thoughts about poetry as a contact between people in different historical periods are clearly expressed in his prose, especially the essay "On the interlocutor" (O sobesednike). But these ideas also run throughout many of his poems, and as we will see, it is precisely in "Našedšij podkovu" that Mandel'štam gives one of the fullest poetic expressions to this concept.

A very important segment of "Našedšij podkovu" is devoted to the image of the dying horse. It concludes the theme of the era coming to an end and serves to introduce the next-to-last section, "He who found a horseshoe." The remnants of an era, in the form of a horseshoe, are found. The horse it comes from will run no more: "A steed covered with lather lies in the dust and snorts" (Kon' ležit v pyli i xrapit v myle). But it preserves the memory of a more glorious past: "And light two-wheeled carts . . ./Break themselves to pieces,/Vying with the snorting favorites of the hippodrome" (I legkie drukolki . . . /Razryvajutsja na časti, /Soperničaja s xrapjaščimi ljubimcami ristališč, my italics). The image of the horse (which raced in the hippodrome) is classical. While there is more than one possible subtext for this, it seems clearly, if only partially, to relate to Pindar. A large number of his odes are devoted to the winners of chariot and horse races. The horse evokes the splendor and wealth of ancient Greece, and for the modern reader it can become the emblem of an era. While Pindar does not neglect the physical beauty of the victorious horse, he frequently pays equal attention to its nonphysical attributes, its character, as it were.[7] In a poetic context, the horse can represent a whole past epoch. The significance of it will be shown in the course of this chapter.

Although it does not relate to "Našedšij podkovu" specifically,

but rather to Mandel'štam's poetry as a whole, it is of interest to show
that both poets had in mind a specific type of addressee for their poetry.
Mandel'štam's concept of the "poetically literate reader" is most clearly
explicated in "Vypad" (II, 270-274). Pindar expressed similar views:
"Full many a swift arrow have I beneath mine arm, within my quiver, many
an arrow that is vocal to the wise; but for the crowd they need interpre-
ters."[8]

"Našedšij podkovu" begins with a straightforward description of a
pine forest which can be used for the construction of ships. Some of the
tall pine trees will be used for masts; in many varieties of pine the
acicular leaves and branches, extending horizontally outward, grow rather
high up on the trunk ("Do samoj verxuški svobodnye ot moxnatoj noši"
[free of their shaggy burden to the very top]). The modifier "rose"
(rozovye) is an accurate description of one of the most common types of
pine in Russia: "The wood of the common pine with a rose or reddish
core."[9] In an earlier Mandel'štam poem we have the opposite image developed: the port, densely filled with the masts of ships, is likened to
a forest:

> O Evropa, novaja Èllada,
> Oxranjaj Akropol' i Pirej!
> Nam podarkov s ostrova ne nado —
> Celyj les nezvanyx korablej.

> O Europe, new Hellas
> Guard the Acropolis and Pireus!
> We do not need gifts from the island —
> A whole forest of unbidden ships.

The choice of pine as the wood for the ships is significant. Russia's
early fleets were built from pine; and pine for shipbuilding is particu-

larly rich in classical associations: "pine-wood ships will cease to
carry merchandise for barter"[10]; "the pine-tree had not yet learned to
scorn the blue sea-waters";[11] etc. The ship, as we will see, is symbolically both the ship of state and the ship of poetry. The ship of
state is sailing in "infuriated" waters ("raz"jarennyj"). Compare, for
example, with Blok: "The [Russian artists] never doubted that Russia is
a large ship which is destined for much sailing."[12] Mandel'štam frequently made use of this metaphor: "Čudoviščna, kak bronenosec v doke,
/Rossija otdyxaet tjaželo" (Monstruous, like a battleship in dock, /Rus-
sia rests heavily). In "Sumerki svobody" the ship symbolically is time
("V kom serdce est', tot dolžen slyšat', vremja, /Kak tvoj korabl' ko dnu
idet" [He who has a heart must hear, O time,/Your ship going to the bot-
tom]), and the ship of state, which is changing its historical course:
"Nu čto ž, poprobuem: ogromnyj, neukljužij/Skripučij povorot rulja./
Zemlja plyvet. Mužajtes', muži" (Well, then, let's try: an enormous,
clumsy,/Creaking turn of the rudder./The earth floats. Courage, men). The
plumb ("otves") has been used by Mandel'štam both in the context of historical thought and of artistic creation. In his essay "Petr Čaadaev,"
he writes: "Mysl' Čaadaeva — strogij perpendikuljar [in 1928 version
"strogij otves"] k tradicionnomu russkomu myšleniju." (II, 331, 604
[Čaadaev's thought is a strict perpendicular [strict plumb] to traditional Russian thinking]). In "Notre Dame" it is the plumb which emerges as
that element of stability, part of the "tajnyj plan" (secret plan) of the
artist, which paradoxically gives the cathedral its seeming movement:

> Stixijnij labirint, nepostižimyj les,
> Duši gotičeskoj rassudočnaja propast',

Egipetskaja mọšč' i xristianstva robost',
S trostinkoj rjadom—dub, i vsjudu car'—otves.

Elemental labyrinth, incomprehensible forest,
Rational abyss of the gothic soul,
Egyptian power and Christian timidity,
Next to a reed — an oak, and king everywhere —
    the plumb.

The navigator ("moreplavatel'") is both the poet and the head of state.

The poetic ship (of inspiration) is a common enough metaphor; it can be

found, for example, in Pindar: "I shall ascend a prow that is crowned

with flowers, while I sound the praise of valour."[13] And it can be found

in Puškin:

Tak dremlet nedvižim korabl' v nedvižnoj vlage,
No ču—matrosy vdrud kidajutsja, polzut
Vverx, vniz—i parusa nadulis', vetra polny;
Gromada dvinulas' i rassekaet volny.

Plyvet. Kuda ž nam plyt'? . . .
           (Osen')

So a ship dozes motionless in still waters,
But hark — suddenly the sailors rush, crawl
Up, down, and the sails fill out, full of wind.
The bulk moved and cleaves the waves.

It sails. Where are we to sail? . . .
           (Autumn)

Mandel'stam uses this metaphor in two ways. In "Notes on Poetry"

(Zametki o poėzii, 1923) he likens new currents in poetry to a ship sail-

ing in unchartered waters (II, 305); in the optimistic "Akter i rabočij"

(Actor and worker) Mandel'štam uses this metaphor throughout the poem.

Most importantly, in "On the Nature of the Word" (O prirode slova, 1922)

Mandel'štam uses the metaphor of the ship of poetry. The passage quoted is particularly relevant to our discussion of "Našedšij podkovu":

Otšumit vek, usnet kul'tura, pereroditsja narod, otdav svoi lučšie
sily novomu obščestvennomu klassu, i ves' ètot potok uvlečet za
soboj xrupkuju lad'ju čelovečeskogo slova v otkrytoe more
grjaduščego, gde net sočuvstvennogo ponimanija, gde unylyj
komentarij zamenjaet svežij veter vraždy i sočuvstvija sovremennikov. Kak že možno snarjadit' ètu lad'ju v dal'nij put', ne
snabdiv ee vsem neobxodimym dlja stol' čužogo i stol' dorogogo
čitatelja? Ešče raz ja upodoblju stixotvorenie egipetskoj lad'e
mertvyx. Vse dlja žizni pripaseno, ničego ne zabyto v ètoj lad'e.

(II, 300-301)

The age will stop stirring, culture will fall asleep, the people
will regenerate, having devoted their best powers to the new social
class, and this whole stream will carry away after it the fragile
bark of the human word into the open sea of the future, where there
is no sympathetic understanding, where doleful commentary replaces
the fresh wind of the hostility and sympathy of contemporaries.
How is it possible to fit out this bark for a distant voyage, without having provided it with everything necessary for so foreign and
so dear a reader? Once again I will liken a poem to an Egyptian
ship for the dead. Everything for life is stored, nothing is forgotten in this bark.

The navigator of the ship of poetry is the poet; the navigator of the

ship of state is Peter I, also its builder. The resinous (pine) boards

have been built into bulkheads "not by the peaceful carpenter of Bethle-

hem, but by the other one/Father of voyages" (ne vifleemskim mirnym

plotnikom, a drugim -- / Otcom putešestvij, drugom morexoda). The Bethle-

hem carpenter is obviously Joseph. In the New Testament, Joseph is fre-

quently referred to as a carpenter, whereas Christ is so referred to only

once (Mark VI, 3); more often Christ is called the "son of a carpenter."

The total poetic context favors Joseph: as Peter I is the father of a new

era of Russian history, so too is Joseph the "father" of a new era

through Christ. Peter I is the head of state; St. Joseph's position is

that of Head of the Holy Family. Finally, we may cite the following as a

possible subtext:

Kto zdes' plotnik, Petr ili Iosif,
Pozdno bylo sprašivat', kogda,
Jakorja u nabereznoj brosiv,
Stali istomlennye suda.[14]

Who is the carpenter here, Peter or Joseph,
It was too late to ask, when,
Having dropped anchor at the quay,
The vessels became exhausted.

As regards Peter I, he has gone into history and poetry as a carpenter, founder of the Russian fleet, and helmsman of the ship of state. In Feofan Prokopovič's funeral oration for Peter, he refers to him as Russia's Japheth, who built and sailed Russia's first fleet of ships. In poetry this tradition begins with Lomonosov's "Petr Velikij" ("Peter the Great"). Most important here, though, is Puškin:

Sej škiper byl tot škiper slavnyj
Kem naša dvignulas' zemlja,
Kto pridal moščno beg deržavnyj
Rulju rodnogo korablja.

(Moja rodoslovnaja)

To akademik, to geroj,
To moreplavatel', to plotnik,
On vseob"emljuščej dušoj
Na trone večnyj byl rabotnik.

(Stansy)

This skipper was that splendid skipper
Who set our land in motion,
Who powerfully gave sovereign movement
To the rudder of our ship.

(My Geneology)

Now an academician, now a hero,
Now a navigator, now a carpenter,
With his all-embracing soul he
Was an eternal worker on the throne.

(Stanzas)

An Enduring Vision /181

By designating Peter I "father of voyages, friend of sea-farers" Mandel'-
štam doubtless has in mind the many explorations that Peter sponsored
(notably those of Vitus Bering), as well as the fact that Peter I called
to his service in Russia a very large number of artists, journeymen, and
artisans.

This section concludes with the metaphoric development of the idea
that the past must be partially rejected in order that new beginnings
might be made: "I oni [= doski = sosny] stojali na zemle / Neudobnoj,
kak xrebet osla / Zabyvaja verxuškami o kornjax" (They too [= boards =
pines] stood on the earth./ Uncomfortable as a donkey's spine, / Their
tops forgetting about their roots). New historical eras imply "forgetting" the previous one; Peter I's reign clearly illustrates this idea.[15]

Sections one and two together, then, broadly speaking introduce
the two major themes of the poem: history and art. They stand as a kind
of prologue to the whole work.

The poem in this sense may be said to begin with the words "S čego
načat'?" (What to begin with?). They clearly echo and complete the above-
cited half line by Puškin, "Kuda ž nam plyt'?" (Where are we to sail?. .)
Section three deals with both art and history; initially the subject is
poetry: "Vozdux drožit ot sravnenij . . . / Zemlja gudit metaforoj"
(The air quivers from similes . . ./ The earth hums with metaphor).
Poetry is not so much part of the air as the air itself -- a life giving
force: "-- vot vse moi prava, -- / I polnoj grud'ju ix vdyxat' ja
dolžen" (Razryvy kruglyx buxt" [These are all my rights, -- /And I must
breathe them with a full chest; Bursts of round bays], 1937); "Esli b
menja lišili vsego v mire -- /Prava dyšat' i otkryvat' dveri" (If I were

deprived of everything in the world -- /The right to breathe and open
doors, 1937); "Vse proizvedenija mirovoj literatury ja delju na razrešen-
nye i napisannye bez razrešenija. Pervye -- èto mraz', vtorye --
vorovannyj vozdux" (I divide all works of world literature into those
permitted and those written without permission. The first are rubbish;
the second -- stolen air, II, 220).

The historical aspect of this section emerges, firstly, in the line
"Vse treščit i kačaetsja" (Everything cracks and rocks) which refers to
the Russian revolution. This idea is reinforced by the image of the
light two-wheeled carts which, together with the above has a clear antecedent in Mandel'štam's "Sumerki svobody": "My v legiony boevye /
Svjazali lastoček . . . vsja stixija / Ščebečet, dvižetsja, živet" (We
have bound swallows into battle legions . . . /the whole element /Twit-
ters, chirps, moves). Not specifically referring to the revolution, but
essentially historical in nature, are similar images in other works by
Mandel'štam:

I promel'knet plamennyx let staja . . .
                    ("Esli b menja naši vragi vzjali," 1937)

And a flock of flaming years will flash by . . .
                    ("If our enemies took me," 1937)

Ostanovit'? Začem? Kto ostanovit solnce, kogda ono mčitsja na
vorob'inoj uprjaži v otčij dom, obujannoe žaždoj vozvrašcenija?
                    (II, 264)

Stop? Why? Who will stop the sun when it speeds along in its
sparrow harness to its paternal home gripped by the desire for
return?

Šumeli v pervyj raz germanskie duby,
Evropa plakala v tenetax.
Kvadrigi černye vstavali na dyby
Na triumfal'nyx povorotax.

                    (Dekabrist)

German oaks stirred for the first time,
Europe wept in hunting nets,
Black quadrigas reared up
On triumphal bends.

                    (Decembrist)

In "breaking themselves to pieces" the carts (chariots) "rival the snorting favorites of the hippodrome." This recalls Pindar's Pythian V to
Arcesilas of Cyrene, winner in the chariot race. The driver was so
skilled that his chariot alone survived whereas forty others crashed.

     "Thrice blessed is the one who will introduce a name into a song":
the significance of the number three requires little comment. Having said
this Mandel'štam introduces a name into the poem twelve lines later,
Neaira. Much more likely, however, is that the name introduced into this
poem is "Našedšij podkovu," the horseshoe finder. It is a generic name
which fits anyone, but particularly the current reader of this poem, who-
ever it may be. "The song adorned with a name /Lives longer among
others": this "song" (cf. Pindar, whose odes were intended to be sung)
is similarly adorned with a name (in the sense of title). Thus, Mandel'-
štam's song (poem), having a name in it and being decorated with a title
will live on longer amid the others. The song with a title is "marked by
a fillet on its forehead"; metaphorically, the title clearly stands in
relation to a poem (on the printed page) as a fillet does to the one who
wears it -- at the top. The fillet ("povjazka") "frees (heals, delivers)
from loss of memory." Mnemosyne, the goddess of memory, wears a fillet

(frontlet, diadem); cf. Pindar, Nemean VII, 15. Mnemosyne is the mother of the Muses, who similarly wear fillets: "Yet we learn that they attained the highest happiness of all mortal men, in that they heard the Muses of the golden snood singing on mount Pelion, and in seven-gated Thebes."[16] Lastly, the Muses exist that man might be freed from ills ("isceljajuščej ot"; cf. "Slovo -- čistoe vesel'e / Iscelen'e ot toski"; "Xudožnik po svoej prirode -- vrač, iscelitel'. Ne esli on nikogo ne vračuet, to komu i na čto on nužen?"[17] [The word is pure joy /The healing of anguish. An artist is by his nature a doctor, a healer. But if he doesn't heal anyone, then for whom and what is he needed?]); "Them [the Olympian Muses] did Mnemosyne (Memory), who reigns over the hills of Eleuther, bear of union with the father, the son of Cronus, a forgetting of ills and a rest from sorrow."[18] A song with these requirements thus frees from absence of memory ("bespamjatstvo"). Another meaning of "bespamjatstvo" is loss of consciousness, faint, which is here caused by "an odor which is too strong and stupefying." The "thrice-blessed" one is paralleled by a list of three kinds of odors; these are respectively human ("blizost' mužčiny"), animal ("zapax šersti sil'nogo zverja"), plant ("dux čobra") odors: the smell of life, of all that is alive in the world.[19]

The air is the subject of section five. It is dark, dense air which is difficult to breathe. This idea is developed through a series of escalated similes. Mandel'štam prepared us for this earlier, "the air quivers from similes." The tenor of these similes is air, although it is twice omitted. The vehicle develops in a logical progression: air like water, air like crystal (= water, too: cf. "Gorjat v portu

tureckix flagov maki, /Trostinki mačt, xrustal' volny uprugij" [The pop-
pies of Turkish flags burn in the port, /Reeds of the masts, the elastic
crystal of the wave] "Feodosija," 1920). The final level, air like earth,
is arrived at through a transitionary simile ("[The air is like] the
moist blackearth of Neaira") which relates to the above and below
similes: "moist" and "Neaira"[20] to water, "blackearth" (černozem) to
earth. Moreover, this moist black earth is ploughed up by four kinds of
tools which correspondingly relate to water and/or earth: the pitchfork
is used on land; the trident is a symbol of mastery over the sea; the hoe
is used on land; the plow is used on land, but is also a common classical
metaphor for the bow of a ship. Mandel'štam himself uses it in "Sumerki
svobody" and in "Admiraltejstvo," anchors are like plows.

Section five essentially deals with the historical air, in much the
same sense that Blok spoke of it in relation to Puškin: "It was not
d'Anthès' bullet which killed Puškin. He was killed by the absence of
air. His culture was dying with him. 'It's time, my friend, it's time.
/The heart asks for peace!' These are Puškin's deep breaths before death
and also the breaths of the culture of Puškin's time.[21] Such air is met
with frequently in Mandel'štam's poetry:

V Petropole prozračnom my umrem,
Gde vlastvuet nad nami Prozerpina.
My v každom vzdoxe smertnyj vozdux p'em,
I každyj čas nam smertnaja godina.

(1916)

In transparent Petropolis we will die
Where Proserpina rules over us.
In every breath we drink deathly air,
And every hour is our time of death.

Nel'zja dyšat', i tverd' kišit červjami,
I ni odna zvezda ne govorit . . .

      ("Koncert na vokzale," 1921)

It's impossible to breathe, and the firmament swarms
    with worms,
And not one star speaks . . .

      ("Concert at the Railroad Station," 1921)

Ja znaju, s každym dnem slabeet žizni vydox . . .

      ("1 janvarja 1924," 1924)

I know, with each day life's exhalation grows weaker

      ("1 January 1924")

Koljut resnicy. V grudi prikipela sleza.
Čuju bez straxa, čto budet i budet groza.
Kto-to čudnoj menja čto-to toropit zabyt'. —
Dušno, i vse-taki do smerti xočetsja žit'.

      (1931)

My eyelashes prick. A tear boiled up in my chest.
I sense without fear that there will be a storm.
Someone strange hurries me to forget something. —
It's suffocating, and still, I'm dying to live.

      (1931)

Mne s každym dnem dyšat' vse tjaželee,
A meždu tem nel'zja povremenit' —
I roždeny dlja naslažden'ja begom
Liš' serdce čeloveka i konja.

      ("Segodnja možno snjat' dekal'komani,
       1931)

With each day it's harder for me to breathe,
However, I can't delay —
And only the heart of man and steed
Are born for the pleasure of running.

      ("Today one can make a decalcomania," 1931)

Tak, čtoby umeret' na samom dele,
Tysjaču raz na dnju lišus' obyčnoj
Svobody vzdoxa i soznan'ja celi.
      (Kak iz odnoj vysokogornoj ščeli," 1934)

So, to actually die,
I will lose a thousand times a day the usual
Freedom of a deep breath and consciousness of the goal.

("How from a mountain crevice," 1934)

Poetry is treated as well in this section, though more subtly than is history. Poetry emerges in the vehicle of the simile "[Vozdux kak] vlažnyj černozem Neery, každuju noč' raspaxannyj zanovo / . . . plugami." ([The air is like] The moist blackearth of Neaira, plowed anew every night/. . . with plows." This recalls an equation which Mandel'štam had made earlier: "Poèzija -- plug, vzryvajuščij vremja tak, čto glubinye sloi vremeni, ego černozem okazyvajutsja sverxu" (Poetry is a plow which blows up time in such a way that the deep layers of time, its blackearth come to the surface, II, 266). "Vozdux . . . kak zemlja" (Air . . . like earth) evokes the earlier "zemlja gudit metaforoj" (The earth hums with metaphor) and together with "vlažnyj černozem" (moist blackearth) appear in one of Mandel'štam's Voronež poems dealing in part with poetry; here as well as the same difficulty breathing:

I ne ograblen ja i ne nadlomlen,
No tol'ko čto vsego pereogromlen--
Kak Slovo o polku, struna moja tuga,
I v golose moem posle uduš'ja
Zvučit zemlja--poslednee oruž'e--
Suxaja vlažnost' černozemnyx ga.

(Stansy, 1935)

I am not robbed, nor broken,
But only made enormous --
Like The Tale of Igor's Campaign, my string is taut,
And in my voice after asthma
The earth is heard -- the last weapon --
The dry dampness of blackearth hectares.

(Stanzas, 1935)

The next section begins with a visual image: "A rustle runs along the trees like a green ball game [lapta]." The children who immediately appear are not playing lapta (the word designating either the game or the bat used in it, the first meaning probably intended in the above simile), but babki (knucklebones). These children have found remnants of the past, but far from understanding their significance, they use the bone fragments in a childish game. This game has ominous associations: in an earlier poem children are playing it at Uglič where the carevič Dmitrij is murdered. The vertebrae for the game come from dead animals. The meaning of this becomes clear from "Vek":

> Vek moj, zver' moj, kto sumeet
> Zagljanut' v tvoi zrački
> I svoeju krov'ju skleit
> Dvux stoletij pozvonki?
> . . . .
> Tvar', pokuda žizn' xvataet,
> Donesti xrebet dolžna,
> I nevidimym igraet
> Pozvonočnikom volna.
> . . . .
> I ešče nabuxut počki,
> Bryznet zeleni pobeg,
> No razbit tvoj pozvonočnik,
> Moj prekrasnyj zalkij vek.
>
>
> My age, my beast, who will be able
> To look into your pupils
> And with his own blood glue together
> The vertebrae of two centuries . . .
>
> A creature, as long as it has enough life,
> Must carry its backbone,
> And a wave plays
> Upon the invisible spine . . .
>
> Buds will again swell,
> A sprout of green will spurt,
> But your backbone is broken,
> My beautiful, pitiful age.

The next two lines are self-explanatory: "Xrupkoe letoisčislenie našej èry podxodit k koncu. /Spasibo za to, čto bylo" (The fragile chronology of our era is coming to an end. /Thanks for what was). What follows is not clear: "Ja sam ošibsja, ja sbilsja, zaputalsja v sčete" (I myself made a mistake, lost count, became confused). Perhaps this refers to a previous forecast. In an earlier essay, Mandel'štam wrote: "Xristianskoe letoisčislenie v opasnosti, xrupkij sčet godov našej èry poterjan" (The Christian chronology is in danger, the fragile counting of the years of our era is lost, II, 366).

The lines, "The era rang like a golden globe. /Hollow, cast, supported by no one," can be explained on the basis of the following:

> Antičnaja mysl' ponimala dobro, kak blago ili blagopolučie; zdes'
> ešče ne bylo <u>vnutrennej pustoty gedonizma</u>. Dobro, blagopoluč'e,
> zdorov'e byli slity v odno predstavlen'e, kak polnovesnyj i
> odnorodnyj zolotoj šar. Vnutri ètogo ponjatija ne bylo pustoty.
> Vot èto-to splošnoj . . . Xarakter antičnoj morali.

(II, 355; my italics)

> Ancient thought understood "good" as happiness or well-being; <u>the</u>
> <u>inner emptiness of hedonism</u> did not yet exist. Good, well-being,
> health were fused into a single notion like a full-weighted and
> uniform golden globe. There was no emptiness in this idea. This
> is the solid . . . nature of classical ethics.

The "golden ball" is at the same time a symbol of power, a symbol always supported,[22] held in the (emperor's, king's) hands, but here "supported by no one":

> The <u>orb</u> [deržava] having the form of a [gold] globe . . . is a sym-
> bol of dominion over the land. Globes having this meaning are
> found on Roman coins of the emperor Augustus. . . . The orb came
> to Russia from Poland where it was called apple (jabłko) and in
> olden times it carried the <u>name</u> <u>apple of the czar's rank</u>, <u>apple of</u>
> <u>command</u>, and simply <u>apple</u>.[23]

Such is the "jabloko" in an earlier poem:

> Zdes', Kapitolija i Forum vdali,
> Sred' uvjadanija spokojnogo prirody,
> Ja slyšu Avgusta i na kraju zemli
> Deržavnym jablokom katjaščiesja gody.

> ("S veselym ržanjem pasutsja tabuny," 1915)

> Here, the Capitolium and Forum far off,
> Amidst the peaceful withering of nature,
> I hear Augustus and on the edge of the earth
> The years rolling like a sovereign apple.

> ("The horses graze with a happy neighing,"
> 1915)

And on this basis the capriciousness of the child's answer ("'I'll give you the apple,' or 'I won't give you the apple'"), echoing the previous "'yes' and 'no'," becomes wholly understandable. As for the last line ("i lico ego točnyj slepok s golosa (And his face is an exact copy of the voice, cf: "Vmesto živyx lic vspominat' slepki golosov. Oslepnut'. Osjazat' i uznavat' sluxom. Pečal'nyj udel! Tak vxodiš' v nastojaščee, v sovremennost', kak v ruslo vysoxšej reki." (To remember the molds of voices instead of living faces. To go blind. To feel and recognize by hearing. A sad fate! Thus does one enter the present, contemporaneity, as one enters the bed of a dried-up river, II, 141).

With the sound of the era still ringing ("xotja pričina zvuka isčezla" [although the cause of the sound disappeared]) we pass to the personification of a past era. As we remarked earlier, the horse can clearly be emblematic of (Pindaric) ancient Greece. At the same time, it calls to mind an other association, notably Czarist Russia. There is a rich literary heritage linking Russia with a galloping horse. We will cite only Puškin:

Ne tak li ty nad samoj bezdnoj,
Na vysote, uzdoj železnoj,
Rossiju podnjal na dyby?

Was it not thus over the very abyss
With an iron bridle
You reared Russia up on its hind legs?

This example could easily be multiplied (Mickiewicz, Annenskij, Blok,
Brjusov, Gogol'). The point is that there is clearly a precedent for
viewing the once galloping horse as an emblem of an entire previous era
of history, evoking Pindaric Greece as well as Czarist Russia. In the
poem we are viewing history in terms of enormous epochs which are now
part of the past. Thus the line "A horse lies in the dust and snorts in
its lather" refers to the death of Czarist Russia (cf. above: "The fragile
chronology of _our era_ is coming to an end" [my italics]) and sounds like
a response to Majakovskij's "Levyj marš (Matrosam)": "Ključu istoriju /
zagonim. / Levoj! / Levoj! / Levoj!" (Left march, To Sailors, Let's
drive the old nag of history. Left! Left! Left!)

The past epochs can be reconstructed, as it were, on the basis of
certain "artifacts" which remain for future generations.

Nastojaščee mgnovenie možet vyderžat' napor stoletij i soxranit'
svoju celost', ostat'sja tem že "sejčas". Nužno tol'ko umet'
vyrvat' ego iz počvy vremeni, ne povrediv ego kornej — inače
ono zavjanet. Villon umel èto delat'. Kolokol Sorbonny,
prervavšij ego rabotu nad Petit Testament, zvučit do six por.

(II, 348)

The present moment can bear the pressure of centuries and preserve its integrity, remain the same "now". One need only know
how to pull it out of the soil of time without harming its
roots, otherwise it will wither. Villon knew how to do this.
The Sorbonne's bell, which cut short his work on the Petit
Testament, still rings.

This, to a large extent, is the significance of the horseshoe. To put it crudely, if the horse represents a past era, then that part of it which is preserved and continues into the future, is its poetry, wrought out as a horseshoe. It is likely that Mandel'štam chose the horseshoe, here identified with poetry,[24] on the basis of a poem by Sologub:

> — Kon' Apollona!
> Ja nedostojna
> Tvoix kopyt.
> Ved' ne takuju
> Skuet podkovu
> Tebe Gefest.
>
> — Molči, podkova!
> Tebja ja vybral,
> Tebja xoču.
> Ja Apollona
> Stremlju s Olimpa
> K zemnym putjam.[25]

> —Horse of Apollo!
> I am not worthy
> Of your hooves.
> Hephestus will not forge
> Such a horseshoe
> For you.
>
> —Quiet, horseshoe!
> I chose you,
> I want you.
> I am heading
> Apollo from Olympus
> To earthly paths.

We might also cite the following, from a poem by Mandel'štam also written in 1923:

> Jazyk bulyžnika mne golubja ponjatnej,
> Zdes' kamni — golubi, doma kak golubjatni,
> I svetlym ručejkom tečet rasskaz podkov
> Po zvučnym mostovym prababki gorodov.

The language of cobblestones is more understandable to
    me than a dove,
Here stones are doves, houses — like dovecotes,
And the horseshoes' story flows like a bright stream
Along the sonorous roadway of the great-grandmother
    of cities.

Perhaps the most important single subtext for this section of the

poem is Mandel'štam's profound essay "O sobesednike" (On the Interlocutor

1913, 1928; II, 275-282):

U každogo čeloveka est' druz'ja. Počemu by poètu ne obraščat'sja
k druz'jam, k estestvenno blizkim emu ljud'jam? Moreplavatel' v
kritičeskuju minutu brosaet v vody okeana zapečatannuju butylku s
imenem svoim i opisaniem svoej sud'by. Spustjas' dolgie gody,
skitajas' po djunam, ja naxožu ee v peske, pročityvaju pis'mo,
uznaju datu sobytija, poslednjuju volju pogibšego. Ja imel pravo
sdelat' èto. Ja ne raspečatal čužogo pis'ma. Pis'mo, zapečatannoe
v butylke, adresovano tomu, kto najdet ee. Našel ja. Značit, ja
i est' tainstvennyj adresat.

    Moj dar ubog, i golos moj ne gromok,
    No ja živu — i na zemli moe
    Komu-nibud' ljubezno bytie:
    Ego najdet dalekij moj potomok
    V moix stixax; kak znat'? duša moja
    S ego dušoj okažetsja v snošen'i,
    I kak našel ja druga v pokolen'i,
    Čitatelja najdu v potomstve ja.

Čitaja stixotvorenie Boratynskogo, ja ispytyvaju to že samoe čuvstvo,
kak esli by v moi ruki popala takaja butylka. Okean vsej svoje
ogromnoj stixiej prošel ej na pomošč', — pomog ispolnit' ee
prednaznačenie, i čuvstvo providencial'nogo oxvatyvaet našedšego.

                    (II, 276-277; my italics)

Every person has friends. Why shouldn't a poet address friends, to
people naturally close to him? At a critical moment a seafarer
throws into the ocean's waters a sealed bottle with his name and a
description of his fate. After long years, wandering along the dunes,
I find it in the sand, read the letter, learn the date of the event,
the last will of the one who perished. I had the right to do this
I did not open somebody else's letter. The letter, sealed in a bottle, is addressed to the one who finds it. I found it. That means
I am the secret addressee.

My gift is poor, and my voice is not loud,
But I live, and on the earth my
Existence is dear to someone:
My distant descendent will _find_ it
In my verses; how can one know? my soul
will be in communication with his,
And as I _found_ a friend in my generation
I will find a reader in posterity.

Reading Boratynskij's poem, I experience the same feeling as if such
a bottle had fallen into my hands. The ocean with its enormous
elements came to its help, — helped to fulfill its destiny, and a
feeling of the providential grips the _one_ _who_ _found_ _it_.

                              (my italics)

This idea is expressed in many of Mandel'štam's poems:

          Ja polučil blažennoe nasledstvo
          Čužix pevcov blužďajuščie sny; . . .

                              (Ja ne slyxal rasskazov Ossiana," 1914)

     I received a blessed inheritance,
     The wandering dreams of other singers. . . .

                    ("I didn't hear Ossian's tales")

          I raskryvaetsj s šuršan'em
          Pečal'nyj veer prošlyx let,
          Tuda, gde s temnym sodrogan'em
          V pesok zarylsja amulet, . . .

                         ("Ešče daleko asfodslej," 1917)

     And the sad fan of past years
     Opens with a rustle toward the place
     Where, with a dark shudder
     The amulet buried itself in the sand.

                    ("Still distant the asphodels'," 1917)

          U kostra my greemsja ot skuki,
          Možet byt' veka projdut,
          I blažennyx žen rodnye ruki
          Legkij pepel soberut.

                    ("V Peterburge my sojdemsja snova"
                     1920)

At the bonfire we warm ourselves out of boredom,
Perhaps ages will pass,
And the dear hands of the blessed women
Will gather the light ashes.

(We will meet again in Petersburg, 1920)

Čtoby rozovoj krovi svjaz',
Ètix suxon'kix trav zvon,
Uvorovannaja našlas'
Čerez vek, senoval, son.

("Ja ne znaju, s kakix por," 1922)

So that the bond of the rose-colored blood,
The ringing of the dry grasses,
Be found stolen
In a century, a hayloft, a dream

("I don't know when," 1922)

The future reader who found the horseshoe, preserves it, cherishes it:

"On sduvaet s nee pyl' [cf. "Kon' ležit v pyli"] / i rastiraet ee

šerst'ju . . ."

   The "human lips, which have nothing more to say" are poetic lips.

In Mandel'štam's poetry this metaphor is not infrequent:

   Ja znaju, s každym dnem
      slabeet žizni vydox,
Ešče nemnogo, — oborvut
Prostuju pesenku o glinjanyx obidax
I guby olovom zal'jut.

("1 janvarja 1924")

I know, with each day life's breath weakens,
A little more — they'll cut short
This simple song about clay wrongs
And pour tin over my lips.

(1 January 1924)

Da, ja ležu v zemle, gubami ševelja,
No to, čto ja skažu, zaučit každyj škol'nik . . .

(1935)

196 / Osip Mandel'štam and His Age

Yes, I lie in the earth, moving my lips,
But what I will say every school boy will memorize.

                    (May, 1935)

Čego dobilis' vy? Blestjaščego rasčeta:
Gub ševeljaščixsja otnjat' vy ne mogli.

                    (1935)

What have you achieved? A brilliant calculation:
You couldn't take away my moving lips.

                    (1935)

The preserved poetic past ("Human lips which have nothing more to say, /
Preserve the form of the last word said") is followed by a tactile image
of remembrance of past things: "And a feeling of heaviness remains in
the hand, /Although the clay pitcher half-spilled while it was being carried home."

     The last section of the poem is somewhat complicated in its
imagery; but here again Mandel'štam has provided subtexts in his prose
for what might otherwise appear to be a surrealistic picture. It is as
if some vast archeological site lies before us, strewn with fossilized
remains and coins. Perhaps the remains of an ancient civilization about
to be discovered.[26] Such are the words of the poet which are dug up, as
so many grains of fossilized wheat. In Mandel'štam's poetry we saw other
instances. The coins become just so many crackers ("lepeški") on which
the era, gnawing at them, has left its tooth prints. Time is hungry. It
eats governments: "Ljudi golodny. Ešče golodnee gosudarstvo. No est'
nečto bolee golodnoe: vremja. Vremja xočet požrat' gosudarstvo" (People
are hungry. The state is hungrier still. But there is something hungrier: time. Time wants to devour the government; II, 267-268). It cuts

the poet. "I menja srezaet vremja, / Kak skosilo tvoj kabluk."
("Xolodok ščekočet temja," And time cuts me, / The way it scythed your
heel; The top of my head tingles with cold, 1922).

In his essay "Gumanizm i sovremennost'" (Humanism and the Present,
1923; II, 394-396) Mandel'štam likens the values of humanism, his values,
to a gold currency not presently in use:

> Perexod na zolotuju valjutu delo buduščego, i v oblasti kul'tury
> predstoit zamena vremennyx idej — bumažnyx vypuskov — zolotym
> čekanom evropejskogo gumanističeskogo nasledstva, i ne pod
> zastupom arxeologa zvjaknut prekrasnye floriny gumanizma, a
> uvidjat svoj den' i, kak xodjačaja zvonkaja moneta, pojdut po
> rukam, kogda nastanet svoj srok.
>
> (II, 396)
>
> The transition to gold currency is the business of the future, and
> in the sphere of culture the replacement of temporary ideas —
> paper issue — by the gold coin of the European humanistic heritage
> is in prospect, and the beautiful florins of humanism will not
> jingle under the archeologist's spade, but will see their day and,
> like hard coin, will go from hand to hand, when their time comes.

Thus, the poet's art and his values are being held in abeyance.
"Čuvstvuju sebja dolžnikom revoljucii, no prinošu ej dary, v kotoryx ona
poka ne nuždaetsja." (I feel myself a debtor to the revolution, but I
bring it gifts which it for the present does not need, 1928; II, 259).
While the essential thrust of what is being said at the end of the poem
is optimistic, — the belief that all this will one day be unearthed
and reach the "reader in posterity," the horseshoe finder, in whom
Mandel'štam had such deep faith — the last two lines are quite pessimistic, with their incessantly recurring ne: "Vremja srezaet mENja, kak
moNEtu, / I mNE uz NE xvataet mENja samogo." (Time cuts me like a coin,
/ And I don't even have enough of myself).

"Našedšij podkovu," then, is a complex synthesis of much of what Mandel'štam has said in other contexts. Essentially, the poet here is concerned with history and art, and the relationship of one to the other. It is difficult to see how one critic could have said of this poem: "What despair in this equation of the world's process and creative impotence."[27] Aside from the fact that there is no such "identification" here, it is clear that the poem asserts rather the opposite; the contrast is not in the impotence of art, but in its permanency, as opposed to history's permutations. For it is, after all, the horseshoe that is found.

Chapter VIII

CONCLUSION

We have examined, then, Mandel'štam's poetic reactions to a wide
variety of events. Some of his poems dealing with World War I display
at times, a rather nationalistic approach to the issues; but in
"Zverinec" (The Menagerie) which must stand as his most complete poetic
statement on the period, he is unequivocally on the side of internationalism and pacifism. The violent antipathy which Mandel'štam initially felt toward the Russian Revolution changed over a period of months
to a kind of restrained acceptance which he expressed in "Sumerki
svobody" (The Dawn of Freedom). Yet the ultimate meaning of "Dekabrist,"
written in the same general period, is enigmatic at best. Does the
resurrection of the Decembrist into the twentieth century suggest a view
of the revolution as a glorious attempt doomed to failure, or that the
inevitable results of any (attempted) revolution are frought with peril
for all concerned? His thoughts on the future of Russia's culture
changed between 1918 and 1920: in "Na strašnoj vysote bluždajuščij
ogon'" (At a fearful height a will-'o-the wisp) Mandel'štam expressed
bleak pessimism at the ability of St. Petersburg, as an emblem of Russia's past, to survive the chaos; however, in "V Peterburge my sojdemsja
snova" (We will meet again in Petersburg) Petersburg's future existence
is not even called into question; it is only unclear who will be "living"
there. Such confidence may be maintained for the length of a poem, yet
a close reading of "Čut' mercaet prizračnaja scena" (The phantasmal
stage barely glimmers), written in the same year as "V Peterburge my

sojdemsja snova," shows that here Mandel'štam is not at all certain that
art can survive in a hostile environment. His view on Czarist Russia as
expressed in "Vek" (The Age) ranges between regret over the irrevocable
end of one era in history and hope that some kind of good will emerge in
a spring which has yet to come. In "Vojna. Opjat' raznogolosica" (War,
Again there is dissonance) Mandel'štam is unequivocal in his opposition
toward the possibility of a new intervention, but he is not at all clear
as to what might be expected to occur within his country in the future.
In "Našedšij podkovu" (The One Who Found a Horseshoe) the chaos of the
moment is juxtaposed to the sweeping changes effected by Peter the
Great's "revolution" and the only certainty which emerges is that Russia's
culture can again survive.

Mandel'štam at various times professed an almost naive belief in,
or perhaps hope for, the existence of a past and future golden age for
humanity. This hope emerges at moments when one might expect the
greatest despair: at the height of World War One ("Zverinec"), during
the Civil War ("Na kamennyx otrogax Pierii" [On the rocky spurs of
Pireus]), at the time of a threatened Allied intervention ("Vojna. Opjat'
raznogolosica"). Yet on the other hand, Mandel'štam sometimes was prey
to a fear of an impending, never clearly delineated, cataclysm ("Koncert
na vokzale," [Concert at the Railway station] "Veter nam utešen'e
prines" [The wind brought us consolation]). In fact, as we have seen,
both the fear of cataclysm and the belief in a golden future were expressed within one and the same poem ("Vojna. Opjat' raznogolosica").
The most optimistic interpretation of such a juxtaposition is that the
cataclysm is the apocalyptic force which might initiate the new golden

age; but Mandel'štam never made such a connection clear.

In examining a number of poems by a single poet, it is almost ir-resistible for the critic to look for a system of thought, a controlling analysis of the world which shaped and governed the artist's work. Cer-tainly one of the primary functions of any poem is to order and give permanent form to experience. But it is more often fruitless to attempt to examine a lyric poet's body of work in terms of any systematic philo-sophy. For a lyric is by definition a personal response to a situation. Its scope and intention is less obviously sweeping than the epic, and rather than attempting to articulate the culture of a people or a nation, the lyric poet speaks in his own voice--although he may insist that he is more or less representative. Indeed, the focus of this genre is directed as much to the poet's response as to the event which occasioned the poem. Certainly a series of lyrics may show development; but it is the develop-ment of a personality--the shifting, modulating, revising of feelings and opinions of a man (who as a poet is more sensitive and aware than most) accommodating reality. Each poem can be seen as a separate attempt to focus and verbalize a complex of emotions and thoughts springing from a particular situation. If an epic may be thought to summarize an age, the lyric chronicles it. What a series of lyric poems written over a period of time lacks in consistency or coherence, it gains in precision or con-creteness, catching the nuance of a year or a season which might be lost a decade later.

Thus, a collection of lyric poems is perhaps the best record of a period of cultural change. Because no widespread agreement on cultural values exists, or they are undergoing change, each poem must contain within it an interpretation and perhaps judgment of events. Rather than merely rephrasing accepted truths as a poet might in an age of stability and peace, in a period of crisis the lyric poet must shape and communicate rather recalcitrant "raw" material, things which in their particular historical form had neither been felt nor expressed before. If such lyric poems have certain dissonance (apparent inconsistencies of belief, etc.) rather than overall harmony, they preserve the complexities of the age, rather than simplifying them.

To avoid chaos and mere emotion, the poet -- and this was particularly true of Mandel'štam -- often relies on tradition to shape his own response. Immediately involved in the moment, the poet is also aware of the continuum in art and history. His effort to understand the present naturally depends on having a perspective of the past.

The lyric poet, as latest representative of a tradition and yet as an individual, develops a certain self-consciousness about his responses. Because he is an individual, the poet has personal, perhaps even unique, feelings about his subject. But because he knows his tradition, the poet is aware that his historical moment bears resemblance to others in a complex variety of ways. His role is to articulate at once both his subjective and objective appraisal of his experience -- both what the moment is to him, immediately, and what it is like, in terms of the rest of history and literature. Emphasizing Mandel'štam's use of images from ancient Greek and Roman sources as if it were the sole content of his poems, Brjusov misses the point that these images serve an essential function of providing a broader historical context.

But first of all, when you've read O. Mandel'štam's "second book,"
idem - his <u>Tristia</u>, the question arises: in what century was the
book written? At times, the present moment seems to flash by,
'our age' is spoken of, the European war is alluded to, 'battle-
ships' and even 'trousers' are mentioned -- an attribute of the
present since neither the ancient Greeks nor the ancient Romans
wore them. But these rays fade behind clouds of all sorts of
Herculeses, Troezens, Piereses, Persephones, Lethean colds, etc.
Less than anyone am I inclined to deny poetry's right to use images
from history and eternal symbols from Greek myths; but, if in a
little book of forty poems into each one some Greek god or hero
climbs and out of each one some allusion to Hellas falls onto the
reader, then, as you wish, this is too much! . . . In an extreme
case, if there is nothing classical in the verses, then there must
be something ancient, or even old; seraphim, priests on the
Euphrates, Valhalla, Scheherezade, Lorelei, etc. All of contemporaneity without fail must be dressed in the apparel of past
ages.[1]

Brjusov is objecting to precisely what is so important to Mandel'štam's

technique. Rather than looking at what is missing, it is instead vital

to look at what Mandel'štam adds to the historical moment from the past.

It is not surprising that the process of simultaneously maintain-

ing an objective distance from events and being nonetheless emotionally

involved results in a certain bifurcation of the self. The heart some-

times would like to believe in something that the intellect knows is im-

possible. Precisely because Mandel'štam's vision is so complex, it is

often ambiguous. Ambiguity derives, not from any failure to focus his

response exactly, but rather from being aware of the variety of possible

responses. Refusing to accept the easy faith of the moment, Mandel'štam

insists on measuring his experience against classical values or histori-

cal antecedents. Because he can comprehend intellectually both sides of

an issue (or especially because in a period of cultural change he is

excruciatingly aware both of what has been gained and what has been

lost), complete emotional commitment to one side or another would be

difficult if not impossible. Mandel'štam's choice instead is for complexity -- to be inclusive rather than exclusive; to articulate all that
he knows and feels, even if that knowledge is more painful to express
than to ignore. Rather than sacrifice his awareness of or allegiance to
one set of values for the sake of another, Mandel'štam remains detached
and may seem aloof.

Faith, in terms of unquestioning allegiance to an idea or value,
seems to depend on simplicity -- an overriding interpretation of experience which resolves contradictions. However much the intellectual would
like to resolve the disharmony of experience, his intellectual honesty
forbids him to ignore the exceptions and contradictions which any simple
philosophy or world view must overlook.

From the beginning, poets have been called vates, or seer, at the
same time they were regarded as makers, or craftsmen. These two titles
are not mutually exclusive and seem especially complementary in the
modern lyric poem. The poet sees more -- his vision encompasses both
present moment and its relation to the past. Likewise, it extends at
times to the future when he conceives of an ideal state which would fulfill the potential of the present, or perhaps would be a desired alterna-
tive. His special gift is a heightened sensitivity which enables him to
see the essential nature of his experience, and historical perspective,
his memory of tradition, which enables him to see an event in a context
much broader than any individual's perception.

But the poet's special awareness would be unnoticed without a
vehicle adequate to express it. The modern lyric poet must be a consum-
mate craftsman, as Mandel'štam's continuing involvement with Acmeism

makes clear. Since Mandel'štam's vision includes the breakdown of a culture, the end of an age, and the beginning of an experiment whose end is unknown, the problem becomes how the poem as an artifact can reflect this fragmentation, confusion, and upheaval and still remain intelligible. If a whole tradition seems to be counterbalanced against a new assessment of man's nature and needs, the poem which can suggest such a tension must be incredibly complex and carefully structured. An era of social change might be diagrammed as two funnels meeting at a single point. The entire past of a nation or culture has gone into the special character of the moment, and the moment has within it the potential for equally diverse, though unknown, future development. Mandel'štam, in order not to be swept away by the dimensions of the immediate upheaval, retains his balance by stepping back. But his move is less to withdraw than to improve his perspective.

Ambiguity may be a concomitant of artistic control. Mandel'štam, in an attempt to be scrupulously exact, to preserve the situation in all its aspects, and to allow a variety of interpretations, may appear to be irresolute, undecided — either unclear in his own mind which interpretation he favored, or else certain himself, but maddeningly obscure to us. But the careful artist, the complex man who sees his own age intensively and can appreciate the past and future imaginatively and intellectually may be ambiguous because it is the only way to be perfectly true to his experience. To recognize the variety of responses may finally be much more demanding than deciding in favor of one set of values or one interpretation of events over another. Thus Mandel'štam's poems are ambiguous not out of perversity but out of accuracy.

Notes

Bibliography

Index

NOTES

I

1. A. Tarasenkov, "Mandel'štam, Osip," Literaturnaja enciklopedija (Leningrad, 1932).

2. A. Selivanovskij, Očerki po istorii russkoj sovetskoj poèzii (Moscow, 1936), p. 60.

3. V. Knjažnin, Pis'ma Aleksandra Bloka (Leningrad, 1925), p. 213.

4. O. Mandel'štam, Sobranie sočinenij v trex tomax, ed. G. Struve, B. Filipoff (Washington, 1967), II, 300. Henceforth, prose (II or III, p.   ) will be cited after the quotation according to this edition. Quotations of Mandel'štam's poetry are from this edition unless otherwise noted.

5. Omry Ronen, "Mandel'štam's Kaščej," Studies Presented to Professor Roman Jakobson by His Students (Cambridge, Mass., 1968), pp. 253-254.

6. "The Social Function of Poetry," On Poetry and Poets (N.Y., 1957), p. 6.

7. Portrety russkix poètov (Berlin, 1922), pp. 104-105.

II

1. Hesiod, "Works and Days," lines 174-192, trans. Hugh G. Evelyn-White, Hesiod, The Homeric Hymns and the Homerica (Cambridge, Mass., 1936).

2. Ovid, Metamorphoses, I, 121-122, trans. Frank J. Miller (Cambridge, Mass. and London, 1960).

3. Lines 1-19, trans. Hugh G. Evelyn-White, The Homeric Hymns; cf. Veresaev's translation:

> S ninfami svetlymi on [Pan]--kozlonogij, dvurogij,
> šumlivyj--
> Brodit po gornym dubravam. . . .
> Nimfy s verxušek skalistyx obryvov ego pri-
> zyvajut. . . .
> Boga veselogo pastbišč. V udel emu otdany skaly,
> Snežnye gornye glavy. . . .
> . . . kak tol'ko že večer nastupit,
> Končiv oxotu, beret on svirel'. . . .
> Zvonkogolosnye k bogu sbirajutsja gornye nimfy.

V. V. Veresaev, Èllinskie poèty (Moscow, 1963), my italics.

4. See A. H. Bryce, Notes on Virgil. Eclogues and Georgics (London, 1856), pp. 21ff.

5. Ecologue 4, 21-24, trans. E. V. Rieu, Virgil, The Pastoral Poems (Baltimore, 1961).

6. Diodorus Siculus, IV, 14, trans. C. H. Oldfather (Cambridge, Mass. 1935).

7. Homeric "Hymn to Heracles," l. 8, trans. Evelyn-White.

8. See Lewis R. Farnell, The Cults of the Greek States (Oxford, 1896), V, 95ff.

9. See, too, "Černozem" (1935).

10. Homeric "Hymn to Demeter," ll. 306-309, trans. Veresaev.

11. Aeschylus. The Prometheus Bound, trans. George Thompson (Cambridge, 1932). See in Merežkoyskij's translation: "Ogon'/ Ja smertnym dal i vot za čto nakazan./ Poxitil ja božestvennuju iskru,/ Sokryl v stvole suxogo trostnika:/ I ljudjam stal ogon' ljubeznym bratom,/ Pomoščnikom, učitelem vo vsem." Prometheus Vinctus (St. Petersburg, 1907), p. 10, my italics.

12. M. Vasmer, Ètimologičeskij slovar' russkogo jazyka (Moscow, 1967), II, 481; I, 316-317.

13. Johann Gottfried Herder, Ideen zur Philosophie der Menschheit, ([Darmstadt] Josef Melzer Verlag, 1966), p. 434.

14. "Ital'janskie obrazy i motivy v poèzii Osipa Mandel'štama," Studi in onore di Ettore Lo Gatto et Giovani Maver (Rome, 1962), p. 608.

15. See, for example, Sergej Gorodeckij, "Rimljane," Sovremennaja vojna v russkoj poèzii (Petrograd, 1915), pp. 245-246.

16. "Classical Motives in the Poetry of Mandel'štam," The Slavic and East European Journal, X, no. 3 (1966), p. 258.

17. My Mission to Russia (Boston, 1923), II, 28.

18. Ibid., I, 183.

19. Slovar' sovremennogo russkogo literaturnogo jazyka (Moscow-Leningrad, 1960), X, 269; see, too, V. V. Vinogradov, "Istorija slova podvig v russkom jazyke," Annaire de l'Institut de Philologie et d'Histoire Orientales et Slaves (Dédié à Boris Unbegaun), XVIII (1966-1967).

20. Cambridge History of Poland, ed. W. F. Reddaway, et al. (Cambridge, 1951), II, 463.

21. Ibid., II, 462.

22. Dated 1 August, 1914, Sem' cvetov radugi (Moscow, 1916), pp. 113-114; originally in "Russkie vedomosti," 1914.

23. M. Zabylin, Russkij narod, ego obyčai, obrjady, predanija sueverija i poèzija (Moscow, 1880), p. 267.

24. See Ed. A. Lippman, Music in Ancient Greece (New York and London), pp. 107ff.

25. Hesiod, Works and Days, 11. 183-184, trans. Evelyn-White.

26. It is interesting to compare Brjusov's reactions in his poem on the same subject, "Tevtonu" (To the Teuton), Sem' cvetov radugi, pp. 132-133; originally in Russkaja mysl', 1915.

III

1. Omry Ronen, "Leksičeskij povtor, podtekst i smysl v poètike Osipa Mandel'štama," Slavic Poetics: Essays in Honor of Kiril Taranovsky (The Hague, 1973), p. 374.

2. See Anna Axmatova, Sočinenija (New York, 1968), II, 174. She indicates that the poem is addressed to her.

3. "As for the poem 'With a half turn,' its history is as follows: In January, 1914, Pronin made a big party for the 'Brodjačaja sobaka,' not in his basement, but in some large hall . . . The usual visitors got lost among the multitude of foreign ones (i.e. foreign to any art). It was hot, crowded, noisy, and rather senseless. We finally grew tired of it and we (20-30 people) went to the 'Sobaka' . . . It was cool and dark there. I was standing on the stage and talking with someone. Some people from the hall began asking me to read some poetry. Not altering my pose, I read something. Osip walked up: 'How you stood, how you read,' and something about a shawl" (ibid., 172-173).

4. Stix i jazyk (Moscow-Leningrad, 1959), p. 235.

5. L. Ginzburg, "O prozaizmax v lirike Bloka," Blokovskij sbornik (Tartu, 1964), p. 164.

6. K. Ryleev, Polnoe sobranie sočinenij (Leningrad, 1934), pp. 41, 42; see also L. Ginzburg, O lirike (Moscow-Leningrad, 1964), pp. 20ff.

7. Ju. Tynjanov, "Argivjane," Arxaisty i novatory (Leningrad, 1929) pp. 300ff; L. Ginzburg, "O probleme narodnosti i ličnosti v poèzii

dekabristov," O russkom realizme XIX veka i voprosax narodnosti literatury (Moscow- Leningrad, 1960), pp. 66ff.

8. Tynjanov, pp. 300, 306.

9. Ivan Jakuškin, Zapiski (Leipzig, 1875), p. 6.

10. See, for example, K. Ryleev, "Nalivajko," "Volynskij"; A. I.
Odoevskij, "Pri izvestii o pol'skoj revoljucii"; V. F. Raevskij, "Smejus'
i plaču (Podražanie Vol'teru)"; N. A. Nekrasov, "Russkie ženščiny." Brutus can be found in Ryleev's "K vremenščiku," "Graždanskoe mužestvo";
Puškin's "Kinžal," and elsewhere.

11. G. A. Gukovskij, Puškin i russkie romantiki (Moscow, 1965),
p. 62; many examples are cited. See also I. Z. Serman, "O poètike
Lomonosova," in AN SSSR, Institute russkoj literatury, Literaturnoe
tvorčestvo M. B. Lomonosova (Moscow-Leningrad, 1962), pp. 125-131.

12. Jakuškin, Zapiski, pp. 5-6; see also A. N. Pypin, Obščestvennoe
dviženie v Rossii pri Aleksandre I, Petrograd, 5th ed., 1918 (vol. 3 of
Issledovanija i stat'i po èpoxe Aleksandra I), p. 366, obviously citing
Jakuškin.

13. P. M. Golobačev, Dekabristy, 86 portretov, vid Petrovskogo
zavoda i 2 bytovyx risunka togo vremeni (Moscow, 1906), p. xxiii,
"Kamera dekabristov v Čitinskom ostroge" (1829).

14. Jakuškin, p. 3.

15. "Kvadrigi . . . na triumfal'nyx povorotax" also suggests
"vorotax" (triumphal arches). The Brandenburger Tor and L'Arc de Tri-
omphe du Carrousel have quadrigae.

16. See D. D. Blagoj, ed., Istorija rosskoj literatury (Moscow-
Leningrad, 1963), II, 156ff.

17. The Slovar' sovremennogo russkogo literaturnogo jazyka (Moscow-
Leningrad, 1950+) provides the following definitions, with examples of
usage, of "sumerki": "1. Polut'ma, nastupajuščaja posle zaxoda solnca.
"Sumerki uže sovsem omračili nebo, i tol'ko na zapade blednel ostatok
alogo sijanija." Gogol', Vij. "Sumerki razvivalis' bystro; edva
možno rasmotret' lica." Pomjalovskij, Očerki bursy.//O predrassvetnom
polumrake. "Tat'jana razbudila ee, kogda v okna izby ešče slepo smotreli
serye sumerki utra." M. Gor'kij, Mat'. Nakonec pojavilis' predrassvetnye sumerki. Tuman sdelalsja serovato-sinim i pasmurnym." Arsen.
Dersu Uzala." Dal' gives the following definition: "Sumerki. Zarja,
polusvet: na vostoke, do vosxoda solnca, a na zapade, po zakate, utrennie i večernie sumerki//voobšče polusvet, ni svet, ni t'ma." Baratynskij's 1842 collection of poetry, Sumerki, clearly refers to evening
twilight, real and metaphoric (see "S knigoju 'Sumerki' S.N.K.": "I
čudotvorno prevratili/V den' jasnyj sumerki moi." [Baratynskij's
italics]). Vjazemskij's poem "Sumerki," similarly, refers to dusk:

"Kogda bledneet den', i sumrak zadymitsja,/I molča na polja za ten'ju
ten' ložitsja,/V poslednem zareve sgorajuščego dnja. . ."

18. Professors Vsevolod Setchkarev (in a personal communication)
and Nils Nilsson (in his talk "Osip Mandel'štam and the Revolution,"
Harvard University Russian Research Center, 5 December 1972) have suggested that the title of Mandel'štam's poem may allude to Wagner's
opera "Die Götterdämmerung." This possibility seems valid, as the opera
concerns the end of one epoch and the beginning of a new one. It has
also been suggested that the editor of Znamja truda, for one, must have
understood 'sumerki' as 'daybreak' or he would probably not have printed
the poem.

19. Sočinenija, II, 174.

20. See Kiril Taranovsky, "Razbor odnogo 'zaumnogo' stixotvorenija
Mandel'štama," Russian Literature, II (1972), pp. 146ff.

21. "Osip Mandel'štam: An Ode and an Elegy," Harvard University
Doctoral Thesis (forthcoming).

22. Sobranie sočinenij (Leningrad, 1932), VIII, 245.

23. See Nils Åke Nilsson, "'Mužajtes', muži!': On the History of a
Poetism," Scando-Slavica, tomus XII (1966), pp. 5-12.

24. Nils Åke Nilsson refers to this book as well in his article
"Ship Metaphors in Mandel'štam's Poetry," To Honor Roman Jakobson (The
Hague, 1968), pp. 1436ff. The conclusions which I draw about Mandel'-
štam's ship metaphors in relation to the Proletkul't poets differ from
Nilsson's.

25. Valer'jan Poljanskij, "Poèzija sovetskoj provincii," Pro-
letarskaja kul'tura, No. 7-8 (1919), p. 56, quoted in Papernyj, p. 200.

26. P. Arskij, quoted in Papernyj, p. 201.

27. Marsirov-Samobytnik, quoted in Papernyj, p. 202.

28. Ibid., p. 203.

29. Proletarskie poèty pervyx let sovetskoj èpoxi (Leningrad,
1959), pp. 227, 233.

30. Professor Kiril Taranovsky has informed me that this is the
punctuation used in the forthcoming Bol'šaja biblioteka poèta edition of
Mandel'štam's poetry. He also notes that part of the problem in understanding this poem is the colloquial syntax, characterized by an abundance of ellipsis, together with the use of noncolloquial vocabulary.
We might compare, for example, the last two lines of the poem with such
a purely colloquial sentence as, "Esli ty umnyj čelovek, èta kniga

nikuda ne goditsja" = "Esli ty umnyj čelovek, ty pojmeš', čto èta kniga nikuda ne goditsja." Similar problems exist in "Čut' mercaet prizračnaja scena" and other poems. See Taranovsky's "Razbor odnogo 'zaumnogo' stixotvorenija Mandel'štama."

31. Cf. Boris Bukhshtab, "The Poetry of Osip Mandel'štam," Russian Literature Triquarterly, no. 1 (1971), pp. 276-277.

32. "Ešče teper' v prostom narode bluždajuščie, bolotnye i svet-jaščiesja na mogilax, vsledstvie fosforičeskix isparenij, ogon'ki priznajutsja za duši usopsix. . . . Donyne vo vsej Germanii suščestvuet pover'e, čto duši, nenasledovavšie blažennogo=lišennye nebesnogo carstva, bluždajut noč'ju poroju po lugam i tolpam ognennymi videnijami. Putnikov, kotorye prinimajut ix za derevenskie ogni, oni sbivajut s nastojaščej dorogi, i to udaljajas', to probližajas'—zavodjat v topkie bolota i truščoby. Javlenie èto izvestno pod nazvanijami: . . . rus. bludjaščij ogon'; teper' èti ogon'ki bol'šeju čast'ju priznajutsja za duši mladen-cev, umeršix bez kreščenijia i potomu nedostoennyx blaženstva." A. Afanas'ev, Poètičeskie vozzrenija slavjan na prirodu (Moskva, 1889), III, 197-198.

33. "Osip Mandel'štam's Poem The Admiralty," Scando-Slavica, tomus XVII (1971), p. 25.

34. Annenskij's "Peterburg," Blok's "Ona strojna i vysoka," "Pri žoltom svete veselilis'," "V èti žoltye dni mež domami"; note also Axmatova's "Vižu vycvetšij flag nad tamožnej/I nad gorodom želtuju mut'."

35. For example. Blok's "Svirel' zapela na mostu," Annenskij's "Mesjac." See to Blok's article "Bezvremen'e" (1906).

36. "Novoe russkoe slovo," 18 April 1971.

37. "Osip Mandel'štam: An Ode and an Elegy." Cf. also, Esenin's "Pevučij zov" ("V mužič'ix jasljax/Rodilos' plamja/K miru vsego mira!/ Novyj Nazaret/Pered vami./Uže slavjat pastyri/Ego utro./Svet za gorami." [Sobranie sočinenij, Moskva, 1966, I, 269-270]); Belyj's "Xristos voskres"; Blok's "Dvenadcat'." Seeing the revolution in terms of New Testament imagery would hardly fit in with a pro-White ideology, directed toward restoration of autocracy; such imagery, however, would be con-sistent with a view of the revolution as a new birth, a new Bethlehem.

38. Vospominanija (New York, 1970), p. 289. Cf. the slightly dif-ferent version given in Vtoraja kniga (Paris, 1972), pp. 539-540.

39. Neobyknovennye sobesedniki Moscow, 1968), pp. 87-88.

IV

1. Taranovsky, "Razbor odnogo 'zaumnogo' stixotvorenija Mandel'-štama," p. 149.

2. Omry Ronen, "An Ode and an Elegy."

3. See "Opernyj teatr," in Mandel'štam, Sobranie sočinenij, III, 402–403.

4. Vospominanija, p. 148.

5. Christophe Gluck, Sämtliche Werke, ed. Ludwig Finscher (Basel, Paris, 1967), I, xxxi. In his essay "Burja i natisk" (1923), Mandel'- štam, writing about Brjusov, singles out "Orfej i Èvridika" (1904) as among his best poems (II, 385). The direct address in l. 30, "—Ty verneš'sja na zelenye luga," does not appear in the opera libretto, but sounds much like Orpheus' words to Euridice in Brjusov's poem: "Vspomni, vspomni! lug zelenyj. . . ."

6. Zapiski mečtatelej, V (1922), p. 82.

7. "Razbor odnogo 'zaumnogo' stixotvorenija Mandel'štama," p. 146.

8. In addition, the swallow here, as Lidija Ginzburg has observed ("Poètika Osipa Mandel'štama," Izvestija Akademii nauk SSSR, Serija literatury i jazyka, XXXI, 4, pp. 323–324; see, too, A. Dymšic, "'Ja v mir vxožu'," Voprosy literatury, No. 3 [1972], pp. 89, 91) may be an al- lusion to Angelina Bosio, the famous Italian opera singer who died of pneumonia contracted on her way from Moscow to Petersburg. Just as the swallow dies, a victim of the cold, so too was Bosio killed by the Rus- sian winter. Ginzburg quotes part of Nekrasov's "O pogode," where Bosio is recalled. It is a very convincing subtext. This allusion to Bosio adds another time plane to the poem. That is, we can see not only con- temporary Petersburg of 1920, but nineteenth century Petersburg as well, when there was an Italian opera. Ginzburg sees stanzas 1–2 as a reminiscence of nineteenth century Petersburg, stanza 4—of twentieth century Petersburg, and stanza 3 "as if on the border of these two plans." Tangential support for this is the line "slašče pen'ja ital'janskoj reči," which suggests that the opera is being performed in Italian, whereas the 1919–1920 production of "Orfeo et Euridice" was probably performed in Russian.

9. Sočinenij, II, 172.

10. Sentimental'noe putešestvie (Moscow–Berlin, 1923), p. 272.

11. See Martyn Lacis [Sudrabs], Črezvyčajnye Komissii po bor'be s kontr-revoljuciej (Moscow, 1921).

12. "Izvestija," 23 February 1918, quoted in A. F. Xackevič, Soldat velikix boev: Žizn' i dejatel'nost' F. È. Dzeržinskogo (Minsk, 1970), p. 233, their italics.

13. I. I. Sreznevskij, Materialy . . . (St. Petersburg, 1902), I, 109.

14. V. Šklovskij, "O poèzii i zaumnon jazyke," Poètika (Petrograd, 1919), p. 24; cf. A. Men'šutin, A. Sinjavskij, Poèzija pervyx let revoljucii (Moscow, 1964), p. 403, for opposite view.

15. Kiril Taranovsky, "Pčely i osy v poèzii Mandel'štama: k voprosu o vlijanii Vjačeslava Ivanova na Mandel'štama,"To Honor Roman Jakobson (The Hague, 1968), p. 1990.

16. Kiril Taranovsky, "The Jewish Theme in the Poetry of Osip Mandel'štam," Russian Literature, no. 7 (forthcoming).

17. Ibid.

18. Quoted from V. Veresaev, Puškin v žizni (Moscow, 1936), II, 442.

19. The change of "sovetskaja noč'" to "janvarskaja noč'" in stanzas one and four seems to me to be well motivated not only for the reasons I suggested above. The timelessness of "janvarskaja noc'" is paralleled by the universality of "vsemirnaja pustota" (11. 6, 30). However, in the second stanza (1. 16: "Ja v noči janvarskoj pomoljus'") the original "sovetskaja nočI" seems more apt, given the specific historical references in this stanza.

As regards the changes in the last stanza, first quatrain: "Gde-to grjadki krasnye partera,/Pyšno vzbity šifon'erki lož;/Zavodnaja kukla oficera;/Ne dlja černyx duš i nizmennyx svjatoš . . ." became in 1928 "Gde-to xory sladkie Orfeja/I rodnye temnye zrački/I na grjadki kresel s galerei/Padajut afikši - golubki." Again, I feel that the second version is on the whole more successful. The visual image of the comparison of fluttering programs to doves seems particularly felicitious. The "sweet choruses of Orpheus" reinforce the connections between this poem and "Čut' mercaet prizračnaja scena." The officer's rigidity is well-conveyed through the metaphor of the wind-up doll, but the image would appear slightly anachronistic in the 1920's. (The subject of the elliptical "Ne dlja černyx duš i nizmennyx svjatoš . . ." remains unstated, but is probably art.)

20. Sočinenija, II, 174.

21. Al. Morozov, "Reminiscenzija," Kratkaja literaturnaja enciklopedija (Moscow, 1971). The Puškin-Blok "borrowing" was first pointed out by Sergej Bobrov, "Zaimstvovanija i vlijanija," Pečat' i revoljucija, no. 8 (1922), p. 77.

22. "Osip Mandel'štam's Poem The Admiralty," p. 22.

23. Cf. in "Telefon" (1918) the complex of theater-darkness-death: "Ves' vozdux vypili tjaželye port'ery,/Na teatral'noj ploščadi temno./Zvonok--i zakružilis' sfery:/Samoubijstvo rešeno" (The heavy portière drank up all the air,/It's dark on the theater square/A bell--and the spheres begin to swirl:/The suicide is decided).

V

1. Op. cit., p. 67.

2. Der Untergang des Abenlandes (Munich, 1920), I, 54.

3. For blood as glue, see Goethe, Faust, I, 2451-2452.

4. Ju. Levin, "O nekotoryx čertax plana soderžanija v poètičeskix tekstax," IJSLP, XII (1969), p. 138.

5. Trans. E. V. Rieu. Cf. Vladimir Solov'ev's translation in Stixotvorenija i šutočnye p'esy (Moscow, 1922).

6. Trans. with commentary, Geoffrey S. Kirk (Prentice-Hall, 1970). Note, too, Annenskij's translation, Vakxanki, tragedija Evridipa (St. Petersburg, 1884). Mandel'štam wrote of Annenskij's translations of Euripides in his 1922 essay "O prirode slova."

7. Quoted from Lewis R. Farnell, The Cults of the Greek States, V, 145.

8. Greek Studies (New York, 1901), p. 10.

9. "Classical Motives," p. 263.

10. These observations are from Diane Burgin's forthcoming paper on Mandel'štam and music.

11. Trans. Frank J. Miller.

12. Trans. E. V. Rieu.

13. Diogenes Laertius, Lives of the Eminent Philosophers, trans. R. D. Hicks (London, 1925), IX, 51.

14. Stixotvorenija (Moscow, 1920); republished in Proletarskie poèty pervyx let revoljucii, pp. 393-394.

VI

1. Il'f and Petrov, 12 stul'ev (Moscow, 1934), p. 168.

2. Reprinted in Polnoe sobranie sočinenij (Moscow, 1939), II, 242ff.

3. Charles S. Terry, Bach (London, 1949), pp. 70, 151.

4. Zavojnen mir (Leningrad, 1925), p. 64.

5. Dymšic, "'Ja v mir vxožu'," p. 78, suggests that they are "symbols of the 'power of the few'" ("vlast' nemnogix").

6. Eclogue IV, 21, trans. E. V. Rieu.

7. Ovid, Met., I: 109–110, trans. Frank J. Miller.

8. V. Kirillov, Proletarskie poèty, pp. 228–229.

9. P. D. Uspenskij, In Search of the Miraculous (New York, 1949), pp. 24ff; quoted in Taranovsky, "Context and Subtext."

10. Cf. in Esenin's "Otčar" (1917) a similar poetic vision: "Zakin' ego v nebo,/Postav' na stolpy!/Tam lunnogo xleba/Zlatjatsja snopy." (Throw it [the unembraceable sphere] into the sky,/Place it on pillars!/ There the sheaves of moon grain shine like gold).

11. Polnoe sobranie sočinenij (Moscow, 1957), IV, 257ff.

12. Other poets used this image as well. S. Tret'jakov, "Vdoxnovenie i benzin," Lët, p. 58; A. Krajskij, "Grani grjaduščego," I. S. Ežov, E. I. Šamurin, Russkaja poèzija XX veka (Moscow, 1925), p. 509.

13. As has been shown by Taranovsky ("Context and Subtext) the dragonflies of death and of the black azure have their source in Belyj's Symphony Kubok metelej (pp. 131–132). The "black azure" might have as its source another poem of Belyj's as well, "Lazuri.Tanka," Stixotvorenija i poèmy (Moscow, 1966), p. 376.

14. Taranovsky, "Context and Subtext."

15. Ronen, "An Ode and an Elegy."

16. Hyginus, XCII, The Myths, trans. ed. Mary Grant (Lawrence, 1960).

17. See Ronen, "Leksičeskij povtor, podtekst i smysl" for a discussion of clouds in Mandel'štam's work.

18. S. V. Šuvalov, "Obrazy v poèzii Gerasimova," Sem' poètov (Moscow, 1927), p. 180.

19. Ivan Filipčenko, Ruki. Stixi i poèmy (Moscow, 1923), p. 133.

20. Aleksej Gastev, "Pervyj luč," in I. S. Ežov, E. I. Šamurin, Russkaja poèzija XX veka (Moscow, 1925), p. 419.

21. Aleksej Gastev, "My posjagnuli," ibid., p. 423.

22. Il'ja Sadof'ev, "Utrennjaja molitva," ibid., p. 502.

23. Samobytnik, "Proletarij," ibid., p. 497.

24. Vasmer, Ètimologičeskij slovar', I, 197.

25. E.g., <u>Slovo o polka Igoreve</u>, Puškin's "Znakomyj pir ix manit vnov'," "Borodinskaja godovščina," Brjusov's "Piršestvo vojny" (In <u>Sem' cvetov radugi</u>).

26. <u>Grani</u>, no 50 (1961), p. 117.

27. In a forthcoming article.

28. "Tri zametki o poèzii Mandel'štama," <u>IJSLP</u>, XII (1969), p. 168.

29. The prototype for this poem again seems to be Puškin, who equates the unpredictability of the wind with the capricious appearance of moments of creativity, in "Osen'" (Autumn), and <u>Egipetskie noči</u> (Egyptian Nights): "Takov poèt; kak Akvilon. . ." (Such is the poet: like Aquilo. . .).

30. Taranovsky, "Pčely i osy," p. 1994.

31. Petr Alekseev, <u>Cerkovnyj slovar'</u> (St. Petersburg, 1818) III, 31; Sreznevskij, <u>Materialy</u>, II, 207.

VII

1. There is no complete translation of Pindar into Russian; but one should note Deržavin's translation of Olympian I and Pythian I (G. R. Deržavin, <u>Sočinenija</u>, ed. Ja. Grot, vol. II, St. Petersburg, 1868); V. V. Majkov's prose translations of Olympian I, II, VII, XIV, Pythian I, II, IV, V (<u>Žurnal ministerstva narodnogo prosveščenija</u>, 1892, 1893, 1896, 1898); Vjačeslav Ivanov's translation of Pythian I (<u>Žurnal ministerstva narodnogo prosveščenija</u>, 1899, and in F. F. Zelinskij [Tadeusz Zieliński], <u>Drevnegrečeskaja literatura èpoxi nezavisimosti</u>, St. Petersburg, 1919-1920); V. V. Majkov's translation of Olympian I, Pythian I, II, III, V. I. Vodovozov's translation of Olympian III, Pythian X, and anonymous translation of Olympian X as well as of several fragments (V. A. Alekseev, <u>Drevnegrečeskie poèty v biografijax i obrazcax</u>, St. Petersburg, 1895); and in Mandel'štam's time: <u>Pindare</u>. Texte ètabli et traduit par A. Puech (Paris 1922); <u>Pindar</u>. Übersetzt und erläutert von Franz Dornseiff (Leipzig, 1921).

2. See Carol Maddison, <u>Apollo and the Nine: A History of the Ode</u> (London, 1960), pp. 2, 4. "The poet is wise because he has a special knowledge, and this not merely how to compose poetry correctly but how to reveal through it matters of first importance of which he is uniquely informed." C. M. Bowra, <u>Pindar</u> (Oxford, 1964), p. 5.

3. Horace, <u>Odes</u>, IV, 2, trans. Joseph P. Clancy (Chicago, 1960).

4. See Bowra, <u>Pindar</u>, pp. 316, 347, 354; Maddison, <u>Apollo and the Nine</u>, p. 7; Rev. R. D. Morice, <u>Pindar</u> (Edinburgh and London, 1879) pp. 72, 76ff.

5. See John H. Finley, Jr., Pindar and Aeschylus (Cambridge, Massachusetts, 1955), p. 120.

6. See Olympian X, 1-7; Nemean VII, 20-21; Isthmian III and IV, 40-42, VI (V) 11-14, VII, 16-19.

7. See Bowra, Pindar, p. 166.

8. Olympian II, trans. Sir John Sandys, The Odes of Pindar (New York, 1927).

9. Bol'šaja sovetskaja enciklopedija (Moscow, 1952), XL, 121. Noteworthy too are the pink pines in I. I. Šiškin's oil painting "Korabel'naja rošča," which hangs in Leningrad.

10. Virgil, Eclogue IV, trans. E. V. Rieu.

11. Tibullus, Elegy I, iii, trans. Constance Carrier (Bloomington, London, 1968).

12. Alexsandr Blok, "Intelligencija i revoljucija" (1918), Sobranie sočinenij (Leningrad, 1936), VIII, 49.

13. Pythian II, 68, trans. Sandys.

14. Benedikt Livšic, "Naberežnaja" (1915), from the cycle "Bolotnaja meduza," Krotonskij polden' (Moscow, 1928), p. 93. I would like to thank Omry Ronen for showing this poem to me.

15. It is difficult to identify for certain the "famous mountain range" which provided the pine for the ship. Perhaps it is Mt. Pelion, which traditionally is a source of ship pine; see Ovid Amores II, 11, 1-4. Euripides Medea, 1-10.

Note Mandel'štam's almost verbatim quotation from Archilichous, in Veresaev's translation: ". . . kak osla xrebet,/Zaros šij dikim lesom, on vzdymaetsja./Nevzračnyj kraj, nemilyj i neradostnyj." (Ronen, Leksičeskij povtor, p. 373).

16. Pythian III, 89-90, trans. Sandys.

17. O. Mandel'štam, "Zapisnye knižki. Zametki 1931-1932 gg.", Voprosy literatury, 1968, no. 4, p. 188.

18. Hesiod, Theogony, 11. 53-55, trans. Evelyn-White.

19. Jurij Levin (in a personal communication) has pointed out that "three" pervades the poem. In addition to "thrice blessed" and the catalogue of three different smells, the poem has three hypostases of air (voda, xrustal', zemlja). There are several groups of three as well; "Ja sam osibsja, ja sbilsja, zaputalsja v sčete"; "polaja, litaja,

niken ne podderživaemaja"; "mednye, zolotye, bronzovye lepeški"; "podkova," "čelovečeskie guby," "oščuščenie tjažesti v ruke." Moreover, the poem as a whole has, as O. Ronen has observed ("An Ode and an Elegy") a triadic structure. Significantly, it is Pindar who is responsible for the metrical system of Greek choral poetry, which consists of triads of strophe, antistrophe, and epode (added by Pindar). Mandel'štam's poem is a close approximation of the triadic arrangement of Pindar's odes. The 92 lines divide into nine stanzas. The sequence of lines is as follows: 13+14+9/+8+8+11/+8+8+13. There is obviously a certain pattern of the strophe, antistrophe, epode type; 13 and 14 (in first triad) are reasonably close, and the rest is accurate—just as in Pindar. Nadežda Mandel'-štam's comments should be quoted here: "Incidentally, O. M. always took into account the number of lines and stanzas in a poem and the number of chapters in prose. 'Is this important?' I expressed amazement. He got angry. For him my incomprehension was nihilism and ignorance: it is not accidental that people have sacred numbers, three, for example, or seven. . . . A number is also culture and is received like an inherited gift from people." (Vospominanija, p. 286)

20. Greek and Roman sources clearly connect Neaira with water. In Hesychius of Alexandria's lexicon, she is called the daughter of Oceanus; interestingly, the phrase "horses of Neaira" also appears there (Hesychii Alexandrini Lexicon, ed. Kurt Latte, Denmark, 1966, II, 700). In Ovid's Amores Neaira is less directly related to water; she is pursued by a river god.

21. Blok, Sočinenija, VIII, 144.

22. See the extensive illustrations in Percy Ernst Schram, Sphaira, Globus, Reichsapfel (Stuttgart, 1958).

23. F. A. Brokgauz and I. A. Efron, Enciklopedičeskij slovar' (St. Petersburg, 1899), XXVI, 445. N.b. Deržava; Podderzivaemaja. See also Sreznevskij, Materialy, III, 1632.

24. The horseshoe, of course, is a symbol of luck as well.

25. F. Sologub, Sobranie sočinenij (St. Petersburg, 1914), XVII, 257. I am most grateful to Omry Ronen for indicating this poem to me. There is a classical antecedent for connecting the horseshoe with poetry: Pegasus, the winged horse, produced Hippocrene, on Mt. Helion, sacred to the Muses, by a stamp of his hoof (cf. Mandel'štam's "Ariosto": "Krylatoj lošadi podkovy tjažely" The winged horse's horseshoes are heavy).

26. It is interesting to consider whether Majakovskij reacted to these lines when writing "Vo ves' golos" (At the Top of My Voice, 1929-1930); cf., for example, Rojas' /v segodnjašnem okamenevšem g[ovne],// našix dnej izučaja potomki . . ."; "Moj stix dojdet, /no on dojdet ne tak — // [. . .] ne kak doxodit /k numizmatu steršijsja pjatak. . . ." (Digging in today's petrified shit,//Studying the progeny of our days. . . ."; "My verse will reach you, /but not like a worn-out five-copeck piece /reaches the numismatist. . . .").

27. S. K. Makovskij, <u>Portrety</u> <u>sovremennikov</u> (New York, 1956), p. 395.

VIII

1. Review of <u>Vtoraja</u> <u>kniga</u>, <u>Pečat' i revoljucija</u>, no. 6 (1923), pp. 64-65.

A SELECTED BIOGRAPHY

Adamovič, G. "Neskol'ko slov o Mandel'štame," Vozdušnye puti, II (1961), 87-101.

Aeschylus. The Prometheus Bound, trans. George Thompson. Cambridge, Cambridge University Press, 1932.

Ancyferov, N. Duša Peterburga. St. Petersburg, Brokganz-Efron, 1922.

Annenskij, Innokentij. Stixotvorenija i tragedii. Leningrad, Biblioteka poèta, 1959.

Aseev, Nikolaj. Sobranie sočinenij v pjati tomax. Moscow, Izd. Xudožestvennoj literatury, 1963.

————— Stixotvorenija i poèmy. Leningrad, Biblioteka poèta, 1967.

Axmatova, Anna. Sočinenija. New York, Inter-Language Library Associates, 1968.

Bal'mont, K. D. Sonety solnca, meda, i luny. Berlin, S. Efron [n.d. 1921].

————— Stixotvorenija. Leningrad, Biblioteka poèta, 1969.

Baratynskij, E. A. Polnoe sobranie stixotvorenij. Leningrad, Biblioteka poèta, 1957.

Barbier, Auguste. Ïambes et Poèmes. Oxford, The Clarendon Press, 1907.

Batjuškov, K. N. Polnoe sobranie stixotvorenij. Moscow-Leningrad, Biblioteka poèta, 1964.

Bekson, O. "O. Mandel'štam. O poèzii," Pečat' i revoljucia, no. 6 (1929), 105-108.

Belyj, Andrej. Četyre simfonii. Munich, W. Fink, 1971.

————— Pepel. Stixi. Moscow, Nikitinskie subbotniki, 1929.

————— Stixotvorenija i poèmy. Moscow-Leningrad, Biblioteka poèta, 1966.

————— Urna. Stixotvorenija. Moscow, Grif, 1909.

————— Zoloto v lazuri. Moscow, Skorpion, 1904.

Bem, A. "O prirode slova," Volja Rossii, no. 6-7 (1923), 159-60.

Berkovskij, N. Tekuščaja literatura. Moscow, Federacija, 1930.

Bezymenskij, A. Vesennjaja preljudija. Izbrannye stixotvorenija. Moscow, Zemlja i fabrika, 1929.

Blok, Aleksandr. Sobranie sočinenij. Leningrad, Izd. pisatelej v Leningrade, 1932.

Bobrov, Sergej. "Tristija," Pečat' i revoljucia, no. 4 (1923), 259-262.

——————. "Zaimstvovanija i vlijanija," Pečat' i revoljucija, no. 8 (1922), 73-99.

Brjusov, Valerij. Krugozor. Izbrannye stixi. Moscow [no pub.], 1922.

—————— Mig. Stixi 1920-1921 gg. Pb.-Berlin, Z. I. Gržebina, 1922.

—————— Neizdannye stixi (1914-1928). Moscow-Leningrad, Gosudarstvennoe, 1928.

—————— Puti i pereput'ja. Sobranie stixov. T.I. (1892-1901), t. II (1892-1905). Moscow, Skorpion, 1908.

—————— Sem' cvetov radugi. Stixi 1912-1915. Moscow, Sirin, 1916.

—————— Stixotvorenija i poèmy. Leningrad, Biblioteka poèta, 1961.

—————— V takie dni. Stixi. 1919-1920. Moscow, Gosudarstvennoe izdalel'stvu, 1921.

—————— "'Vtoraja kniga' Mandel'štama," Pečat' i revoljucija, no. 6 (1923), 63-66.

Brown, Clarence. "Into the Heart of Darkness: Mandel'štam's Ode to Stalin," Slavic Review, no. 4 (Dec., 1967), 584-604.

—————— Mandelstam. Cambridge, Cambridge University Press, 1972.

Bukhshtab, B. "The Poetry of Mandel'štam," Russian Literature Triquarterly, no. 1 (1971), 262-282.

Bušman, I. Poetičeskoe iskusstvo Mandel'štama. Munich, Institut po izučeniju SSSR, 1964.

Činnov, I. "Pozdnij Mandel'štam," Novyj žurnal, no. 88 (1967), 125-137.

Čukovskij, N. "Vstreči s Mandel'štamom," Moskva, no. 8 (1964), 143-152.

Deržavin, G. P. Sočinenija, ed. Ja. Grot. St. Petersburg, Imperatorskaja Akademija nauk, 1868.

Drozda, Miroslav. "Literární Názory Osipa Mandelštama," Acta Universitatis Carolinae, Slavica Pragensia, XI (1969), 211-221.

Dymšic, A. "'Ja v mir vxožu' (Zametki o tvorčestve O. Mandel'štama)", Voprosy literatury, no. 3 (1972), 67-93.

Eliot, T. S. On Poetry and Poets. New York, Farrar, Straus and Cadahy, 1957.

---------- Selected Essays, 1917-1932. New York, Harcourt, Brace, 1934.

Èrenburg, I. Ljudi, gody, žizn' (vol. 8 of Sobranie sočinenij v devjati tomax). Moscow-Leningrad, Xudožestvennaja literatura, 1967.

---------- Portrety russkix poètov. Berlin, Argonavty, 1922.

Esenin, Sergej. Sobranie sočinenij. Moscow, Xudožestvennaja literatura, 1966.

Euripides. The Bacchae, trans. with commentary G. S. Kirk, Englewood Cliffs, Prentice Hall, New Jersey, 1970.

Ežov, I. S., E. A. Šamurin. Russkaja poèzija XX veka. Moscow, Centrifuga, 1925.

Farnell, Lewis R. The Cults of the Greek States. 5 vols. Oxford, The Clarendon Press, 1896.

Fet, A. A. Polnoe sobranie stixotvorenij. St. Petersburg, A. F. Marks, 1912.

Footman, David. Civil War in Russia. London, Faber and Faber, 1961.

Gerasimov, Mixail. Neugasimaja sila. Moscow [no pub.], 1922.

Geršenzon, M. A. "A. M. Bartel', Zavojuem mir! Per. O. Mandel'štama," Pečat' i revoljucija, no. 8 (1925), 252-254.

Ginzburg, L. O lirike. Moscow-Leningrad, Sovetskij pisatel', 1964.

---------- "O probleme narodnosti i ličnosti v poèzii dekabristov," O russkom realizme XIX veka i voprosax narodnosti literatury. Moscow-Leningrad, Nauka, 1960.

---------- "Poètika Osipa Mandel'štama," Izvestija Akademii nauk SSSR. Serija literatury i jazyka, XXXI (July-August 1972, vyp. 4) 309-327.

Gnedič, N. I. Stixotvorenija. Leningrad, Biblioteka poèta, 1956.

Gromov, P. A. Blok, ego predšestvenniki i sovremenniki. Moscow-Leningrad, Sovetskij pisatel', 1966.

Gumilev, N. Sobranie sočinenij v četyrex tomax. Washington, 1964.

Herder, Johann Goltfried. Ideen zur Philosophie der Menshheit. Darm-
stadt, Josef Melzer, 1966.

Hesiod, The Homeric Hymns, The Homerica, with Eng. trans. Hugh G. Evelyn-
White, Cambridge, Mass., Harvard University Press, 1936.

Horace. Carmina, trans., ed. A. A. Fet. Moscow, M. P. Ščepkin, 1883.

---------- Odes and Epodes, trans. Joseph P. Clancy. Chicago, University of Chicago Press, 1960.

Hyginus. The Myths, trans., ed. Mary Grant, Lawrence, University of
Kansas Press, 1960.

Ivanov, G. "Osip Mandel'štam," Novyj Žurnal, no. 43 (1955), 273-284.

---------- Peterburgskie zimy. New York, Izd. imeni Čexova, 1953.

---------- "Voennye stixi," Apollon, nos. 4-5 (1915), 84-87.

Ivanov, V. "O literaturnyx gruppirovkax i tečenijax 1920-x godov,"
Znamja, no. 5 (1958), 190-208; no. 6 (1958), 179-198.

Ivanov, Vjačeslav. Cor Ardens. Moscow, Skorpion, 1911.

---------- Prozračnost'. Moscow, Skorpion, 1904.

Ivask, Ju. "Epoxa Bloka i Mandel'štama," Mosty, nos. 13-14 (1968),
209-235.

---------- "Xristianskaja poèzija Mandel'štama," Novyj Žurnal, no. 103,
(1971), 109-123.

Jíša, Jan. "Osip Emiljevič Mandelštam," Československa Rusistika, XI
no. 3 (1966), 153-157.

Karpovič, M. "Moe znakomstvo s Mandel'štamom," Novyj Žurnal, no. 49
(1957), 258-261.

Kataev, V. "Trava zabvenija," Novyj mir. no. 3 (1967), 3-129.

Kerenskij, A. Russia and History's Turning Point. New York, Duell, Sloan
and Pearce, 1965.

Kirillov, Vladimir. Stixotvorenija i poèmy. Moscow, Xudožestvennaja
literatura, 1970.

Knjažnin, V. Pis'ma Aleksandra Bloka. Leningrad, Kolos, 1925.

Kurbatov, V. Peterburg. St. Petersburg, Izd. Obščiny sv. Evgenii, 1913.

Lacis [Sudrabs], Martyn Ivanovič. Črezvyčajnye komissii po bor'be s kontr-revoljucij. Moscow, Gosudarstvennoe izdatel'stvo, 1921.

Lět, Sbornik stixov, ed. N. Aseev. Moscow, Krasnaja nov', 1923.

Levin, Ju. "O nekototyx čertax plana soderžanija v poěticeskix tekstax," Strukturnaja tipologija jazykov, 195-215. Moscow, Nauka, 1966.

—————— "O častotnom slovare jazyka poěta: Imena suščestvitel'nye u O. Mandel'štama," Russian Literature, no. 2 (1972), 5-36.

—————— "O nekotoryx čertax plana soderžanija v poěticeskix tekstax. Materialy k izučeniju poětiki O. Mandel'štama," International Journal of Slavic Linguistics and Poetics, XII (1969), 106-164.

—————— Razbor dvux stixotvorenij O. È. Mandel'štama," Russian Literature, no. 2 (1972), 37-48.

Lur'e, A. "Detskij raj," Vozdušnye puti, III (1963), 161-172.

Maddison, Carol. Apollo and the Nine: A History of the Ode. London, Routeledge, Kegan Paul, 1960.

Maguire, Robert. Red Virgin Soil. Soviet Literature in the Twenties. Princeton, Princeton University Press, 1968.

Majakovskij, V. V. Polnoe sobranie sočinenij. Moscow, Xudožestvennaja literatura, 1937.

—————— Polnoe sobranie sočinenij. Moscow, Goslitizdat, 1956.

Makovskij, S. Portrety sovremennikov. New York, Izd. imeni Čexova, 1955.

Mandel'štam, Nadežda. Vospominanija. New York, Izd. imeni Čexova, 1970.

—————— Vtoraja kniga. Paris, YMCA Press, 1972.

Mandel'štam, Osip. "Dva neizdannyx stixotvorenija," Vestnik russkogo studenčeskogo xristianskogo dviženija, IV, no. 98, (1970), 68.

—————— "Dvadcat' dva neizdannyx stixotvorenija," VRSXD, III, no. 97 (1970), 107-144.

—————— Kamen'. St. Petersburg, Akmè, 1913.

—————— Kamen'. Petrograd, Giperborej, 1916.

—————— Kamen'. Pervaja kniga stixov. Moscow-Petrograd, Gosudarstvennoe izdatel'stvo, 1923.

Mandel'štam, Osip. The Prose of Osip Mandelstam, ed., trans. Clarence
   Brown. Princeton, Princeton University Press, 1965.

————————— Razgovor o Dante. Moscow, Iskusstvo, 1967.

————————— Sobranie sočinenij, ed. G. Struve, B. Filipoff. New York,
   Izd. imeni čexova, 1955.

————————— Sobranie sočinenij v trex tomax, ed. G. Struve, B. Filipoff.
   Washington, D.C., Inter-Language Library Associates, 1967.

————————— Stixotvorenija. Moscow-Leningrad, Gosudarstvennoe izdatel'-
   stvo, 1928.

————————— Tristia. Petersburg-Berlin, Petropolis, 1922.

————————— Vtoraja kniga. Moscow-Petrograd, Krug, 1923.

————————— trans. of Maks Bartel'. Zavojuem mir! Izbrannye stixi. Moscow, Gosudorstvennoe izdatel'stvo, 1925.

Margvelašvili, G. "Ob Osipe Mandel'štame," Literaturnaja Gruzija, no. 1
   (1967), 75-96.

Men'šutin, A., A. Sinjavskij. Poèzija pervyx let revoljucii. Moscow,
   Nauka, 1964.

Meyer, Herman. The Poetics of Quotation in the European Novel. Princeton, Princeton University Press, 1968.

Mindlin, Em. Neobyknovennye sobesedniki. Moscow, Sovetskij pisatel',
   1968.

Morozov, Al. "Mandel'štam, Osip," Kratkaja literaturnaja enciklopedija,
   IV, 568-570. Moscow, Gosudarstvennoe naučnoe izdatel'stvo, 1967.

————————— "Reminiscenzija," Kratkaja literaturnaja enciklopedija, VI,
   254. Moscow, Gosudarstvennoe naučnoe izdatel'stvo, 1967.

Nilsson, Nils Åke. "The Dead Bees: Notes on a poem by Gumilev," Orbis
   Scriptus. Dmitrij Tschizewskij zum 70 Geburtstag, pp. 573-580.
   Munich, W. Fink, 1966.

————————— "Mandel'štam and the Revolution," Scando-Slavica XIX (1973),
   7-16.

————————— "Mužajtes' muži!" On the History of a Poetism," Scando-
   Slavica, XII (1966), 5-12.

————————— "Osip Mandel'štam and His Poetry," Scando-Slavica, IX
   (1963), 37-52.

Nilsson, Nils Åke. "Osip Mandel'štam's 'Insomnia Poem," IJSLP, X (1966), 148-153.

────────── "Osip Mandel'štam's Poem The Admiralty," Scando-Slavica, XVII (1971), 21-26.

────────── The Russian Imaginists. Stockholm, Almquist and Wiksell, 1970.

────────── "Ship Metaphors in Mandel'štam's Poetry," To Honor Roman Jakobson, pp. 1436-1444. s'Gravenhage, Mouton, 1968.

Odoevcova, I. Na beregax Nevy. Washington, V. P. Kamkin, 1967.

Orlov, Vl. "Na rubeže dvux epox (Iz istorii russkoj poèzii načala našego veka)," Voprosy literatury, no. 10 (1966), 111-143.

Ovid. Tristia, Pontic Epistles, ed., with Eng. trans. Henry T. Riley. London, H. G. Bohn, 1851.

Papernyj, Z. Poètičeskij obraz u Majakovskogo. Moscow, Akademija Nauk, 1961.

Pavlov, Vl. "Istoričeskie vzgljady Osipa Mandel'štama," Grani, XXV, no. 78 (1970), 197-211.

Pindar. The Odes, with trans. Sir John Sandys. New York, London, Putnam, 1927.

Poèty "Pravdy": Stixotvorenija, 1911-1922. Moscow, Xudožestvennaja literatura, 1967.

Pomorska, Krystyna. Russian Formalist Theory and Its Poetic Ambiance. The Hague, Mouton, 1968.

Proletarskie poèty pervyx let sovetskoj èpoxi. Leningrad, Biblioteka poèta, 1959.

Przybylski, R. "Arcadia Osipa Mandelsztama," Slavia Orientalis XIII, no. 3 (1964), 243-262.

────────── "Osip Mandel'štam i muzyka," Russian Literature, no. 2 (1972), 103-125.

Puškin, A. S. Polnoe sobranie sočinenij. Moscow, Izd. Akademii Nauk SSSR, 1964.

Revoljucionnaja poèzija (1890-1917). Leningrad, Sovetskij pisatel, 1959.

Ronen, Omry. Osip Mandel'štam: An Ode and an Elegy. Harvard University Doctoral Dissertation, forthcoming.

Ronen, Omry. "Leksičeskij povtor, podtekst i smysl v poètike Osipa Mandel'štama," Slavic Poetics: Essays in Honor of Kiril Taranovsky. The Hague, Mouton, 1973.

————— "Mandel'štam's Kaščej," Studies Presented to Professor Roman Jakobson by his Students. Cambridge, Mass., Slavica Publishers, 1968.

Ryleev, K. Polnoe sobranie sočinenij. Leningrad, Izd. pisatelej v Leningrade, 1934.

Selivanovskij, A. Očerki po istorii russkoj sovetskoj poèzii. Moscow, Xudožestvennaj literatura, 1936.

Sellar, W. Y. The Roman Poets of the Augustan Age: Virgil. Oxford, The Clarendon Press, 1883.

Segal, D. M. "Mikrosemantika odnogo stixotvorenija," Slavic Poetics: Essays in Honor of Kiril Taranovsky. The Hague, Mouton, 1973.

————— "Nabljudenija nad semantičeskoj strukturoj poètičeskogo proizvedenija," IJSLP, XI (1968), 159-171.

————— "O nekotoryx aspektax smyslovoj struktury 'Grifel'noj ody' O. E. Mandel'štama," Russian Literature, no. 2 (1972), 49-102.

Semenko, P. "Mandel'štam—perevodčik Petrarki," Voprosy literatury, no. 10 (1970), 153-169.

Sil'man, T. I. "Podtekst kak lingvističeskoe javlenie," Naučnye doklady vysšej školy, no. 1 (1969), 84-90.

Šklovskij, V. Sentimental'noe putešestvie. Leningrad, Gelikon, 1924.

Sobranie stixotvorenij Dekabristov. Moscow, I. I. Fomin, 1906.

Solov'ev, Vl. S. Stixotvorenija i šutočnye p'esy. Moscow, W. Fink, 1968.

Sovremennaja vojna v russkoj poèzii. Petrograd, [ed. V. Glinskij, no. pub.], 1915.

Struve, G. "Ital'janskie obrazy i motivy v poèzii Osipa Mandel'štama," Studi in onore di Ettore Lo Gatto et Giovanni Maver, pp. 601-614. Rome, Sansoni, 1962.

Svjatopolk-Mirskij, D. "Šum vremeni," Sovremennye zapiski, no. 25 (1925), 541-543.

Taranovsky, Kiril. "Dva molčanija Osipa Mandel'štama," Russian Literature, no. 2 (1972), 126-131.

Taranovsky, Kiril. "Mandel'štam's Monument not Wrought by Hands," <u>Cali</u>-<u>fornia</u> <u>Slavic</u> <u>Studies</u>, VI (1971), 43-48.

---------- "O zamknutoj i otkrytoj interpretacii poètičeskogo teksta," <u>American</u> <u>Contributions</u> <u>to</u> <u>the</u> <u>Seventh</u> <u>International</u> <u>Congress</u> <u>of</u> <u>Slavists</u>, Vol. I <u>Linguistics</u> <u>and</u> <u>Poetics</u>. The Hague, Mouton, 1974.

---------- "Pčely i osy v poèzii Mandel'štama: k voprosu o vlijanii Vjačeslava Ivanova na Mandel'štama," <u>To</u> <u>Honor</u> <u>Roman</u> <u>Jakobson</u>, pp. 1973-1995. The Hauge, Mouton, 1968.

---------- "The Problem of Context and Subtext in the Poetry of Osip Mandel'štam," <u>Slavic</u> <u>Forum</u>: <u>Essays</u> <u>in</u> <u>Linguistics</u> <u>and</u> <u>Literature</u> (in press).

---------- "Razbor odnogo 'zaumnogo' stixotvorenija Mandel'štama," <u>Russian</u> <u>Literature</u>, no. 2 (1972), 132-151.

---------- "Stixosloženie Osipa Mandel'štama (s 1908 po 1925 god)." <u>IJSLP</u>, V (1962), 97-125.

---------- "The Jewish Theme in the Poetry of Osip Mandel'štam" <u>Russian</u> <u>Literature</u> No. 7 (forthcoming).

---------- "Tri zanetki o poèzii Mandel'štama," <u>IJSLP</u>, XII (1969), 165-170.

Tarasenkov, A. "Mandel'štam, Osip," <u>Literaturnaja</u> <u>enciklopedija</u>, VI, 756-759. Leningrad, Izd. kommunističeskoj akademii, 1932.

Terapiano, Ju. "Osip Mandel'štam," <u>Grani</u>, no. 50 (1961), 102-122.

Terras, Victor. "Classical Motives in the Poetry of Mandel'štam," <u>Slavic</u> <u>and</u> <u>East</u> <u>European</u> <u>Journal</u>, X, no. 3 (1966), 251-267.

---------- "'Grifel'naja oda' O. Mandel'štama," <u>Novyj</u> <u>zurnal</u>, no. 92 (1968), 163-171.

---------- "The Time Philosophy of Osip Mandel'štam," <u>The</u> <u>Slavic</u> <u>and</u> <u>East</u> <u>European</u> <u>Review</u>, XLVI, no. 109 (1969), 344-54.

Tibullus. <u>The</u> <u>Poems</u>, trans. Constance Carrier. Bloomington, Indiana University Press, 1968.

Tjutčev, F. I. <u>Lirika</u>. 2 vols. Moscow, Nauka, 1965.

Tynjanov, Ju. <u>Kjuxlja</u>. Moscow, Sovetskij pisatel', 1947.

---------- <u>Arxaisty</u> <u>i</u> <u>novatory</u>. Leningrad, Priboj, 1929.

Vasmer, Maks. *Etimologičeskij slovar' russkogo jazyka*. Moscow, Progress, 1964.

Vejdle, V. O. "O poslednix stixax Mandel'štama," *Vozdusnye puti*, II (1961), 70-86.

Veresaev, V. V., trans. *Èllinskie poèty*. Moscow, Biblioteka antičnoj literatury, 1963.

Virgil. *Bucolica et Georgica*, ed. Archibald H. Bryce. London, Glasgow, T. Nelson, Sons, 1856.

---------- *The Pastoral Poems*, with trans. E. V. Rieu, Baltimore, Maryland, Penguin Books, 1961.

Volkov, A. *Poèzija russkogo imperializma*. Moscow-Leningrad, Xudožestvennaja literatura, 1935.

Volosin, M. *Demony gluxonemye*. Berlin, Knigoizdatel'stvo pisatelej, 1923.

---------- *Stixi o terrore*. Berlin, Knigoizdatel'stvo pisatelej, 1923.

Weisgerber, Jean. "The Use of Quotations in Recent Literature," *Comparative Literature*, no. 1 (1970), 36-45.

Žirmunskij, V. *Voprosy teorii literatury*. Leningrad, Academia, 1928.

INDEX

"A nebo buduščim beremenno." See "But the sky is pregnant with the future"

"Actor and Worker" (1922), 73-75, 179-180

Admiralty, the, 66-67

Age, the, Mandel'štam's treatment of, 104-119

"Age, The" (1923), 11, 103-119, 189, 201

Air: concept of, 10-11; in "He who found a horseshoe," 185-188

Airplanes: Blok on, 132, 134; Mandel'štam on, 132-134; as dragonflies, 143-145; in "War. Again there is dissonance," 160

Air warfare, focus of "War. Again there is dissonance," 121-122, 129

"Akter i rabočij." See "Actor and Worker"

Ambiguity in Mandel'štam's work, 6, 200, 204-206

"Among the priests a young Levite" (1917), 90

Annenskij, Innokentij, 68, 192

Arcesilas of Cyrene, 184

Aseev, N. N., 49, 121; editor of Lët, 120; "Guard the clouds," 122-123

Assyrian, use of, 143-145

"At a fearful height a will-o'-the-wisp" (1918), 4, 62-70, 200

Austria, 26

"Aviator" (Blok), 132

Axmatova, A. A., 86, 97

Azrael, 149, 166

Azure, the, use of by Blok and Mandel'štam, 141-143, 166

"Bach" (1913), 131, 150, 151-152

"Badger Hole" (Blok), 67

Bal'mont, K. D., 58

Baratynskij, E. A., 195

Barbier, Auguste, 52

"Barsuč'ja nora." See "Badger Hole"

Barthel, Max, 133

Batjuškov, K. N., 95

Baudelaire, Pierre Charles, 143

"Bax." See "Bach"

"Est' cennostej nezyblemaja skála." See "There is an unshakeable scale
   of values"
Ether, imagery of, 135-136, 139
Eugene Onegin, 69
Euripides, 95, 111
"Europe" (1914), 2
Euterpe, 111, 112
"Even now on Mt. Athos" (1915), 2
"Evrope." See "Europe"

"Feodosija" (1920), 186
Fioraventi, Rodolfo, 131
"Flejty grečeskoj tèta i jota." See "Theta and iota of a Greek flute"
Flight, Collection of Poetry (Aseev), 120
Flute, 111-112

"Gay banquet" (Puškin), 41
Germany: military might of, 22; and the Decembrists, 38-39, 41
"Give Tjutčev a dragonfly," 146
Glinka, Mixhail Ivanovič, 35
Gluck, Christoph, 83
Gofman, V., 35
Gogol', Nikolaj, 51, 192
Golden Age: in "The menagerie," 9-11, 14, 16; in "War. Again. . ." 135,
   139, 140, 158, 165, 168; Mandel'štam's hope for, 201
Gorodeckij, Sergej, 121
Grey, Sir Edward, 10
"Gumanizm i sovremennost'." See "Humanism and the present"
Gurdžiev, G. I., 138-139

Hades, 17
"Hagia Sophia" (1912), 164
"He who found a horseshoe: a Pindaric fragment" (1923), 1, 4, 88, 164,
   201; analyzed, 169-199; text, 169-174; as Pindaric ode, 174-176;
   imagery of ships in, 177-182; themes of history and art, 182-184, 199;
   concept of air, 185-188; concept of poetry, 188; galloping horse, 191-
   192; horseshoe and finder, 193-198

Heine, Heinrich, 45-46

Hellenism, 90

Hephaestus, 15

Heracles, 15-16, 17, 18

Herder, Johann Gottfried, 106

Hesiod, 9

Historical events, reaction to, 4-6

Horace, 164; on the Pindaric ode, 174

Horse, image of: in Pindar, 176; Russia linked to, 191-192

"Horses graze with a happy neighing" (1915), 191

"How from a high mountain crevice" (1934), 187-188

"How the leavened dough rises" (1922), 137

"Humanism and the present" (1923), 114, 144-145, 198

Hyginus, 153

"I am cold" (1916), 64-66

"I bathed at night in the courtyard" (1921), 149

"I climbed the step ladder" (1922), 164

"I didn't hear Ossian's tales" (1914), 88, 195

"I don't know when" (1922), 164, 196

"I forgot the word I wanted to say" (1920), 85

"I hate the light" (1912), 150

"I ponyne na Afone." See "Even now on Mt. Athos"

"I won't see the famous 'Phèdre'" (1915), 76, 82, 100

"If our enemies took me" (1937), 183

Iliad, 95

"In the dissonance of a girls' chorus" (1916), 131

"In transparent Petropolis we will die" (1916), 64-65, 66-67

Internationalism, 200

Intervention, theme of, 120, 164-165, 201

Isaiah, 109; on the Golden Age, 14, 135

Italy, 20-21

"Ja nenavižu svet." See "I hate the light"

"Ja ne slyxal rasskazov Ossiana." See "I didn't hear Ossian's tales"

"Ja ne uvižu znamenitoj 'Fedry'." See "I won't see the famous 'Phèdre'"

"Ja ne znaju s kakix por." _See_ "I don't know when"
"Ja po lesenke pristavnoj." _See_ "I climbed the step ladder"
"Ja slovo pozabyl, čto ja xotel skazat'." _See_ "I forgot the word I wanted to say"
Jakuškin, Ivan, 37, 39
Japheth, 181
"Joyfully take from my palms" (1920), 120, 165
Judaism, 90

"Kak iz odnoj vysokogornoj ščeli." _See_ "How from a high mountain crevice"
"Kak rastet xlebov opara." _See_ "How the leavened dough rises"
"Kak tel'ce malen'koe krylyškom." _See_ "Like a little body with a small wing"
Kamen'. _See_ Stone
"Kassandre". _See_ "To Cassandra"
Kataev, I., "Swan's nest," 123–124
Kerenskij, Aleksandr, 29, 30, 36
"Kinžal." _See_ "Dagger, The"
Kirillov, V. T., 50, 59–60, 61
Kjuxel'beker, V. K., 35
Kljuev, N. A., 72
"Kogda Psixeja–Žizn' spuskaetsja k tenjam." _See_ "When Psyche–Life descends to the shades"
"Kogda v temnoj noči zamiraet." _See_ "When in dark night dies"
Kolokolov, N. I., 118–119
"Kometa." _See_ "Comet, The"
"Koncert na vokzale." _See_ "Concert at the railroad station"
Kraevskij, A. A., 90
"Krivcovu." _See_ "To Krivcov"
"Krovavaja misterija 9-go janvarja." _See_ "Bloody mystery play of January 9"
"Kuvšin." _See_ "Pitcher"
Kuzmin, M., 72

Leben, Otto Heinrich von, 45

"Na kamennyx otrogax Pierii." See "On the stony spurs of Pieria"

"Na rozval'njax uložennyx solomoj." See "On a sledge piled with straw"

"Na strašnoj vysote bluždajuščij ogon'." See "At a fearful height a will-o'-the-wisp"

"Našedšij podkovu." See "He who found a horseshoe"

"Ne verja voskresen'ja čudu." See "Not believing in the miracle of resurrection

Neaira, 184

"Neither triumph nor war" (1913), 2

Nekrasov, N. A., 41

"Neskol'ko slov o graždanskoj poėzii." See "Some words about civic poetry"

Neva, the, 65–66

"Ni triumfa ni vojny." See "Neither triumph nor war"

Night, theme of, 148–149, 154

Nilsson, Nils Åke, 57, 65, 99

"XIX Century," 54, 143–144

"1914," 22

"Noise of Time, The," 115

"Not believing in the miracle of resurrection" (1916), 164

"Notes on poetry" (1923), 179

"O prirode slova." See "On the nature of the word"

"O sobesednike." See "On the interlocutor"

"Oda Betxovenu." See "Ode to Beethoven"

Ode, Pindaric, 174–175; rapid transitions of, 175

"Ode to Beethoven" (1914), 27

Offended era, meanings of, 9–10

"On the interlocutor," 176, 194

"On the nature of the word" (1922), 2, 85

"On a sledge piled with straw" (1916), 108

"On the stony spurs of Pieria" (1920), 165, 201

"1 January 1924," 105, 113, 187, 196

"Orfeo et Euridice" (Gluck), 83–84

"Otčego duša tak pevuča." See "Why is my soul so melodious"

Puškin, A. B., 34, 70, 84, 90, 164, 191–192; on Lenskij, 39; "Gay banquet," 41; "In the depth of Siberian mines," 42; on Cypris and roses, 95–96; motifs from, 162–163; on metaphor of ships, 179; on Peter I, 181–182

"Puškin and Skrjabin," 91–92

Raevskij, V. F., 35

"Rakovina." See "Seashell"

"Razgovor o Dante." See "Talking about Dante"

"Razryvy kruglyx buxt i xrjašč i sineva." See "Breaches of round bays, and gravel, and blue"

Red Terror, 87

"Rejms i Kel'n." See "Rheims and Cologne"

"Retribution" (Blok), 132

"Return to the incestuous womb" (1920), 89–90

Revolution, 29–75, 200; concept of people in, 50

"Rheims and Cologne" (1915), 28

Romains, Jules, 114

Ronen, Omry, 53, 72

Ryleev, K., 35–36

"S veselym ržaniem pasutsja tabuny." See "Horses graze with a happy neighing"

Sadyker, P., 122

St. Joseph, the carpenter, 180

"Seashell" (1911), 149

"Segodnja možno snjat' s dekal'komanii." See "Today one can make a decalcomania"

"Segodnjašnij Berlin." See "Today's Berlin"

"Sestry – – tjažest' i nežnost'." See "Sisters – – heaviness and tenderness"

Ship imagery, 58–59; in Pindar, 178–179; in Mandel'štam, 179–182

Siberia, 38

"Sisters – – heaviness and tenderness" (1920), 90, 94

Šklovskij, V., 87

Sky, theme of, 141–143, 166–168

"Vojna, Opjat' raznogolosica." See "War. Again there is dissonance"
"Vozmezdie." See "Retribution"
"Voz'mi na radost' iz moix ladonej." See "Joyfully take from my palms"

"War. Again there is dissonance" (1923), 120-168, 201; dating of, 121;
    setting of, 122; other poems in anthology, 122-125; text of, 125-129;
    composition of, 129-130; analysis of, 130-168; lines 1-11, 130-135;
    image of wheat in, 135-139; lines 13-20, 140-141; "Wind brought us
    comfort," 141-149; section I, 149-159; section II, 159-164; section
    IV, 164-165; section V, 165-168
"We will meet again in Petersburg" (1920), 1, 4, 57, 76, 80, 81, 195-
    196, 200; compared with "Phantasmal stage," 82; themes of, 86-102
"What is the grasshopper-clock singing" (1917), 85
Wheat, imagery of, 135-139
"When in dark night dies" (1918), 76-78
"When Psyche-life descends to the shades" (1920), 85
Whitman, Walt, 114
"Why is my soul so melodious" (1911), 141, 163
Will of the People (Volja naroda), 29, 32
"Wind brought us comfort, The" (1922 and 1923), 120, 127-128, 201;
    analyzed, 141-149
Wings, image of, 143
Witte, Count, 23
"Word and culture, The" (1920), 94, 137-138, 139-140
Word signals, 35
World War I, 7-28, 200; "The Menagerie," 7-28
Wrangel, P. N., 75

"Xolodnoe leto." See "Cold summer"

Zadonščina, 87
"Zametki o poèzii." See "Notes on poetry"
Zamjatin, Evgenij, 84
"Zverinec." See "The Menagerie"